Frauds Against the Elderly

Frauds Against the Elderly

Charles C. Sharpe

McFarland & Company, Inc., Publishers
Jefferson, North Carolina, and London

Library of Congress Cataloguing-in-Publication Data

Sharpe, Charles C., 1935–
    Frauds against the elderly / Charles C. Sharpe
      p.   cm.
    Includes bibliographical references and index.

    ISBN 0-7864-1855-9 (softcover : 50# alkaline paper)

    1. Aged—Crimes against—United States.   2. Fraud—
United States.   3. Swindlers and swindling—United States.
4. Consumer protection—United States.   I. Title.
HV6250.4.A34S53   2004
364.16'3—dc22   2004006359

British Library cataloguing data are available

Cover photograph ©2004 Creatas

Manufactured in the United States of America

McFarland & Company, Inc., Publishers
  Box 611, Jefferson, North Carolina 28640
    www.mcfarlandpub.com

10/09

Table of Contents

Preface

The tragedy of fraud against the senior citizens in our society is that its perpetrators target as victims those who have contributed so much to that society. They rob the elderly of assets accumulated over lifetimes, of their independence, and of the dignity to which they are entitled. The inevitable depredations of old age rob them of the physical and mental acuity needed to ward off the plunderer.

The scams, schemes, and frauds described in this book do not prey on senior citizens exclusively; members of any age or socioeconomic group can become victims. The young have the law and time to help them recover; the old often have only the law. An inordinate number of older Americans are victimized at a time in life when they are particularly vulnerable to the callous exploitation of their trust, sympathy, loneliness, and, sadly, indigence. So often these elders become trapped in a downward spiral of repeated victimization as they grow increasingly desperate to recoup their losses. Their desperation is compounded by the fear of being perceived as no longer responsible enough to manage their own lives.

The reader will note what may seem to be a disproportionate number of citations of documents issued by the Federal Trade Commission (FTC). There are three reasons for this. First, the FTC is the primary, virtually the sole, source of research and published reports on the topic of fraud against senior citizens. Second, those media reports and discussions of the topic by senior citizen organizations and advocacy groups which address the problem in their publications or on their websites derive almost exclusively from materials published by the FTC—sometimes quoted, but usually paraphrased without attribution. Third, the

research reports and publications of the FTC are in the public domain—
paid for by the American taxpayers who are encouraged to copy and
disseminate this material among those citizens for whom it is most relevant but perhaps inaccessible.

There are no tragic case histories recited here. Almost daily the
media report these. Rather, the purpose of this book is to focus on the
most prevalent frauds, schemes, and scams that victimize the elderly in
an effort to inform senior citizens and to alert them, their families, and
caregivers to the unscrupulous opportunists whom they may confront.

Acronyms

AARP	Prior to 1999, The American Association of Retired Persons
AF	Advance-fee
AG	Attorney General
AMA	American Medical Association
AoA	Administration on Aging
ATM	Automated teller machine
BBB	Better Business Bureau
CD	Certificate of deposit
CFA	Call for Action
CFTC	Commodities Futures Trading Commission
CMRA	Commercial mail receiving agency
DMA	Direct Marketing Association
DOJ	Department of Justice
EIN	Employer Identification Number
FBI	U.S. Federal Bureau of Investigation
FCA	Funeral Consumers Alliance
FCC	Federal Communications Commission
FDA	Food and Drug Administration
FDIC	Federal Deposit Insurance Corporation
FTC	Federal Trade Commission
GAO	General Accounting Office

3

HUD	Department of Housing and Urban Development
ICFA	International Cemetery and Funeral Association
IRS	Internal Revenue Service
ISP	Internet service provider
MLM	Multilevel marketing
NAAG	National Association of Attorneys General
NCLC	National Consumer Law Center
NFIC	National Fraud Information Center
PIN	Personal identification number
RM	Reverse mortgage
SEC	Securities and Exchange Commission
SPRY	Setting Priorities for Retirement Years
SSN	Social Security number
USPIS	United States Postal Inspection Service
USPTO	United States Patent and Trademark Office

I

Introduction

Definition of Fraud

> The easiest thing of all is to deceive one's self;
> for what a man wishes, he generally believes to be true.
> —Demosthenes

The word fraud comes from the Latin *fraus*—cheating, deceit. It is any form of intentional perversion of truth, or trickery deliberately practiced in order to gain some advantage or end, unfairly and dishonestly, in order to deprive another person of his or her property, legal rights, or interests, or to induce another person to relinquish something of value, and which causes that person to suffer a loss.

As defined in *Merriam-Webster's Dictionary of Law*, fraud is:

1. Any act, expression, omission, or concealment calculated to deceive another to his or her disadvantage. It is a misrepresentation or concealment with reference to some fact material to a transaction that is made with knowledge of its falsity or in reckless disregard of its truth or falsity and with the intent to deceive another and that is reasonably relied on by the other who is injured thereby.

2. The crime or tort of committing fraud. A tort (civil) action based on fraud is also referred to as an action of deceit. Actual fraud is fraud committed with the actual intent to deceive and thereby injure another—it is also called fraud in fact. Constructive fraud is conduct that is considered fraud under the law despite the absence of an intent to deceive because it has the same conse-

5

quences as an actual fraud would have and it is against public interests (because of the violation of a public or private trust or confidence, the breach of a fiduciary duty, or the use of undue influence) This is also called legal fraud.

Fraud in the factum is that in which the deception causes the other party to misunderstand the nature of the transaction in which he or she is engaging especially with regard to the contents of an instrument such as a contract or promissory note.

Fraud in the inducement is that in which the deception leads the other party to engage in a transaction the nature of which he or she understands [Merriam-Webster 1996].

Proving Fraud

A party who has lost something due to fraud is entitled to file a civil lawsuit for damages against the party acting fraudulently, and the damages may include punitive damages as a punishment or public example due to the malicious nature of the fraud. Quite often there are several persons involved in a scheme to commit fraud and each and all may be liable for the total damages.

Even though a person has suffered a financial loss—compensible damages under tort law—it is not always easy to prove that he or she was a victim of fraud. Their loss could have been the result of using poor judgment or due to a variety of other factors. Greed and ignorance can be very conducive to fraud.

To sustain an action in law for alleged fraud several requirements must be met. There must be proof by a preponderance of evidence that:

- The accused made false or deceptive statements;
- he or she knew that these statements were false and untrue;
- there was a deliberate intent to deceive;
- the victim was in fact deceived; and
- the victim suffered financial damage and is legally entitled to recovery of those damages.

In a criminal lawsuit, the accused could be found *guilty* and be fined and or could go to prison. In a civil lawsuit, he or she could be found *liable* for damages.

Fraud and Deception: There Is a Difference

Deception can take many forms. It is the intent that can define it as fraud.

- In *The Wizard of Oz*, Dorothy accused the Wizard of being a "humbug." Such puffery, boasting, or bragging is not criminal fraud. These are common tactics used in advertising media. They are not illegal—ridiculous, ludicrous, and implausible perhaps, but not illegal. The intent is to persuade the gullible, to deceive but not victimize them. The average person can recognize humbug for what it is and ignore it.
- Misrepresentation is the reporting of inaccurate information. This can be the result of an innocent mistake, incorrect information, hyperbole, or the omission of relevant facts. Misrepresentation can be in error or by a deliberate statement or action—fraud.
- Deception is a form of trickery. It is embellishment with the intent to bamboozle. The deception may be through exaggeration, or by omission—not telling the whole truth. Deception may border on puffery—which is legal. However, deception is an inherent element of fraud—which is not legal. In this circumstance, the degree of the deception is irrelevant. What will be is the degree of any injury to the victim of the deception (Source: Harrison, "Don't Get Gypped," 1999).

Scope of Fraud Against Senior Citizens

The Victims

There are many predators in society who look at gray hair and see gold. Studies have shown that the elderly in our population who have retired from working many years during some of the most prosperous times in America hold a major part of the nation's assets. Many legitimate business enterprises hope to share that wealth—as do many thieves. These con artists got their name from their skill at winning the confidence of their victims of all ages.

Most senior citizens readily recognize the dangers posed by muggers and burglars, but fail to perceive the threat of the rapacious con artist with a friendly face, ingratiating manner, glib pitch, and black heart. These scam artists not only know where the money is, they also know how to exploit the weaknesses and insecurities of the elderly—isolation, loneliness, impairment, fears of losing their independence, the shame and humiliation of having been easily duped—all of the factors that enable the thieves to escape prosecution and move on to their next victim.

In view of the anticipated growth in the number of senior citizens in the U.S. population (as discussed in "The Numbers" which follows), and considering the alarming increase in the types and frequency of fraud perpetrated against them, there is growing concern among advocates for the elderly and the various regulatory and law enforcement agencies. Unfortunately, their efforts have not always been entirely successful in protecting this most vulnerable segment of our society.

In her remarks before the Senate Judiciary Committee on July 21, 1999, Susan Herman, then Executive Director, National Center for Victims of Crime, stated:

> The elderly in this country are ignored. We live in a fast-paced, youth-oriented society. Elder issues are not high on the social agenda. Many of our parents and grandparents live their twilight years in isolation and loneliness. Policy debates about crime and its victims focus on victims of violent crime, virtually to the exclusion of victims of nonviolent property crimes. Every crime has a victim and every victim needs this nation's help. Nonviolent crime can be emotionally, physically, and spiritually devastating. And, because they have particular difficulty being their own advocates, elderly victims have a special claim on our social conscience.
>
> Elderly victims of fraud are among the most underserved of any victim group. Every day there are thousands of cases of elderly people scammed by home services, defrauded by caregivers, exploited by neighbors or family members, or tricked by the unscrupulous. Best estimates are that 20% of the elderly have been victims of some kind of fraud.
>
> The impact of fraud on elders can be profound and life altering. Elders, more often than not, live on fixed incomes, many at or below the poverty level. Too often, fraud means elderly Americans go without food, medication or other necessities. As elders lose their savings, go into debt, mortgage property, or take out credit card advances to pay those exploiting them, even comfortable lifestyles collapse.

Generally, senior citizens do not have the time or opportunity for financial recovery; their prime earning years are behind them. At a time in life when one tries to conserve assets, a blow to financial security is often a permanent and life-threatening setback.

Elder fraud victims often find their trust shattered. They doubt their judgment. They feel isolated, depressed, angry, and ashamed. These violations of trust compounded with the subsequent uncertainty about paying bills, often lead to illness. In fact, 78% of elderly victims develop acute and chronic anxiety. Even when elders do reach out, help is rarely available. As a nation, we don't address the needs of victims of nonviolent crime. Every state in this country has a financial compensation system that pays for medical and counseling expenses, and other costs of a crime. None cover elder fraud....

We must do better, we must do more, and we must act soon.

Older Americans served this country well. They deserve dignity and financial security, and yet they are too frequently robbed of both. Our elders deserve no less [National Center for Victims of Crime, "Elder Fraud," 1999].

The Administration on Aging (AoA) affirms that "The advent of telecommunications has increased public interest in government intervention and protection against unscrupulous business practices. Older adults are thought to be particularly vulnerable to solicitation schemes through the mail and telephone, as they were in previous decades to door-to-door salesmen and are feared to be in the near future to the Internet. Aging advocacy organizations are urging Federal agencies and Congress to support greater public awareness of popular scams and greater enforcement of existing laws restricting prohibited practices" (Administration on Aging, "Consumer Protection & the Elderly," 2002).

The Many Faces of Fraud

The con artists who prey on the elderly are not always easy to recognize. They do not look or act like thieves. Their schemes and scams would not be as successful as they are if their victims could readily identify them. Invariably they are amiable, ingratiating, even unctuous. They are slick, smooth operators who are very adept at gaining their victims' trust and they have a vast repertoire of practiced skills to draw upon in victimizing senior citizens. They have become masters of exploiting the socioeconomic conditions and concerns common among this population of our society. They target the physical frailties of the elderly person and those of human nature; this is their niche.

Modes and Types of Fraud Against Senior Citizens

There are many modes of operation that con artists employ to defraud the elderly, but most are variations of these three:

1. Telemarketing
2. Mail
3. Door-to-door sales

Many fraudulent scams involve both mailings—including e-mail—and telemarketing. Some employ all three methods.

There are seven broad areas of fraud against seniors identified by the Federal Trade Commission as being frequently employed by grifters.

1. Health
2. Credit, including credit card fraud and credit "repair"
3. Telemarketing and direct marketing, including mail order
4. Investments
5. Home improvement/maintenance and sales
6. Insurance
7. New and used car sales and auto repair

(Source: United States Federal Trade Commission, "Fraud Against Seniors," 2000).

There are many other types of fraud but these seven are the most frequent cause of consumer complaints and affect the aged more often than any others.

In an extensive report dated January 1997, the FTC discussed protection activities in four areas of fraud against consumers:

1. Telemarketing
2. Investment
3. Business opportunity and job placement
4. Consumer finance.

(Source: United States Federal Trade Commission, "Fighting Consumer Fraud," 1997).

The findings in this FTC report relevant to fraud against senior citizens are cited in the relevant sections of this book.

The Reasons for Targeting Senior Citizens

The disproportionate number of the elderly who are victims of consumer fraud is partly attributable to two factors: 1. generational and 2. economic. Senior citizens can be subverted by their most admirable traits—their traditional values and norms can make them highly vulnerable. Many may have grown up in more refined, genteel times. They are loath to simply hang up the telephone on a glib telemarketer, or shut the door in a con artist's face.

In a statement before the Senate Special Committee on Aging, 104th Congress, 2nd Session, on March 31, 1996, Edward Bruce Gould, Jr., a *convicted telemarketer*, testified: "In the case of senior citizens, who in most cases had their lives affected by having lived as children or younger adults through the Great Depression, the key is to work on the greed and insecurity caused by those times.... Because most senior citizens are more trusting of supposedly 'caring' strangers, because they grew and matured in less threatening times, they are incredibly easy to con out of everything they have" (United States Federal Trade Commission, "Fighting Consumer Fraud," 1997).

Data from the FTC (cited in United States Federal Trade Commission, "Fraud Against Seniors," 2000) and numerous state and local authorities have shown consistently that the elderly are targeted for an array of frauds for a variety of reasons. These include:

- Trust
    "Everyone is subject to fraudulent schemes and con games. Older people in particular seem to be frequently targeted, perhaps because as a group they tend to be more trusting of others and assume the same sincerity in return" (Federal Reserve Bank of San Francisco).
    "Individuals who grew up in the 1930s, 1940s, and 1950s were generally raised to be polite and trusting. Two very important and positive personality traits, except when it comes to dealing with a con man. The con man will exploit these traits knowing that it is difficult or impossible for these individuals

to say 'no' or just hang up the phone" (United States Federal Bureau of Investigation, 2001).

Many are trusting to a fault—they can be very reluctant to believe that a well-dressed, well-spoken, solicitous young man or woman could be attempting to deceive and defraud them. Scam artists often target older people, knowing they tend to be trusting and polite toward strangers. Many were raised on the belief that a person's word was his or her bond, and that a handshake was all that was required to guarantee a promise. Good manners are paramount to many older Americans, who were raised in a far more civil society than the one they inhabit today. However, graciousness can cost them. To the con artist there really is "no fool like an old fool."

- Accessibility

    Being retired or suffering from physical problems, seniors are the group of people most likely to be at home during the day and evening and therefore receive telemarketers' calls or visits from door-to-door salespersons—and to listen to their pitches.

- Isolation and Loneliness

    Con artists prey on vulnerability and loneliness. Isolation is an increasingly sad fact of life for seniors. Typically they are home alone, lonely, and welcome an opportunity to speak to another person or meet new friends. They are likely to be more than willing to talk at length to someone on the phone or who comes to their door. To them, the person who may actually be promoting a scam can be welcome "company" to whom they may reach out.

    Often, seniors may not have regular contact with relatives and friends with whom they can discuss prospective investment or financial affairs. They often have no one that they can confide in or rely on for guidance. The con artists often attempt to substitute their guidance for that of distant family or friends.

    While anyone age 60 or older is likely to be on at least one "mooch" (sucker) list, a woman 70 or older is virtually guaranteed to be. Such women are often widows, lonely and suffering from ills that make them desperate for someone to talk to. Con artists avidly read obituaries to identify the names of recent widows and target them during their period of mourning, hoping they will be less vigilant against scams. Mourning the loss of a spouse can make one particularly predisposed to listen to the smooth talk of a sympathetic sounding grifter who will commiserate to win their trust and who may spend hours talking to a prospective victim. These scammers are masters of such psychological stratagems.

- Declining Physical Health or Mental Acuity

    Older persons become vulnerable to fraud with advancing age and concomitant health problems. Health improvement scams and medical quackery frauds are proving to be very lucrative for their operators. The Federal Bureau of Investigation (FBI) remarks, "When it comes to products that promise increased cognitive function, virility, physical conditioning, anti-cancer properties and so on, older Americans make up the segment of the population most concerned about these issues. In a country where new cures and vaccinations for old diseases have given every American hope for a long and fruitful life, it is not so unbelievable that the products offered by these con men can do what they say they can do" (United States Federal Bureau of Investigation, "Fraud Against the Elderly," 2001).

    Declining health makes it difficult for some seniors to leave their homes and also deprives them of their ability to perform even the simplest household repairs and maintenance. This can make the offer of doing such tasks from a traveling company or handyman very difficult to resist. Declining mental health due to Alzheimer's disease or other conditions may challenge seniors to remember whether or not they agreed to make a particular purchase, investment, or donation.

- Assets

    It used to be that to be old was to be poor, but older people now typically have greater resources than their own children and certainly more than the generation or two before them. Scam artists' growing interest in older Americans arises largely from the fact that, unlike previous generations, seniors are most likely to have "nest-eggs" thanks to better retirement plans. Senior citizens usually have funds from Social Security and employer pensions, IRAs or 401(k) savings, and, if they are widows, the proceeds of their late husband's life insurance. Many have invested wisely or saved their money, and as a result may have accumulated substantial assets.

It is not surprising that fraud perpetrators would solicit older Americans in their efforts to capture a significant amount of this money. In a March 25, 2002, NBC news report, Lisa Myers confirmed that "Crooks prey on trusting people who have money in the bank. Increasingly, America's seniors are the target of common scams, from unscrupulous car dealers to dishonest telemarketers. Nearly one third of all fraud complaints are filed by older Americans, who tend to be more trusting and have savings" (Myers, "Older Americans Targeted for Scams," 2002).

Senior citizens usually own their home and have excellent credit—all of which the con artist will try to tap into. The fraudster will focus his or her efforts on the segment of the population most likely to be in a financial position to buy into a scam.

The FBI confirms reports that "Cons target seniors because they have the perception that seniors have a ready and large supply of money from their life's savings or they have valuable property. Investment schemes may appear particularly tempting to seniors because they are frequently on a fixed income but would like to make more money for the sake of their future security" (United States Federal Bureau of Investigation).

Promoters of investment schemes often troll for prospects by visiting churches, country clubs or senior citizen centers. The scammers often perform a legitimate service, such as income tax preparation, to win the confidence of an elderly customer before pitching a fraudulent investment.

Senior citizens realize that they are likely to live much longer than their predecessors—maybe long enough to deplete their nest-egg. Many are fiercely determined never to become an economic or physical burden to their children. Sadly, that combination makes them easy prey for fraud. Persons who, after retirement, find themselves on smaller, fixed incomes may look for ways to supplement their pensions and the fraud-ulent schemes can sound very alluring.

The Victims' Responses

Unfortunately, older Americans are less likely to report a fraud because they do not know where or how to report it; are too ashamed at having been scammed; or do not fully realize they have been scammed. In some cases, an elderly victim may not report the crime because he or she is concerned that relatives may come to the conclusion that he or she no longer has the mental capacity to take care of his or her own financial affairs.

"Even after older people recognize they've been the victimized, they often resist taking action against the perpetrator. Often, experts say, an elderly person is embarrassed to report the crime because it jeop-ardizes their sense of themselves as independent and in control. They're forced to rely on somebody else. That goes against the grain for so many people" (CNN, "Investment Scams Targeting the Elderly," 2000).

Typically they admit that they feared telling their children about their predicament. Many senior citizens have said "I got into it, and I couldn't get out." They believe that they are trapped. This type of fear and anxiety keeps many fraud victims falling for new scams in the hope of replacing some of the lost money so their sons and daughters will never know what has happened. They fear that their children will say they can't handle their finances and they'll be put in a nursing home. Elder fraud has torn victims' families apart as relatives try to intervene, or have reacted unsympathetically as vindictive, deprived likely heirs.

According to The National Center for Victims of Crime, "Unfor-tunately, many elder victims are too embarrassed to report [a fraud]. Sometimes the perpetrator is a loved one or their caregiver, and they don't want to get them in trouble. Sometimes, elders are not aware they have been defrauded or feel that reporting will do no good, or they don't want to bother the police. Sometimes, they are reluctant to con-front their greatest fear—that they will be considered incompetent to handle their own financial affairs. By reporting, many feel they risk their independence" (National Center for Victims of Crime, "Elder Fraud," 1999).

Often the victims do not even realize what has happened until the situation has been explained to them in detail. Even then they are often reluctant to admit that they have been defrauded. The victim's realization that he or she has been victimized may take weeks or, more likely, months after contact with the con man. This extended time frame will test the memory of almost anyone—especially an elderly person. When an elderly victim does report the crime, he or she often makes a poor witness. The con man knows the effects of age on memory and is counting on the fact that the elderly victim will not be able to supply enough detailed information to investigators such as:

- How many times did the scammer call?
- What time of day did he or she call?
- Did he or she provide a call-back number or an address?
- Was it always the same person?
- Did you meet in person?
- What did the person(s) look like?
- Did he or she have recognizable accent?
- Where did you send the money?
- How did you send the money?
- What did you receive if anything and how was it delivered?
- What promises were made and when?
- Did you keep any notes of your conversations?

The Consequences of Fraud Against the Elderly

The economic consequences older citizens in the U.S. suffer at the hands of these thieves can be devastating. In many cases, an older person's victimization has consumed his or her life savings. Social Security is often the principal source of income for many older citizens in the U.S. With monthly Social Security or pension checks, in relatively fixed and modest amounts, and given the limits of a victim's advanced age and life expectancy, it is virtually impossible for elderly victims to ever replace assets lost as a result of fraud.

The psychological consequences can be equally devastating. Many elderly victims have plunged into such a state of despair that they have lost their will to live; they become severely depressed; they consider— or actually commit—suicide. Elder fraud can exact a terrible financial, emotional, and human toll.

The Numbers

On August 26, 2002, the nation's chief postal inspector warned senior citizens, their families, and their caregivers that older Americans are increasingly becoming the targets of con artists. "Fraud complaints are on the rise, and more people aged 60 and over are becoming victims. In uncertain financial times, people are looking for a secure place to invest their retirement money.... These conditions make it easier for con artists to swindle investors, especially senior citizens, out of their entire life savings" (United States Postal Inspection Service, "Senior Citizens Targeted," 2002).

Fraud, in its many forms and various extents, is an age-old problem. It has increasingly become a problem in old age. Unfortunately, accurate statistics on the number of elderly persons victimized by the many forms of fraud are difficult to derive, since research has shown that approximately only one in fourteen cases is reported. However, data from a number of studies confirm that older Americans are being increasingly targeted by predators who view them as easy marks. As the numbers of senior citizens will increase, inevitably so too will the number of victims.

On the basis of the Bureau of the Census population projections released following the national census in 2000, we can anticipate a moderate increase in the elderly population until about 2010; a rapid increase for the next twenty years to 2030; and then a return to a moderate increase between 2030 and 2050. By 2030, there will be about 70 million older persons, more than twice their number in 2000. Persons 65 years of age and over represented 12.4 percent of the population in the year 2000 but are expected to grow to be 20 percent of the population by 2030 (Sources: Administration on Aging, *A Profile of Older Americans, 2001,* 2001; United States Bureau of the Census, *Population Projections,* 2000).

The rapid growth of the elderly population, particularly the oldest (80 years and over), represents in part a triumph of the efforts of science and technology to extend human life, but these age groups also require a disproportionately large share of special services and public support. Many areas of public life will be greatly affected by these changing demographics of aging, and many new concerns will arise from three conditions linked closely to one another.

1. The proportion of elderly in the total population is now substantial (estimated at 13–14 percent in 2003.)
2. The number of elderly and the rate of aging are expected to increase steeply, with implications for a vast increase in the numbers of persons requiring special services (health, recreation, housing, nutrition, and the like); participating in various entitlement programs; and requiring formal and informal care.
3. There is a recognition of the possible implications of an aging society for the whole range of our social institutions, from education and family to business and government. Protection must also be included. The increasing numbers of elderly will inevitably produce and increasing number of victims of fraud and abuse—particularly among those senior citizens living alone (Source: Administration on Aging, *A Profile of Older Americans: 2001*, 2001).

The Internet and Telemarketing Fraud

Senior citizens have increasingly become targets for both Internet and telemarketing scams. When senior citizens have access to computers and the Internet they immediately become potential victims. Although they can be victimized in a number of ways, the Internet is emerging as a primary medium—the scammers are lurking for senior citizens in cyberspace. The National Consumers League's Internet Fraud Watch maintains a website called "Internet Fraud Tips." It presents general Internet fraud prevention tips and discusses 21 of the major Internet frauds. This information can be found at: http://www.fraud.org/internet/inttip/inttip.htm.

Senior citizens are increasingly going online. According to data from the 2000 census, among the 21.8 million households where a householder was age 60 or older, 5.3 million households (24.3 percent) had a computer, slightly less than half the figure for the general population (51.6 percent). Internet access was present in 3.9 million (17.7 percent) of these households which is 42.6 percent of the figure for the general population (41.5 percent). On an individual basis, 9.3 million (28.4 percent) of the older persons had home computer access and 4.2 million (12.8 percent) used the Internet at home, which is 34 percent of the figure for the general population (Source: United States Bureau of the Census, "Home Computers and Internet Use," 2001).

The Cost to Victims of Internet and Telemarketing Fraud

It is estimated by the U.S. Office of Consumer Affairs that $100 billion or more are taken each year from American consumers by fraud despite major law enforcement efforts to stop the theft. Because of their particular vulnerability, an overly large segment of those who fall victim to the con artists fall in the 60 years of age and over group.

Telemarketing fraud alone costs Americans consumers an estimated $40 billion annually. About 37 percent, or $15 billion, of that is bilked from persons over 50 years of age who are especially susceptible and account for about 56 percent of all victims (Source: United States Federal Trade Commission, "Consumer Fraud against the Elderly," no date). The repeated victimization of the elderly, according to federal law enforcement, is the cornerstone of illegal telemarketing. Seniors lose untold billions more through mail fraud—deceptive mailings with carefully placed small print—home improvement scams, and dozens of other swindles designed to deceive or mislead. "Scam artists from around the world are preying on seniors at an alarming rate. The FBI estimates that seniors got ripped off over $40 billion in the last year [2000] from an estimated 14,000 illegal telemarketing operations. A recent report suggests that seniors 55 and older in the United States alone have 77 percent of the available disposable income. It's no wonder these predators target the elderly" (United States Federal Bureau of Investigation, 2001).

On September 10, 2001, in testimony before a congressional committee, Dennis M. Lormel, Chief Financial Crimes Section of the Federal Bureau of Investigation, stated:

> [T]he FBI has identified elder fraud and fraud against those suffering from serious illness as two of the most insidious of all white collar crimes being perpetrated by today's modern and high tech con man. The Internet, high speed dialers, mail drops, and computers are just some of the tools available to the fraudster to separate a victim from his money. Many elderly citizens rely on pensions, social security and life savings to support themselves. The seriously ill and their families are desperate to find some glimmer of hope. The losses inflicted by these unscrupulous con men and their organizations are both financially and emotionally devastating to these victims [United States Federal Bureau of Investigation, "Fraud Against the Elderly," 2001].

II

Frauds, Scams, and Schemes

Advance-Fee Loans

Advance-Fee Loan Scams

The vast majority of lending institutions and loan companies are owned and managed by reputable professionals. However, there are many fraudulent loan brokers and other individuals in business who misrepresent the availability and terms of credit. In addition to the many obstacles a senior citizen may already encounter in obtaining or retaining credit in times of financial need, he or she may become highly vulnerable to the various scams and schemes that opportunistic thieves will attempt. "Clever con artists will offer to find financing arrangements for their clients who pay a 'finder's fee' in advance. They require their clients to sign contracts in which they agree to pay the fee when they are introduced to the financing source. Victims often learn that they are ineligible for financing only after they have paid the 'finder' according to the contract. Such agreements may be legal unless it can be shown that the 'finder' never had the intention or the ability to provide financing for the victims" (United States Federal Bureau of Investigation, "What Is an Advance-Fee Scheme?" no date).

This fee may range from $100 to several hundred dollars. The swindlers frequently demand a percentage of the gross amount of the loan as their fee. Small businesses have been charged as much as several thousand dollars as such a fee. Whether you are an individual consumer or an owner of a small business, the result is the same: You do not get any money; the con artist does—and once they do, he or she vanishes, as does the money you have paid.

The advance-fee swindler will claim to be able to obtain a "guaranteed" loan for you from a legitimate, reputable lending institution, such as a bank or a savings and loan association. However, the swindler has neither the ability nor the intent to obtain a loan for you. Instead, he or she either pockets the fee you paid and disappears, or remains in the area to bilk other unsuspecting victims while stalling you with various excuses as to why your loan has not been approved, or repeated promises that it is being "reviewed."

However, do not confuse a legitimate pre-approved credit offer with a legitimate pre-qualified offer from mortgage brokers, banks, savings and loans, and credit unions. A pre-approved offer requires only your oral or written acceptance of the terms. A pre-qualified offer means you've been selected to *apply*; you still must go through the normal application process, and you still can be turned down.

The Scope of the Problem

The senior citizen on a fixed income who is experiencing financial difficulties and cannot make ends meet, and who may have had difficulty obtaining a loan through normal channels, can be a primary target for an advance-fee loan scheme. In addition to such financial problems seniors may also have heavy debt, poor credit, and are often in desperate need of substantial help with their personal finances. They are the least able to absorb the economic injury caused by such scams and schemes. Fraud promoters know that these individuals are willing to pay small amounts of money to process loans, arrange financing, or help locate sources of credit that promise to cure their financial woes. Usually, these loans are offered by "offshore banks."

There are many variants of the advance-fee scam. Individuals often respond to advertisements that generally appear in the classified section of local and national newspapers and magazines and on the Internet. E-mail messages offer home-equity loans that do not require equity in your home, as well as solicitations for "guaranteed," unsecured loans regardless of the applicant's financial situation or credit history. These pitches may also be made in radio advertisements, on local cable stations, and in flyers circulated in neighborhoods and shopping centers. Unfortunately, such advertising in respected media outlets or on the Internet does not guarantee the legitimacy of the company behind the advertisement (Source: United States Federal Trade Commission, "Easy Credit? Not So Fast," 1999).

The prospective loan applicant is reassured that he or she has "nothing to lose" because the fee will be refunded if his or her loan application is turned down. The lenders seniors are directed to are merely lists of financial institutions who will turn down any applicant who does not meet their particular loan qualifications. The fee they have paid for this useless information will not be refunded; applicants invariably receive nothing—no loan, no refund. Recent FTC law enforcement efforts demonstrate that fraud promoters who promise financial services or assistance for a fee invariably do not deliver. Instead, they take millions of dollars from consumers without providing any services at all. Frequently, applicants are referred to other companies that require additional payments. These "turn down rooms" do not make good on their promises to deliver refunds. They are operating another scam!

The Telemarketing Sales Rule

According to the Telemarketing Sales Rule, if someone guarantees or suggests that there is a strong chance they can get or arrange a loan or other form of credit for you, it is illegal to ask you to pay—or for them to accept payment—for their service until you actually receive your loan or line of credit. Otherwise they are violating the law (16 CFR Part 310). The FTC confirms that legitimate, guaranteed offers of credit do not require payments up front. Although lenders may require you to pay application, appraisal, or credit report fees, these fees seldom are necessary before the lender is identified and the application completed. What is more, says the FTC, these fees are paid to the lender, not to an intermediary who is arranging the loan. The FTC's Consumer Counsel advises you not pay for a promise.

Tips and Advice

Here are some points to keep in mind before you respond to ads that promise loans or easy credit, regardless of your credit his-tory:

- Legitimate lenders never "guarantee" or say that you are likely to get a loan before you apply, especially if you have no credit history, a poor credit history, or a recent record of bankruptcy.
- If you apply for a real estate loan, it is common business practice for lenders to request payment for a credit report or appraisal. However, legitimate lenders should not ask you to pay in advance for processing your application.
- If you do not have the offer in hand or confirmed in writing and you are asked to pay, do not do it. It is fraud and it is against the law (Source: United States Federal Trade Commission, "Easy Credit? Not So Fast," 1999).

If you are not dealing directly with a lending institution on your own behalf, the following guidelines will help you avoid being victimized by an advance-fee scam.

- Know with whom you are doing business. Obtain the name of the loan representative and the name, address, and telephone number of the company he or she claims to represent.
- Do not accept the agent's claims of guaranteed loan services at their face value. Always be skeptical.
- Insist on being told the name of the lending institution which purportedly will fund your loan.
- Verify with the lender all oral and written representations made by the agent or broker regarding their affiliation with the lender.
- Ask for the names, addresses, and phone numbers of other clients of the agent. Contact them to see if they received loans. (Beware of shills!)
- *Always* consider consulting an attorney or business advisor for guidance.

Remember: Ask yourself why this broker can obtain a loan for you from a legitimate lender when you yourself have already been turned down, perhaps many times.

"Bank Examiner"

Bank examiner schemes are resurfacing throughout the country.

The most recent schemes are targeting the elderly and many have been swindled, sometimes out of their life savings.

Citing a 1995 AARP bulletin, no longer online but still highly relevant, Don McLeod reported:

> Older Americans across the country are losing millions of dollars in a high-tech revival of an age-old fraud—the "bank examiner" scam. Total losses must be at least $5 to $10 million a year.... The actual numbers could be much higher because so many cases go unreported.... There's not a city in the country that hasn't been hit.... [The problem is] worse now than ever before, and it's especially bad in places like Florida, where you have so many elderly living.... But there has been a resurgence of it since 1991. No one knows exactly why this type of fraud is on the rise. But some experts cite the proliferation of computers—through which hackers can gain confidential bank information about people—and more cunning use of the telephone. Whatever the reasons for the trend, swindlers prey largely on older people, usually widows, who grew up in an era when people respected authority. These individuals often are quite willing, even eager, to do a good deed.... After using the phone to set up a meeting, the impostors dress and groom themselves to look believable in their roles as cops or bankers. They flash badges and credentials that look real enough. And they employ the solicitous "customer relations" manner that one might expect from such officials. Scare tactics are commonly used to rattle the victim and cloud his thinking. He is told of a "problem" with his account, that it's being drained by crooked employees and he must act soon or all the money will be gone. The "bank examiners" have special tricks for those who require more persuading [cited in McLeod, "High Tech Swindlers Filen Millions," 1995].

The Scam

As described by McLeod, the targeted victim, who is usually an elderly female, is contacted, usually by phone, by a person claiming to be an officer of the bank at which she has her account. The call may sound very official, intimidating, or perhaps a little threatening, depending on the mark's response. The objective is to convince the intended victim to help catch a "dishonest employee" at the bank. The scam can have several variations, but the objective is the same: persuade the victim to withdraw funds from her bank account and give them to the scam artist—with no questions asked.

In a variation of the scam, the con artists may pose as FBI agents, bank auditors, or other bank officials, police officers or detectives who state that the victim's help is needed to conduct an investigation to apprehend an employee, usually a teller, suspected of theft. Whatever the caller's persona, the message rarely varies, as the prospective victim—as a "responsible citizen"—is asked for help in catching a dishonest person. The potential victim may be told that her checking or savings account has had some unusual withdrawals and that a bank employee is under suspicion of fraudulent activity, and that the bank is conducting an "internal investigation" of the suspect. They then ask for her help in catching the suspect in the act. She might even be told that the bank will reimburse her as a "reward" for her cooperation in the investigation. The victim can do a "good deed," the "official" says. "You can even be a hero." All she needs to do is go down to the bank and withdraw some money so the transaction can be monitored and the bank's suspicions can be confirmed.

After this part of the pitch, the con artist waits to see if you will take the bait—he or she waits for your reaction to see if you are skeptical or if you might believe that the caller is really a bank examiner who is trying to help you. Once the con artist has your interest, the scam will unfold very quickly. The victim, wanting to help nab the crook, often agrees and is then given the "plan of action" by the phony bank officer. As a valued bank customer you are asked to withdraw a large sum of money in cash and hand it over to an "investigator" who will be waiting for you outside the bank or at another predetermined location—typically a parking lot. The caller might instead propose that a representative of the bank will come to your home, pick up the money, and redeposit it in your account to test the employee's honesty. He explains that the deposit must be in cash so that serial numbers on the bills can be "checked" which involves marking and recording the serial numbers on the bills. The supposed investigator will put on an elaborate show of doing this as part of the ruse. You will be guaranteed to have your money returned for redeposit so the marked bills will make their case against the allegedly dishonest teller—exactly how will not be revealed—"Security," you know. You are in potential trouble if you do not interrupt the con artist to ask: "How can you possibly trace individual bills through your banking system?" (In this part of the scam the envelope in which the scam artist has placed the cash is often switched for an identical one with only scrap paper inside, and the victim is directed to go to the bank to make the redeposit personally.)

The victim is assured that her account is fully insured by the Federal Deposit Insurance Corporation (FDIC), and that she will suffer no loss due to a bank employee's dishonesty, the only statement made in the scam that is true—irrelevant in this scenario, but true. The scam obviates both assertions.

The victim follows through with the plan and withdraws the agreed amount and then meets the phony bank official. The impersonator then takes the money from the victim, telling her that it will be held as evidence. She is reassured the money will be immediately redeposited in her account, after the investigation has been completed. She is given an official-looking receipt for the exact amount of the money. The funds are deposited into the scam artist's pockets. The victim never sees his or her money again.

The success of the bank examiner scam depends on the victim's gullibility, passivity, trust, and eagerness to do a good deed without questioning or asserting him or herself in the face of perceived authority. The con artists rely on these traits of human nature to control and manipulate their victims and exploit them to effect the fraud and prevent them from thinking clearly and rationally. Victims have reported that they became more excited as they became more involved in the plot.

In another variation—the easiest for the con artist—the caller may claim that due to some "computer error" or other internal problem, the bank must verify certain data regarding the victim's accounts. The caller then attempts to elicit the "necessary information" about the victim's accounts—particularly the numbers. The caller may also try to ascertain if the victim lives alone, and to elicit other personal information. If the phony bank officer succeeds in getting the information, he will thank the victim profusely, and tell him or her that he will call back if there are any further problems. The next problem for the victim: His or her accounts are immediately cleaned out. In the speed and confusion of these subterfuges, con artists keep the victim sufficiently distracted to prevent him or her from realizing just how implausible the whole scenario really is.

Prevention

The bank examiner scam is a very common one, and any phone call asking for the withdrawal of funds from your bank account should be viewed with a high degree of suspicion, regardless of how persuasive or authoritative the caller may sound. No bank is ever going to ask you to simply take money out of your account for *any* reason. Therefore, if someone calls you and asks you to withdraw money and give it to him or her under any pretext, you should realize immediately that it's a scam. Law enforcement and bank officials suggest several actions you can take to protect yourself:

- Call your police or sheriff's department immediately and report the attempt.
- Call or visit your bank immediately to report the contact and alert the proper official to the possibility of other potential victims. Look up the bank's phone number on your own. Any number the "bank examiner" suggests you call will be answered by an accomplice in the scheme.
- Give the police and the bank personnel all the information you can, including any unusual characteristics of the caller's voice, speech patterns, or accents, or a full description if you have had a personal encounter.
- Fully cooperate with the bank and the police during any investigation. Your only reward will be knowing that you may prevent the victimization of another senior citizen. You truly can be a hero.
- Hang up before the scam artist has a chance to go to work on you. End the conversation immediately, no matter what the so-called bank examiner tells you. If you stay on the line and allow the con artist to continue to talk, you risk losing a considerable sum of money.
- If the scenario he or she presents seems unusual, or if you feel uncomfortable, just hang up.
- Trust only people you know. Do not trust someone because he or she has a friendly voice or appears to be an authoritative figure. Swindlers usually are friendly and have honest faces and pleasant personalities. That is how they gain your trust—and steal your money.
- Remember, no financial institution or government agency routinely uses private citizens in the conduct of internal investigations.

Many financial institutions now request that their customers first read and sign an affidavit when they wish to withdraw a large amount of cash. The document alerts consumers to the scams described here and encourages them to speak to a bank representative or law enforcement officer in such situations. This is not an attempt to keep your money or control how you spend it—it is an effort to protect you and every other citizen from fraud. Increasingly, banks, credit unions, and savings and loan associations are training their personnel to spot possible victims— especially among the elderly. But once a customer has been persuaded that a bank employee may be a thief, it can be difficult, if not futile, to dissuade that person from making a withdrawal and doing his or her "duty" to catch the swindler in the act. Remember, mental acuity and knowledge about how these schemes work are your best defense against them. These fraud artists are very clever and resourceful in devising ways to trick people out of their money. Do not let them trap you.

Business Opportunities

Business Opportunity Fraud

Many consumers, particularly recent retirees, are attracted to advertisements touting opportunities for individuals to operate their own small businesses or to work at home. Calls from would-be entrepreneurs responding to these advertisements are usually directed to a telemarketer, who glowingly describes the business opportunity and the amount of money that can be made by following the company's business plan. To clinch the sale the telemarketer often provides the consumer with the names and telephone numbers of other "satisfied investors" who have purportedly profited in the venture, and from whom the prospective investor can receive an unbiased opinion. In fact, they are "singers" —shills who are paid by the promoter to lie about their "success."

After the consumer pays anywhere from hundreds to tens of thousand of dollars to become a distributor or to receive the "business plan," he or she learns that the revenue projections of the telemarketer were highly inflated and that the only people who make money in the so-called business opportunity are the promoters themselves. Every year, the FTC brings numerous cases against purveyors of such fraudulent business opportunities. Business opportunities fall into two general types: 1. franchises and 2. work-at-home. We will focus here on those businesses operating at a location *outside* a person's residence, and not those operating entirely on their premises or from an individual's residence. These will be discussed in "Work-at-Home," which—along with franchises—comes under the definition, statutes, regulations, and rules covering any business opportunity. In the eyes of the law, and the rules and regulations of the FTC, they are all treated equally.

THE SCAMS HAVE BECOME EPIDEMIC

Past and current reports of investigations from the FTC have confirmed that a growing national epidemic of business opportunity scams is preying on would-be entrepreneurs and that they include the elderly in increasing numbers. (United States Federal Trade Commission, "Business Opportunity Scam Epidemic," 1995) Though business opportunity scams are not a new problem, the swindles have skyrocketed recently due to the introduction of high-pressure telemarketing tactics previously used to tout travel and sweepstakes rip-offs. And there has been a surge in swindlers seeking to take advantage of changing job markets and the demographics of American society. Business opportunities have received considerable attention in recent years, owing in large part to the decline of traditional job security, the large number of individuals who have lost jobs due to corporate "downsizing," and the trends in early retirement.

The scam artists offer a wide array of "get rich quick" and self-employment schemes that target consumers of all ages and socioeconomic groups who are looking for an investment opportunity, part-time employment, or the chance to start their own business—the persons who have always hoped for success and "making it big." They all share the dream of owning their own business and being their own boss. Unfortunately the majority of these dreams become nightmares. The odds of success are about the same as playing a national lottery. There are very many potential dangers and traps for the desperate and the unwary—young or old. All age groups are vulnerable, the elderly especially so.

Every year, thousands of consumers across the nation fall prey to fraudulent business opportunity promoters, even though many potential entrepreneurs are diligent about meeting with the promoters, checking references, and verifying the business' financial and legal status before they invest. Indeed, the FTC says that fraudulent business opportunities consistently rank in the top ten categories in its database of consumer fraud complaints. Increasingly, the experiences of senior citizens who have been cheated are being included in the database.

Based on the findings of a 1995 coordinated law enforcement effort known as "Project Telesweep," state and federal officials estimate that well over $100 million a year is being lost to swindlers promising quick, easy money in a wide variety of scams and schemes which offer the aspiring, unsuspecting entrepreneurs pre-packaged businesses. The FTC has warned repeatedly that many of these business opportunities are scams that promise more than they can possibly deliver (Source: United States Federal Trade Commission, "Business Opportunity Scam Epidemic," 1995).

THE TARGETED VICTIMS

In a brief article, "Economics of the Aging Revolution," published on the website of the Department of Sociology of Trinity University in San Antonio, an unnamed author, discussing retirement, comments: "The processes of 'modernization' have regularized the structural unemployment of the older cohorts of workers. Corresponding with this development has been the emergence of ideological justifications which have, in turn, modified the very meaningfulness of old as a status attribute. 'Retirement' is supposedly the old age status that individuals earn in exchange for their lifetimes of social contributions—a time for leisure, individualism, and self-fulfillment. But there are other ways of perceiving this new life-cycle state wherein individuals are no longer expected to be social contributors" (Trinity University, "Economics of the Aging Revolution," no date).

Scam artists have found many other ways for senior citizens to achieve the "individualism and self-fulfillment" the unnamed author describes. Fraudulent business opportunities are just one of them. Always quick to seize on a new way to make an illicit dollar, con artists have picked up on the changes in the traditional American job market. The result: Fraudulent operators are relentlessly pushing overhyped and worthless business opportunities to an often desperate and susceptible public. If you are a recent retiree or a downsized worker who may suddenly be in possession of a large retirement or severance package, you are a prime target.

Senior workers who have reached retirement age (sometimes mandatory) often are not ready or willing to retire. They believe that they have many productive years left. They may not have received a "golden parachute." They usually experience a drastic decrease in their income and a subsequent change in lifestyle. Frequently, these retirees need a second income simply to make ends meet—and in many instances, just to survive.

For those considering going back to work, their age is a major factor working against them. They soon learn that, with the exception of consulting, there simply are no jobs that pay what they were making before retirement. In desperation or determination they may see an answer in self-employment—in a business opportunity. However, a repertoire of business skills and experience accumulated over a lifetime is no guarantee of success.

In the last ten years, many Americans have succumbed to hopes that entrepreneurial or technological ventures could help them launch small businesses. The fraud promoters target these consumers with false claims of lucrative franchise and business opportunities, guarantees of security or stable employment, and promises that their services or products will provide them with sustained income. They have bilked millions of dollars from such consumers through these dubious but cleverly crafted and marketed promises. Such business opportunity scams and work-at-home schemes are frauds that have cost consumers their life savings and destroyed their dreams. These swindlers are looting the American dream.

THE OFFERS AND THE COME-ONS

The promises: "Effortless income," "easy money," "get rich quick." The reality: *Go broke quick!* That's the unfortunate truth usually learned too late by the thousands of individuals who fall victim every year to swindlers peddling a variety of money-making opportunities. Be wary if the salesperson makes the work sound too easy. The thought of easy money may be appealing, but success generally requires hard work.

The con artists often locate their marks through trade shows, television infomercials, print advertisements, websites, e-mail, and telephone solicitations. Once touted almost strictly on a face-to-face basis, business opportunities are increasingly being promoted through slick and aggressive telemarketing campaigns. They attempt to persuade the prospective investors that interest by the public in a specific market niche is very high and that the window of opportunity will soon close.

Typically these promoters make promises that sound exciting but simply are not truthful. As many consumers who have answered these ads have learned, and as the FTC has confirmed, very many of these business opportunity promotions are nothing but scams that take consumers' money up front and fail to deliver on the promises. They pressure investors to make a quick decision and hand over their investment. Consequently consumers are getting ripped off, losing large amounts money instead of making it.

It is not difficult to see why consumers would be drawn to tempting ads that promise "proven" and "lucrative" opportunities and use similar bait. Such statements as "Broke? Out of a job? Need a second income?"; "Want to work from home?"; "No skills? No experience?"; "Good pay for little effort!"; "Set your own hours!"; and the usual "Be your own boss" and "You can start right away" are familiar promises. If you can answer "yes" to any of these rhetorical questions, then you are likely to be attracted by such advertisements.

New venture or not, some old advice applies: The promise of substantial earnings with minimal effort or training is a sure warning sign of fraud. The obvious question is: "If these business systems produce the results described and promised, why isn't everyone using them?" What these ads do not say is that the individuals behind these schemes are not really interested in helping you run a successful business: Their primary interest is getting your money. And to get you to invest, they will mislead you about the earnings potential and promote a phantom opportunity that has little or no chance of succeeding. Unfortunately, the crooks behind the fraudulent scams are the only ones who get rich quick.

Their offers are short on details but long on promises. A franchise or business opportunity may sound appealing, especially if you have limited resources or business experience. However, you could lose a significant amount of money if you do not carefully investigate a proposal before you invest.

THE USUAL SUSPECTS

The scam artists are highly sophisticated. They know exactly how to keep consumers from guessing the true nature of their operation. While the scams can be difficult to detect, there are tell-tale signs of fraud that the consumer can learn to spot. It may not be an easy task, but consistently there are certain clues. Most of the business opportunity schemes and scams:

- Claim "we are not just selling you a business, we want to put you *in* a business." (They want to *give* you the business!)
- Usually list an 800-number and urge the prospect to call for more information. Invariably, you will be told to leave your name and telephone number so that an "associate" (salesperson) can call you back with the "further information" (a high-pressure sales pitch). Exercise caution when it comes to advertisements that contain little more than glowing promises and an 800-number. This is very likely a come-on to lure you into calling a telemarketing "boiler room" operation! Keep in mind that just because an ad appears in a reputable newspaper or magazine, or on national television does not mean that the information it contains is accurate or the offer is legitimate.
- Promise instant riches, easy money. They make wild and completely unsubstantiated claims about potential earnings and "proven" concepts and "guaranteed" winners." (They say "GUARANTEED" very often, usually followed by several exclamation points!!!)
- Assert that "no experience" or "no training" is necessary.
- Promise exclusive locations and territories.
- Rely on high-pressure sales techniques to coerce a potential victim to make a quick financial commitment.
- Proffer references ("singers") specially selected by the promoter.
- Fail to provide prospective investors with a disclosure document as required by law (Source: United States Federal Trade Commission, *Franchise and Business Opportunites*, 2000).

While fraudulent business opportunities prey on consumers, they also harm legitimate businesses. To evade the law, promoters of fraudulent business opportunities often jump from one city to the next, leaving behind unpaid bills for newspaper ads, office rent, phone bills, supplies, and services.

Franchises

Want to be your own boss? A franchise opportunity may sound appealing, especially if you have limited resources or business experience. However, you could lose a significant amount of money if you do not investigate a franchise offering carefully before you buy. The FTC has stated: "Many people dream of being an entrepreneur. By purchasing a franchise, you often can sell goods and services that have instant name recognition and can obtain training and ongoing support to help you succeed. But be cautious. Like any investment, purchasing a franchise is not a guarantee of success" (United States Federal Trade Commission, *A Consumer Guide to Buying a Franchise*, 1994).

Many, if not most, business opportunities meet the FTC's definition of a franchise. If the following three elements accurately describe a business opportunity, it is considered a franchise.

1. If the goods you will market will be supplied entirely by the parent company or suppliers it designates, or services you will provide will be only those prescribed by the parent company, and in accordance with their training and manuals of procedure.
2. If the company will assist you in securing locations or clients.
3. If you are required to provide a cash investment at the time you sign the franchise contract or within a designated time thereafter.

If the proposed business opportunity incorporates these three elements, the FTC's Franchise and Business Opportunity Rule (the Franchise Rule) requires franchisors to provide specific information to help you make an informed decision. A franchise or business opportunity seller must furnish you with a copy of the "Franchise Disclosure" (also called a "Franchise Offering Circular") document at least ten business days before you pay any money or legally commit yourself to a purchase. You can use these disclosures to compare a particular business with others you may be considering or simply for information. The disclosure document includes:

- The names, addresses and telephone numbers of at least ten previous purchasers who live closest to you;
- a fully audited financial statement of the seller;
- background and experience of the business' key executives;
- the anticipated cost of starting and maintaining the business;
- and the responsibilities you and the seller will have to each other once you have invested in the opportunity.

Under the FTC rule, the seller must wait at least ten business days *after* giving you the required documents before accepting your money or signature on an agreement. To help you evaluate whether owning a franchise is right for you, the FTC has prepared the booklets *A Consumer Guide to Buying a Franchise* and *Franchise and Business Opportunities*. Both documents are available online at the URLs shown in the main sources. They are recommended reading. These informative publications will help you understand your obligations as a franchise owner; how to shop for franchise opportunities; how to ask the right questions before you invest; and how to avoid franchise frauds. They include a detailed discussion of the Franchise Rule and the required content of a Disclosure Document.

"Unfortunately, not all franchise opportunities are legitimate. Con artists seeking to capitalize on the franchise boom create their own 'investment' opportunities, which they promote to inexperienced investors. To induce the unwary to invest, these con artists promise the world, but deliver little to nothing" (United States Postal Inspection Service, Distributoship and Franchise Fraud, no date).

Before investing in any franchise system or in any business opportunity, be sure to obtain a copy of the Disclosure Document and study it very carefully. Make sure you understand all of the provisions. Get a clarification or answer to your concerns before you invest.

The Seminar Pitch: A Real Curve Ball

Thousands of consumers throughout the country have attended business opportunity seminars in hotel conference centers or other public venues where they are persuaded to invest in fraudulent business opportunities or other highly dubious ventures. Typically, consumers are lured to the seminars by infomercials, e-mails, or letters promising invaluable information on how to operate a home-based business, how to buy and sell real estate, trade in securities, invest in foreign currencies, and an array of other ventures promising large income. At the seminars, however, consumers learn very little, if anything, about how to run a profitable business. Instead, the virtually captive audience is treated to relentless and slick sales pitches for schemes that are essentially worthless. Often consumers succumb to these pitches because the seminar hucksters create the impression that anyone, regardless of abilities or experience, can buy their program and earn a lot of money.

Seminar scam artists are smooth operators. Most have the gracious manner and impeccable grooming that project an image of respectability, legitimacy and prosperity. And they should appear prosperous, because in the past few years such seminar hucksters have bilked consumers out of millions of dollars—and they are claiming new victims every day.

Generally, seminar programs are conducted in sessions over a period of several hours in an environment conducive to gaining consumer confidence, and which end with an enthusiastic pitch to buy the huckster's phony deal. A common ploy of these pitchmen is to lace their carefully rehearsed sales presentations with seemingly off-hand folksy yarns, ingratiating personal anecdotes and "success stories." The sole objective is to establish rapport with their gullible audiences and reinforce the notion that they too can become successful and earn substantial income.

The FTC wants to alert the public to the secrets of the seminar squeeze. Be wary of promotional materials or sales pitches that make these claims:

- "Absolutely no obligation." ("Absolutely" is a favorite word; as is "guaranteed," and, *ad nauseum*, "great.")
- "You can earn big money fast, regardless of your lack of experience or training."
- The program or business opportunity is offered for a "short time only."
- The deal is a "sure thing" that will deliver "security for years to come."
- You will reap "financial rewards by working part time or at home."
- "You'll be coached each step of the way to success."
- "The program has worked for thousands of other participants—even the organizers" (Source: United States Federal Trade Commission, "The Seminar Pitch," 1998).

Promises of quick, easy money can be powerful lures. If you buy into a franchise or business opportunity at a seminar, you may find that the products and information you purchased are worthless and that your money is gone. Don't get hit by the pitch—the fast pitch, the curve ball that will make you strike out in the business opportunity game.

Business opportunity scams and schemes really hurt. They inflict major economic hardship. Generally, when promises of profits seem to be exceptionally attractive or when there is a hard sell to sign up immediately or risk losing the opportunity, just say no, walk away, or hang up. Before you make a commitment ask: "Could these 'biz opp' offers be out for your coffers?" "Are these business opportunities really flopportunities?" What you may see as the knock of opportunity may knock you down and out.

Charity Fundraising

Telefunders and Bogus Charities

Beggars can be choosers, and senior citizens are their first choice when it comes to charity fraud. This area of telemarketing fraud, sometimes referred to as "telefunding," targets consumers, very often older citizens, willing to donate money to spurious charitable causes. The telefunders, often employing prize promotions, either raise money for bogus charities, misrepresent the amount of donations that go to a bona-fide charity, or make other material misrepresentations about how the donor's contribution will be used.

There are thousands of recognized charities that solicit for contributions. Many are legitimate, but not all of them are. A legitimate charity readily provides information about its mission, how your donation will be used, and proof that your contribution is tax-deductible. The problem: Some phony charities use names that sound like, or materials and logos that look like, those of respected national and international organizations.

Throughout the year, and especially during the holiday seasons, you probably receive appeals by mail, e-mail, or telephone urging you to contribute to any number of good causes. But the U.S. Postal Inspection Service and the FTC warn those who want to give that there are plenty of fraud operators out there who are scheming for your money— and the last thing on their mind is charity. Not only do such come-ons bilk you of donations, but they also put money you intended for a worthwhile cause into the coffers of con artists.

CHARITABLE DONATIONS: GIVE OR TAKE

Over a decade ago it was estimated that over $1.5 billion of the amount raised for charities in the U.S. is misused or ends up in the pockets of fraudulent solicitors. Much of this money comes from senior citizens. It pays to be cautious when making a donation. Asking questions about the nature and activities of the organization is the only way you can be sure the money you contribute will support worthwhile causes (Source: Seniors.gov, "Charitable Donations," 1991).

PAID FUND RAISERS

Many legitimate charities find it more efficient to utilize professional fund-raising operations to handle large-scale mailings, telephone drives, and other solicitations rather than using their own paid staff or volunteers. These professional fund raisers are in business to generate money, and can legally keep a portion of the funds they collect. If you are solicited for a donation, ask if the caller is a paid fund raiser and what percentage of your donation he or she will retain as compensation for their services. If you are not comfortable with the numbers, you may want to consider other options for donating.

CHARITY CHECKLIST

But just how do you know who is legitimate and who is not? If you are thinking about donating to one of the more than 700,000 federally recognized charities soliciting for contributions, the FTC advises taking certain precautions. To guard against being taken advantage of, consider the following guidelines and precautions to ensure that your donations will benefit the individuals and organizations you intend to support.

- Be wary of appeals that endeavor to tug at your heartstrings, especially pleas involving patriotism and catastrophic current events.
- Ask for identification. Many states require paid fund raisers to immediately identify themselves as such.
- Ask for the exact name of the charity for which they are soliciting.
- Watch out for similar sounding names. Do not be fooled by names that closely resemble those of legitimate, respected orga-

nizations. Sound-alike names are a common tactic of phony charities.

- If the solicitor claims that the charity will support local organizations, call these local groups to verify those claims. Confirm that the organization is aware of the solicitation and has authorized the use of its name. If not, you are likely dealing with a fraudulent solicitor.
- If in doubt, or if you're unfamiliar with the charity, ask the caller to send you written information about the organization—including the charity's name, address, and telephone number. Ask for its annual report and or financial statements. If the solicitor is not willing to provide this information, you should be highly suspicious.
- Ask how your donation will be distributed—what percentage of your contribution will go directly to the organization's cause. What percentage will be allocated to cover the charity's administrative costs? If the proportion is highly skewed in favor of the latter, be skeptical.
- Be suspicious of solicitors who say they will accept your donation in cash only. (Con artists want cash so there will be no paper trail for authorities to follow.)
- Be very wary of any proposal to send a courier to pick up your donation, or to use an overnight delivery service to send it.
- *Never* send cash gifts that can be lost or stolen. For security and tax record purposes, it's best to pay by check. Use the official full name of the charity—not an acronym—on your check.
- Make checks payable to the beneficiary organization only—*never* to an individual solicitor.
- As always, do not give out personal or financial information over the phone. Do not provide any credit card or bank account information until you have reviewed all information from the charity and made the decision to donate.
- Watch out for solicitors who insist that you act immediately. Refuse any high-pressure appeals. Legitimate fund raisers will not push you to donate.
- Do not give in to solicitors who continually call after you have refused to donate. Legitimate organizations will take no for an answer and remove your name from their call lists as you direct.

- Beware of organizations that use meaningless terms to suggest they are tax exempt charities. The fact that an organization has a tax "identification number" does not mean it is a charity. All nonprofit and for profit organizations must have an Employer Identification Number (EIN). Any qualified individual can easily obtain one from the IRS.
- Understand that contributions made to a "tax exempt" organization are not necessarily "tax deductible." Know the difference. Tax exempt means the organization does not have to pay taxes. Tax deductible means you can deduct your contribution on your federal income tax return. Even though an organization is tax exempt, your contribution may not be tax deductible.
- If deductibility is important to you, ask for a receipt showing the amount of your contribution and stating that it is tax deductible. A receipt that instructs you to "keep this receipt for your tax records" means only that.
- Be skeptical if someone thanks you for a pledge you cannot remember having made. If you have any doubt whether you have made a pledge or previously contributed, check your records. Be on the alert for invoices claiming you've made a pledge when you know you haven't. Some unscrupulous solicitors use this approach to get your money.
- Consider the costs. When purchasing merchandise or tickets for special events, or when receiving free goods in exchange for giving, remember that these items cost money and generally are paid for out of your contribution. Although this can be an effective fund-raising tool, in the end, less money may be available for the charity's cause.
- Be wary of "guaranteed" winnings or prizes in exchange for a contribution. You should never have to donate money to be eligible to win. This is just another form of the advance-fee scam.

If you feel overwhelmed by direct mail requests for donations, you can help to reduce the number of those solicitations. Include a note with your donation directing the charity not to rent, sell, or exchange your personal information and donation history. You can also ask a nonprofit organization to limit its donation requests to once or twice a year. If the organization fails to honor your requests, you may want to find a different charity to support.

Many charities use your donations wisely. Others may spend much of your contribution on administrative expenses or increased fund-raising efforts. Some may misrepresent their fund-raising intentions or solicit for phony causes. Do not be discouraged from giving others a helping hand, but be cautious and take care to make sure that the organization you are giving to is a legitimate charity, and not one that was set up for the sole purpose of bilking the public (Sources: Seniors.gov, "Charitable Donations," 2001; United States Federal Trade Commission, "Protecting Yourself," 2003).

Credit Cards

Senior Citizens and Credit Card Fraud

There are three primary types of fraud involving credit cards that can victimize the senior citizen; we will examine them in this order:

1. Stolen cards and/or numbers resulting in fraudulent usage of the cardholder's account;
2. phony credit card offers—an actual card may never be involved but an advance-fee surely will be; and
3. credit card "loss protection" insurance.

Regarding senior citizens and credit cards, the National Consumer Law Center has said that:

> Credit card payment problems are the leading cause of Chapter 7 consumer bankruptcy filings. Many low-income consumers take advantage of minimum payment provisions, multiple opportunities to obtain new cards, "teaser" rates, and high credit limits to meet pressing financial needs. Older Americans are by no means immune from this problem. Since 1993, more than a million people aged 50 and older have filed for bankruptcy. In a recent survey of these senior bankruptcy filers, the number one reason cited for filing bankruptcy was loss of jobs, followed by medical debt problems. The third most important reason cited for filing bankruptcy was to escape creditors' (most commonly credit card issuers) harassing debt collection tactics. In addition to the more than three billion credit card offers that are mailed to con-

sumers each year, credit cards are advertised everywhere. While this increase in access to credit for low and moderate income debtors is generally a good thing, many debtors, including many seniors, have not been educated to resist the overwhelming marketing of credit which has pervaded our society in recent years. Effective financial education may help debtors avoid new problems in the future [National Consumer Law Center,"Advice for Seniors," 1999].

Stolen Credit Cards or Card Numbers

Many of the elderly in our society were brought up in a socioeconomic climate where consumers traditionally paid cash for all merchandise and services. Today, more and more senior citizens prefer to use credit cards which are more convenient but not necessarily safer. Credit cards, or, increasingly, credit card numbers, can be readily stolen from the unwary or unsuspecting senior. Although financial liability may be limited, the emotional stress can be beyond measure.

The companies which issue credit cards are continuously developing and implementing means to assure the security of and protection for their users and their cards. Many now include a photograph of the cardholder so that criminals might be thwarted in making face-to-face purchases with a stolen card. More and more credit card companies are incorporating holograms, coded imprints, or hidden images or devices which make it extremely difficult for counterfeiters to duplicate cards the companies have issued. However, despite these technological improvements, the senior citizen—or anyone else—can still become a victim of credit card fraud.

AVOIDING FRAUD FROM STOLEN CARDS OR ACCOUNT NUMBERS

According to the FTC, "Credit and charge card fraud costs cardholders and issuers hundreds of millions of dollars each year. While theft is the most obvious form of fraud, it can occur in other ways. For example, someone may use your card number without your knowledge. It's not always possible to prevent credit or charge card fraud from happening. But there are a few steps you can take to make it more difficult for a crook to capture your card or card numbers and minimize the possibility" (United States Federal Trade Commission, "Avoiding Credit and Charge Card Fraud," 1997).

Guard your card numbers very carefully. Remember, a thief does not need your card itself to charge goods or services to your account; they need only your card number. This can be readily used to make purchases over the telephone, on the Internet, or through the mail. Duplicating a card with your number can be done also, although technology has made that increasingly challenging for would-be thieves.

Here are some tips from AARP and the FTC to help you protect yourself from credit card fraud.

- Do not leave cards, purchase receipts, or statements lying around—even in your home. Do not leave them in your car.
- Secure all credit card bills and receipts. These can divulge your credit card number to whomever may find them. Thieves ("dumpster divers") rummage through trash to find discarded receipts, or credit card and bank statements. Seniors who live in apartment buildings or condominiums where trash is placed in common areas to await removal must be particularly careful in this respect.
- Never routinely lend your card(s) to anyone. They may not be as careful.
- Sign your new credit cards as soon as you receive them.
- If convenient, carry your cards separately from your wallet or purse in a zippered compartment, a card holder, or other secure repository.
- Do not carry more cards than you would routinely need and use. There is rarely a good reason to carry more than one or two credit cards; the more you carry and or display, the greater the risk of loss or theft.
- Keep a record of your account numbers, their expiration dates, and the phone number and address of each company in a secure place.
- Be vigilant in handling your credit cards. Try to keep the card under surveillance at all times. Observe your card during each transaction, and retrieve it as quickly as possible. It is not unheard of for a dishonest salesclerk to make an extra imprint of a credit card and then sell the information or use it to make personal charges.
- Be aware of persons around you when you are using your card.

Shield the card from the eyes of someone who could be looking over your shoulder. Thieves have trained themselves to memorize card numbers. They may even be carrying small cameras. You need not be paranoid, but you do need to be alert and careful.

- Always check the amounts on your charge slip before you sign it. If there is any dispute, refuse to sign. *Never* sign a blank receipt or one with any blank spaces; additional charges can be inserted. When you sign a receipt, draw a line through any blank spaces in which an amount could be written.
- Assure that each and every credit card transaction is complete and correct at the time it is made. Dishonest merchants—particularly those you might encounter while traveling—may alter your charge slip after you have signed it. If you determine later that any were altered, notify the credit card company immediately.
- Assure that all incorrect receipts are voided and destroyed; also destroy any unneeded duplicate copies.
- Save all receipts to compare with monthly billing statements.
- Open monthly statements promptly and reconcile the account, just as you would your checking account. Carefully review the statements to confirm that you made or authorized each of the purchases indicated. If you note any that you know you did not make or authorize, immediately report these to the credit card issuer.
- Notify card companies at least thirty days in advance of a change in your mailing address.
- Do not write your account number on a postcard or on the outside of an envelope. You really should not write it on checks either, as usually requested on payment remittance portions of many bills.
- *Never* write your personal identification (PIN) number on your credit card. With this number and the card, a potential thief can easily access the funds in your bank account using an ATM.
- Do not provide a telemarketer—or anyone—with your credit card number unless you are certain that he or she represents a reputable business or unless you have called them to initiate an

order. A con artist will attempt to sell you fictitious goods or services as a device to elicit your credit card number.

- Be careful of this common ploy: You respond to a mailing asking you to call a long-distance number to claim a free trip or bargain-priced travel package. You are told you must join a "travel club" first and you are asked for a credit card number for billing purposes. The catch: You will indeed be billed! Charges you did not authorize will appear on your statement. You never get to take a trip, but you have been taken for a ride!

- Be especially wary if you receive a phone call from someone who claims to be a representative of a vendor, a bank, or even the card issuer. They may state that they are from the "security department" and they want to "activate the protection feature" on the holder's card. Or they may advise you that there has been a "mix-up" with your credit card. They will request the holder's credit card number and its expiration date to "verify our records." Among scam operators, this is known as "phishing. " As reported in the media, it has recently become a prime method of identity theft. (We will discuss it again in a later section.)

- Another scam involves your checking account number. It typically begins with a letter advertising easy credit approval or low credit card interest rates. When consumers call, they are asked for their checking account number, supposedly as part of the "approval" process (Sources: AARP, "Credit Card Fraud," 2002; United States Federal Trade Commission, "Avoiding Credit and Charge Card Fraud," 1997).

Phony Credit Card Offers

Do you have poor credit? Are you having trouble obtaining a major credit card because of a poor credit rating or other reason? Beware of con artists and their offers of phony credit cards or the credit repair scam. Typically, the promoters of these phony card offers indicate that your card is "pre-approved" and that it can be obtained "without any credit check." If you do have a poor credit history, be skeptical if you are offered such a deal. Some seemingly legitimate programs to extend you credit will end up costing you a great deal of money, and you will not get the credit cards that you think are being offered.

If those credit card companies get you a card at all, it will be a "secured" bank credit card with high up-front "application" fees that requires you to deposit and maintain a balance of several hundred dollars in a savings account or it will be a "catalog" card from a business that you probably never heard of. You can apply for a secured credit card by yourself. To find banks that do not charge application fees for secured cards, check the BankRate web site at www.bankrate.com. Such companies try to get consumers to get a credit card by encouraging them apply using financial information of other people with good credit histories. Be aware that it is a criminal act to apply for credit using someone else's name and credit history! Remember instant credit is like instant coffee; both require a measure of liquidity!

The scam can start with an e-mail, phone call, postcard, or a letter—still the principal means of contact—which claims that for a fee (always payable in advance and which typically ranges from $35 to $200) you can obtain an unsecured major credit card with a credit limit of $5,000 or more. For your money you are likely to receive a plastic "catalog card" that is not a bank card and can be used only to pay for purchases from the catalog of a specific merchandiser, which is likely owned by the company that issued the card and which may offer products or merchandise that may be of absolutely no interest or use to you. This concept of a "single-use" credit card is not new, but recently unwary victims of this scam are being sold these cards by con artists who misrepresent them as being all-purpose bank credit cards. At times, the deception is magnified by the fact that the merchandise in the catalog from which you must choose your purchases is either inferior or grossly overpriced. Be sure that you know the specific purpose and any limitations of the card you are being offered. If you are not satisfied with the information provided by those marketing the cards, do not pay the required fee; otherwise, you may become a victim. Such credit card scams are another trap for senior citizens in difficult or desperate financial circumstances. The U.S. Postal Inspection Service affirms that "Seniors can protect themselves against the phony 'one-shot' credit card offers by being very careful when they are considering opening a new credit card account" (United States Postal Inspection Service, "Credit Card Schemes," no date).

PROTECTING YOURSELF

The FTC has taken action against companies that deceptively advertise major credit cards through television, newspapers, and mailings. The advertisements may offer unsecured credit cards, secured credit cards, or not specify a card type. They usually lead you to believe you can get a credit card simply by calling the number shown. To avoid being victimized, look for the following signs:

- Offers of easy credit. No one can guarantee to get you credit. Before deciding whether to give you a credit card, legitimate credit providers retrieve and examine your credit report;
- a required "security deposit," "processing," or "application" fee—payable in advance of course;
- credit cards offered by "credit repair" companies or "credit clinics";
- or directives to call to a 900-number for which you are billed for just making the call. A recorded message may instruct you to give your name and address to receive a credit application, or send you a list of banks offering secured cards—a list available from any telephone book. It also may tell you to call another 900 number—at an additional toll charge—for more information—yet *another* scam!

These deceptive advertisements for credit cards often leave out such essential information as:

- There are eligibility requirements such as income or age;
- there is a relatively high annual fee;
- or the secured card has a higher than average interest rate on any balance.

In a report released on August 6, 2002, Carol McKay of the National Consumers League stated: "Phony credit cards offers have become the #1 telemarketing fraud, accounting for more than a quarter of all telemarketing fraud reported to NFIC and outpacing prizes and sweepstakes scams, which usually top the list. Targeting consumers with financial problems, these crooks typically ask for payment upfront by arranging to debit victims' bank accounts. They guarantee you a credit card, even if you have a bad credit history.... But the only real guarantee is that you'll lose your money. Most legitimate credit card issuers don't charge in advance, and if there is a fee to get a card, it is usually very small, not the hundreds of dollars that con artists demand" (McKay, "Credit Card Scams," 2002).

Telemarketing is not the only marketing means, however. In their publication "Advice for Seniors About Credit Cards," the National Consumer Law Center (NCLC) reports: "More than three billion credit card offers are mailed to consumers each year. These offers can be very enticing. Nearly every offer promises some special benefit to a new card. In some cases, the offer is for a low rate. In others, no annual fee is promised. These offers, however, never discuss the down-side of a new card or the potential risks" (National Consumer Law Center, "Advice for Seniors About Credit Cards," 1999).

THE GOLD AND PLATINUM CARD FLEECE

Beware of promotions for "gold" or "platinum" cards that promise to get you credit and or repair your credit rating even if your credit history has been very poor. What customers do get is a gold or platinum colored plastic card (cardboard if you pay less)—but it's not a credit card at all. It comes with a catalog of overpriced junk merchandise. Consumers can use the card to buy these products only and only if they put cash down first. In other words, the card is pretty much good for nothing. You may also find that ads for these cards direct you to call a 900 number for more information.

Credit Card Loss Protection Offers: They're the Real Steal

You may get a call from a person who firmly asserts that you need credit card "loss protection" insurance. Do not buy the pitch—and definitely do not buy the so-called loss protection insurance. It is worthless! It is yet another scam. The promoters, who prey on the elderly and young adults, scare consumers with false stories, telling them that they are liable for far more than $50 in unauthorized charges on their credit card accounts and that they need credit card loss protection because computer hackers can access their credit card numbers through the Internet and charge thousands of dollars to their account.

This type of fraud affects senior citizens in particular. The National Consumer's League reported that a recent study of telemarketing fraud showed that 71 percent of the credit card loss protection plan complaints received by the National Fraud Information Center (NFIC) were made by consumers age 50 and older (Source: United States Federal Trade Commission, "Fraud Against Seniors," 2000).

These scam artists are simply lying to get people to buy specious and worthless protection and insurance coverage. If you did not authorize a charge, simply do not pay it. Follow your credit card issuer's procedures for disputing charges you have not authorized. The FTC has confirmed that such offers are popular among fraudulent promoters who are trying to exploit consumers' uncertainty. Its advice: Remember that federal law limits your liability for unauthorized changes to $50, so "ditch the pitch" for credit card loss protection (Source: United States Federal Trade Commission, "Credit Card Loss Protection Offers," 2000).

Credit Repair

Credit Repair Scams

In the past several years, the FTC has taken legal action against numerous companies that deceptively advertised credit repair services on the Internet. In one of the most recent cases, on August 11, 2003, Nationwide Credit Repair, one of the country's largest credit repair operations, agreed to pay more than $1.15 million in consumer redress to settle FTC charges that it violated federal law by engaging in fraudulent credit repair activities sold through a multilevel marketing organization. Their nationwide network of approximately 50,000 sales representatives regularly told consumers that they were able to remove all negative items such as bankruptcies, foreclosures, and late-payments from individual credit reports.

To convince consumers that they actually could do this, they purported to use a "one-of-a-kind" computer disk that they claimed could search for and identify errors in the entry process used by the credit reporting agencies to enter negative items onto consumers' credit reports. They told consumers that the computer disk was so unique and amazing that it had been valued at more than $200 million in an independent appraisal, and had once been insured by Lloyd's of London for $15 million. They allegedly also told consumers that the credit reporting agencies themselves wanted the disk so badly that one of them offered $10 million for it. The Commission's complaint alleged that all of these representations were false and deceptive and that the defendants did not have a computer disk or any type of software program that was able to do the things they represented to consumers.

According to the Commission's complaint, the defendants' credit repair "service" simply entailed mailing letters to the major credit reporting agencies challenging each negative item that appears on a particular consumer's credit report—an action any consumer can take without cost. The complaint alleged that, just like any consumer, the defendants were not able to remove negative items from credit reports that are accurate, verifiable, and current.

In addition to these core misrepresentations, the Commission's complaint alleged that the defendants violated federal law by requiring consumers to pay in advance for the credit repair service; by misrepresenting the terms of their 110 percent money back guarantee; by making untrue and misleading statements about their customer's credit standing to the credit reporting agencies; and by failing to provide their customers with a written notice as required by federal law (Sources: United States Federal Trade Commission, "National Credit Repair," 2003; and *Fighting Consumer Fraud*, 1997).

You see the advertisements in newspapers, on TV, and on the Internet; you hear them on the radio. You may even get calls from telemarketers offering these types of services. However, such advertisements may violate Section 5 of the Federal Trade Commission Act which prohibits deceptive advertising. Credit repair advertisements, products, and services may also violate the Credit Repair Organizations Act (CROA), the federal Telemarketing Sales Rule, and all applicable criminal statutes—federal and state.

The Claims

Your mail and e-mail may also be filled with offers from such services and from credit "clinics" that make these common claims:

• "Credit problems? No problem!" There are potential problems here for the unwary—*big* problems!
• "We can clean up your credit history!" Be alert if you are told that accurate information will be changed or erased, or that only the credit repair company can remove old or inaccurate information. Such claims are patently false. The promoters of these scams cannot deliver.
• "We can erase bad credit information—*guaranteed!*" The truth is that no one can erase bad credit information from your report if it is accurate.
• "Only we can remove old or inaccurate information!" If there are legitimate errors on your report or information that is old, you can take steps to correct the report yourself without paying a lot of money to one of these companies. "Legitimate errors" means that the information is inaccurate, not just that it is information you do not like or not want divulged. "Old information" means credit information that is older than seven years, or bankruptcy information older than ten years.
• "We can remove bankruptcies, judgments, liens, and bad loans from your credit file *forever!*" It cannot be done on demand.
• "The information on your report is accurate but we'll erase it anyway!" If this involves lying to the credit reporting agency, it is illegal.
• "You can create a new credit identity—legally." You may get a new identity—a number in a state or federal prison!

Credit Counseling Organizations

The for-profit credit repair operations should not be confused with nonprofit credit counseling services that help consumers reduce their debts and pay bills on time. Many consumers seek help from non-profit credit counseling organizations in managing their debt or repairing damaged credit. In October 2003, the Federal Trade Commission, the Internal Revenue Service, and state regulators issued a consumer alert for those seeking assistance from tax-exempt credit counseling organizations. They urged consumers to be cautious when choosing a credit counseling organization. Many credit counseling organizations provide valuable advice, education, and assistance to those seeking to better manage their debt.

But an increasing number of complaints to federal and state agencies indicate that some organizations are engaging in questionable activities. These regulators are concerned that some credit counseling organizations using questionable practices may seek tax-exempt status in order to circumvent state and federal consumer protection laws. State and federal statutes regulating credit counseling agencies often do not apply to tax-exempt organizations. Many of these groups provide a valuable service to consumers, but some use the tax code to skirt consumer-protection laws.

Unscrupulous credit counseling groups, exploiting gaps in the law, take unfair advantage of desperate taxpayers struggling with financial problems. Consumers need to be wary of the "quick fixes" offered by some of these organizations. They need to be careful not to lose even more money to someone offering a quick and easy way to fix credit problems. Very simply, consumers seeking help must take some common sense precautions. Consumers can help protect themselves from deceptive credit counseling practices by following these tips:

- Check that the organization will help you manage your finances better through counseling and education.
- Carefully read through any written agreement that a credit counseling organization offers. It should describe in detail the services to be performed; the payment terms for these services, including their total cost; how long it will take to achieve results; any guarantees offered; and the organization's business name and address.
- Beware of high fees or required "voluntary contributions" that, with high monthly service charges, may add to your debt and defeat your efforts to pay your bills. It is illegal to represent that negative information, such as bankruptcy, can be removed from your credit report. Promises to "help you get out of debt easily" are a red flag.
- Make sure that your creditors are willing to work with the agency you choose. If they are, follow up with those creditors regularly to make sure your debt is being paid off.
- Check with state agencies and your local Better Business Bureau to find out about a specific credit counseling organization's record.

The Consumer Credit Counseling Service assists consumers who have problems in paying their bills—before their good credit ratings suffer. Your local Consumer Credit office can help you work out flexible payment plans to make debt repayment more feasible. Call 1-800-388-CCCS for an interactive recording that will provide you with the phone number of the office nearest to you.

Advice

If you are a senior citizen (or anyone) who has credit problems and is trying to find a way out, the glowing promises are aimed at you. These scam artists are doing a thriving business offering their so-called credit repair services which—for a fee ranging from $50 to $1,000 or more—promise to "fix" an unfavorable credit report. Be very wary if you are asked for a large sum of money in advance. The problem: It is illegal to charge an up-front fee for credit repair and such companies cannot require you to pay their fee until they have delivered the promised services. The truth is, they cannot deliver. A "money-back guarantee" will not protect you if the company is dishonest. After they accept the illegal up-front fees, they do nothing to improve the applicant's credit report. They often simply abscond—vanish with the money (Source: United States Federal Trade Commission, "Credit Repair: Self-Help," 1998). Remember that only time and good credit habits will restore your credit worthiness.

Dance Studios

Dancing can provide senior citizens with diversion, exercise, companionship, and a great deal of pleasure. However, dance lessons can prove far more costly than the elderly person had planned or expected, especially when they do not know how to protect themselves against some dance studios' unscrupulous sales practices.

To help make consumers aware of some of these deceptive tactics, in February 1989 the Federal Trade Commission issued the brochure "Dancing for Dollars"; the publication is no longer available but its content is summarized in this chapter and presented in more detail in the sources cited. The brochure described several of the techniques that dance studio sales staffs might use to pressure potential students into spending more money on contracts than they intended or could afford. In its brochure the FTC provided tips to protect yourself from such tactics.

Sales Techniques

If you are considering, or are already taking, dance lessons, you should understand the sales techniques that some studios may use to persuade you to sign up, or to keep you coming back. Be wary if a dance studio tries to utilize any of the following high-pressure sales tactics and prohibited techniques in an attempt to induce you to purchase lessons or extend contracts:

- "Relay salesmanship" or consecutive sales talks by more than one sales representative; the objective of this tactic is to put you under heavy pressure to sign a contract, and persuade you to buy lessons that you may later realize you did not want or cannot afford;
- requests you to sign an incomplete contract—*never* do this!;
- misrepresentation of the total cost of the program;
- false claims that dancing prowess will enable you to attain an enhanced degree social status;
- and flattery.

Some studio instructors, using such tactics, exploit a student's emotions or personal vulnerabilities to oversell lessons. Sometimes, when students refuse to purchase additional prepaid lessons, instructors will embarrass or neglect them in classes, or assign them to a less skilled instructor. Awareness about the possible use of these sales techniques can help you avoid potential problems. In addition, you may avoid problems if you comparison shop for dance lessons.

Contracts

As a precaution against buying long-term, prepaid contracts, consumers are advised not to sign contracts—*any contracts*—immediately, especially if they may have concerns about the reputation or stability of the business, or are asked to prepay a large amount of money for a "lifetime" membership, an "exclusive club" membership, or a dance/cruise package offer. You are cautioned to take adequate time to consider the move and discuss such contracts with a friend, family member, or even an attorney before making any commitment. Beware of signing a long-term contract which requires you to prepay thousands of dollars for lessons you may be unable to complete or wish to cancel. Before entering into such an agreement, offer to pay in advance for only a specified number of lessons to determine if you are satisfied with them. You are advised to start small and be cautious. Try it out first to see if you like it!

You may get a discount if you make a large prepayment on a long-term contract, but it will have little value if later you are unable to take the classes, you want to cancel them, or the studio closes before your lessons are completed. Only a few states require studios to post bonds to protect consumers' prepayments. Even if the contract offers you a refund or cancellation option, you may be unable to get your money back in the event that the studio should suddenly close or go bankrupt (a common experience) or its refund check bounces. Prepay only as much as you can afford to lose. Typically dance lessons at private, commercial studios are relatively expensive compared to those offered through local senior citizen centers—which usually are free or quite inexpensive and do not require a long-term commitment.

OVERLAPPING CONTRACTS

Some studio instructors try to convince their students during the course of the initial lessons to sign additional contracts before completing those in effect. These overlapping contracts may obligate you to purchase additional lessons that extend beyond your means, interest, physical fitness, or even your life expectancy!

ORAL PROMISES

Before you sign, carefully review the contract and insist that it clearly state in writing all oral promises made to you including:

- The cost per hour of each lesson;
- will the lessons be private or group;
- the number of lessons you are agreeing to;

- the aggregate cost;
- your rights regarding cancellation and refund; (these are important in case you change your mind about lessons, relocate, or become ill);
- and any prepayment protections if required by state law (Sources: The Consumer Law Page, "Dance Studios," 1992; Crime Watch, "How to Protect Yourself," 1996).

Tips to Protect Yourself

There are two primary ways in which you can protect yourself. Before signing or renewing a contract for dance lessons, consider taking the following measures:

1. Research the company. Confirm that the dance studio holds, and prominently exhibits, a current license from the state and or a local jurisdiction. Try to determine if the studio is accredited or approved by any professional organization(s), and how long it has been in operation. Request references from persons in your community. Contact your local Better Business Bureau (BBB), your state's Attorney General's office, and even the FTC to determine whether any complaints or lawsuits are pending against the business. If its headquarters are located out-of-state, you may wish to contact the appropriate agencies and authorities in the state of jurisdiction.
2. Determine your legal rights. As an additional precaution, when you do contact your local or state consumer protection office, confirm your legal rights under local or state law with regard to maximum costs for contracts, cancellation and refunds, requirements for bonding, and the "cooling off" rule which will give you a specified number of days to reconsider your decision after you sign your contract. Determine that the contract you are offered clearly and conspicuously describes your legal rights under the laws of your state or locality.

Direct Mail

Frauds and Scams in Your Mailbox

Many swindles are perpetrated through the U.S. mail. Marketing solicitations of all types are among the 180 billion pieces of mail the U.S. Postal Service delivers each year. While most are for legitimate products, services, and charities, others definitely are not. They are scams, sent by bandits to capitalize on your financial needs, naiveté, generosity, optimism, or everyone's fantasy of hitting the jackpot. Fraudulent promoters sometimes use the language and advertising techniques of legitimate mail-order businesses and respected publications as covers to promote their own illegal schemes. Certain key words are used alone or in combinations to entice the reader to respond favorably to an advertisement. Identifying the danger signs can limit losses and protect consumers.

The U.S. Postal Inspection Service has reported that they responded to 66,000 mail-fraud complaints in 2001, and postal inspectors had already responded to more than 68,000 complaints by mid 2002—an increase of 27 percent. Unfortunately, it is nearly impossible to stop the delivery of unsolicited mail. The Postal Service can only help you prevent the delivery of sexually-oriented advertising and pornographic material (Sources: United States Postal Inspection Service, *2001 Annual Report of Inspections*, 2001; and *2002 Annual Report of Inspections*, 2002).

Government Look-Alike Mail

This is a pervasive and insidious tactic of mail-fraud promoters. You might receive a manila envelope in the mail or by a private carrier service which, at first glance, may appear to be an official document that has come from a government agency. The name and address of the sender might confirm that impression, and an official-looking facsimile seal will be very convincing. To make the mailing look even more authentic, messages such as "Important Notice," "Official Business," or "Open Immediately" are often displayed on the envelopes in large type and red ink. Such mailings are carefully designed to be deceptive and confusing, but, primarily, to get attention. They are often illegal. Rather than official government documents, they typically contain sweepstakes promotions or requests for donations to bogus charities.

The problems caused by these look-alike mailings led to the passage of the Deceptive Mailings Prevention Act of 1990. This law (Title 39, United States Code, Sections 3001(f) and (g)), places certain restrictions on these types of mailings and, under the Act, they are no longer permitted, unless:

- The sending entity actually has a certifiable government connection, approval, or endorsement;
- the material and the envelope it is sent in bear a prominent notice as prescribed by the U.S. Postal Service which disclaims such connection, approval, or endorsement;
- or the material is contained in a publication purchased or requested by, and mailed to, the addressee.

If you are uncertain about a mailing, carefully examine the envelope and the material enclosed. If the mailing entity is not being totally deceptive, it should be readily apparent whether or not the mailing is artful government look-alike material from a private organization not connected with any government agency or program. If you receive such an unsolicited mailing and the required disclaimer as described is not present, advise your local postmaster (Source: United States Postal Inspection Service, "Government Look-Alike Mail," no date).

Catch the Bandit in Your Mailbox

What can you do to protect yourself? The FTC says "Boot the bandit out of your mailbox!" Develop good habits, including a healthy skepticism. Thoroughly and carefully read all of the material you receive in the mail. Determine the legitimacy of the offer before signing anything or sending a remittance. If you are tempted to send any money for a product or service that is being touted, and it is a company you have never heard of, take your time and check it out.

How can you tell the difference between an offer from a legitimate organization and one from an outfit that is just out to steal your money? It is not an easy task. Sham promotions and solicitations are slick looking, skillfully written, and can be very convincing. But according to the

FTC and the U.S. Postal Inspection Service a savvy consumer can learn to see through a scam and avoid becoming victimized by heeding the following suggestions:

- Discard any solicitation that asks for payment for a "free" gift. If it is free or a gift, you should not have to pay. Free is *free*!
- Toss any solicitation that does not clearly identify the sender and includes a street address and a phone number.
- Pay particular attention if you are directed to call a toll-free number for more information about a product or service. Often, when you dial a toll-free number in response to a bogus solicitation, you are surreptitiously connected to a pay-per-call 900-number. Then you are charged to listen to a promotion for a product, service, prize, contest, or sweepstakes.
- Ignore any solicitation that looks like a government document and suggests contest winnings or unclaimed assets are yours for a small fee. The government does *not* solicit money from citizens.
- Disregard any solicitation for a "prepaid" or "special deal" with a nominal monthly "processing fee." You will save yourself years of monthly payments for products or services you no longer want or could pay less for elsewhere.
- Beware of such assertions as: "Final offer—you must send your money by tomorrow!" "Last chance!" or "A bargain that nobody else can match!"
- Be suspicious about extraordinary promises or unusually high monetary returns. The swindlers rely on human greed to accept such promises at face value.
- Be cautious and do not rush into anything until you investigate.
- Always read the fine print carefully. *Very carefully*!! (Source: United States Federal Trade Commission Bureau of Consumer Protection, "Catch the Bandit in Your Mailbox," no date).

"Do Not Call" Registries

Senior citizens plagued by unwelcome and intrusive telemarketers now have a new resource available to largely eliminate such nuisance calls—"do not call" registries. Nearly fifty million consumers had already registered with the National Do Not Call Registry by mid September 2003; nine million of these names had been transferred from state registries. Many others had put their names and telephone numbers on the Direct Marketing Association's Telemarketing Preference Service list, or on individual company lists.

A do not call registry does not prevent calls from political organizations, charities, or telephone surveyors. Also, telemarketers can call individuals with whom they have an existing business relationship; an existing business relationship includes voluntarily giving your phone number or address to a business when you make a purchase or redeem a coupon for an offer of a free sample of a product (read the fine print!).

Consumer protection officials are advising that identity thieves and rip-off artists, not missing any opportunities, have seized on and begun to take advantage of the popularity of these registries—particularly the national registry—to trick consumers into divulging personal information or to con them out of fees to register for them. The FTC has warned consumers to be wary of scams related to these registries.

How the Scams Work

If you receive a call asking you to "confirm your registration" on the National Do Not Call Registry, you are the target of a scam according to the FTC, the federal agency that created and maintains it. The phony "official" who asks for your personal information, supposedly to verify that you are, or want to be on the list, is a con artist who could use your personal information to run up debts in your name or otherwise steal your identity. Some of these operators are pushing a similar scam through spam e-mail.

The FTC affirms that once a consumer becomes listed on any actual registry, there is absolutely no further need to submit or confirm any personal information. None is requested to register initially; the individual's name and telephone number is the *only* information required. No government official—state or federal—will call people to put them on a registry or confirm that they are on one.

The FTC reminds consumers that all registrations on the national registry can be done free, and confirmed at any time, online at: http://www.donotcall.gov/ (Sources: United States Federal Trade Commission, "FTC Warns Consumers," 2003, "Fraud on the Line," 2003, and "Scam Artists Use Do Not Call," 2002). They can do this them-selves—directly, or through some state governments, quickly, easily, and securely—but *never* through private companies. However, scams involv-ing payment of fees to register popped up almost as soon as the national registry was announced, and consumers began receiving calls from pri-vate companies soliciting them to register using their services. On August 21, 2003, the FTC warned consumers not to be duped into responding to national advertisements urging them to call "1-800-DONOTCALL." Consumers calling this commercial number are con-nected, for a $2.95 fee, to the FTC's Do Not Call sign-up system. Connecting to the FTC's sign-up procedure through this commercial number takes approximately seven minutes. Signing up directly on the FTC's online site, at the URL shown above, is free and takes less than two minutes.

"The FTC does not allow private companies or other third parties to 'pre-register' consumers for the[national] registry. Web sites or phone solicitors that claim they can or will register a consumer's name or phone number on a national list—especially those who charge a fee—are a scam" (Source: United States Federal Trade Commission, "FTC Warns Consumers," 2003, and "Fraud on the Line," 2003).

Avoiding the "Do Not Call" Scams

The FTC's Bureau of Consumer Protection says consumers can avoid these scams. Here's how:

- Keep information about your bank accounts and credit cards to yourself—including the numbers—unless you know who you're dealing with.
- Never share your Social Security number with a person you don't know.
- Don't share your personal information if someone calls you claim-ing to represent a "Do Not Call" registry, an organization to stop fraud or even the FTC itself.
- If you get such a call, either hang up immediately or write down the caller's organization and phone number and report it to the FTC at www.ftc.gov or 1-877-FTC-HELP, or to your state

attorney general (United States Federal Trade Commission, "FTC Warns Consumers," 2003, and "Fraud on the Line," 2003).

To Learn More about the National Do Not Call Registry

The reader who would like additional information about the National Do Not Call Registry may go to the FTC website: http://www.donotcall.gov/. You can register a phone number (effective for five years), or verify or a delete a registration. The site also lists those entities that are exempt from the FTC rules and can still telephone you.

DMA's Telemarketing Preference Service

The Direct Marketing Association (DMA) maintains a list of persons who do not want telemarketing calls. You can write to the DMA at:

> Direct Marketing Association
> Telephone Preference Service
> P.O. Box 9014
> Farmingdale, NY 11735-9014.

To receive fewer sweepstakes offers in the mail, write to:

> Direct Marketing Association
> Mail Preference Service
> P.O. Box 9014
> Farmingdale, NY 11735-9014.

When contacting the DMA, you must provide your name, address, phone number, and signature.

Door-to-Door Sales

As confirmed frequently in the media, an inordinate number of senior citizens regularly fall victim to door-to-door sales fraud. Although comparatively few in number, these dishonest sales people cause the elderly much suffering and financial loss. Many different kinds of goods, services, and business opportunities are sold door-to-door. Some are licit; many are illicit. Virtually any type of fraud, scheme, or scam can be presented at the senior citizen's door. Home repairs and phony "inspectors" are the primary ones. Senior citizens who live in warm climates such as Florida, Arizona, or California are particularly vulnerable because while the pitchmen may be unscrupulous, they do not like traipsing around in the cold and are inclined to be more active when and where it is warm.

If you are home during the day, you are more likely to have an encounter with door-to-door salespersons. While some of them are reputable (like Willie Lohman, a vanishing breed), it is important to be wary and protect yourself from being scammed. The salesperson may be pitching anything from home improvements to funeral services, living trusts, books, magazines, or household equipment and supplies. Be vigilant. You can choose those stores you wish to shop in and can walk out and not return if you are not satisfied with the merchandise or service, but you have little choice about the type of salesperson who comes to your door. These con artists are charming and friendly. Their smiles are ingratiating. They are successful in their efforts because they appear so trustworthy.

What to Be Alert For

The door-to-door con artists typically:

- Offer a personal greeting—they will most likely use your last name which they may have noted on the mailbox, house sign, or obtained from city directories available at most public libraries.
- Are invariably charming and friendly, oozing warmth and sincerity.
- Engage in some ruse or stratagem to attempt to gain access to your residence. Frequently, scam artists say they are attempting to find an address, and need to use the telephone to assist them in their search. State very simply and firmly that it is your home and that they cannot enter it, and that if they attempt to do so, you will call the police.

- Assert that they represent your electric, telephone, water company, or other state or local agency that has sent them to "check" or "test" one thing or another.
- Attempt to accost you while you are outside your home—sitting on the porch or working in the garden. (They know you will not be able to shut the door in their face.) Retreat to the house and shut the door in their face!
- Insist on payment in cash. If you protest that you do not have the required amount on hand, they will most willingly volunteer to take you to the bank and wait outside for you until you can make a withdrawal. (If your are lucky, they may even take you back home!) Should they agree to accept your check they are certain to go to your bank immediately to attempt to cash it.
- Try to convince you that your family (or neighbors) will be disappointed or even angry if you do not take their suggestions and buy their products or services—particularly a home improvement.
- Maintain that they have been doing the same work or providing the same services to "satisfied customers in the neighborhood." Do not waste your time asking them for references.

Protect Yourself

A number of precautions are in order:

- Do not buy a product or sign a contract for a service on impulse.
- Do not succumb to high-pressure sales pitches, or those that appeal to your emotions.
- Do not permit entry to any person that you do not know or who has not properly identified themselves.
- Demand identification. If in doubt—which you certainly should be—go into the house (alone!) and call the office of the company or agency they claim to represent. Insist on proper credentials, preferably a photo ID. Most local laws mandate that door-to-door salespersons or solicitors obtain a permit before they can approach residents in the community. You can confirm that they are in compliance by calling the number on their credentials.

• Thoroughly investigate the product or service being offered and the vendor before you make a commitment. Affirm that you will make a final decision after, and only after, you have had the opportunity to review the details of the offer.

• Review the materials which they have given to you (if any). Compare the cost with other vendors or service providers. Confirm to your own satisfaction what the quoted price or fee includes. For a product, will there be any additional charges for shipping or installation?

• Check with your local BBB or consumer protection office to check out the company or vendor.

If You Change Your Mind

Door-to-door sales transactions are subject to the FTC's "Cooling-Off Rule" (explained in the following section). In the event that you do change your mind, you can rescind the contract and receive a full refund of any deposit. The other party is obliged to advise you that you have the right to cancel any contract until midnight of the third business day following the transaction.

Simply stated: If the seller does not provide the mandated disclosures concerning the right to cancel the transaction within three days, or if they attempt to or actually install the product or perform the service prior to the end of the cooling off period, the consumer may still be able to cancel the deal, or secure damages under applicable laws, rules and regulations.

THE COOLING-OFF RULE

The Federal Trade Commission's Cooling-Off Rule gives you three days to cancel purchases of $25 or more. Under the Rule, your right to cancel for a full refund extends until midnight of the third business day after the sale. The salesperson must tell you about your cancellation rights at the time of sale. He or she also must give you two copies of a cancellation form (one to keep and one to send) and a copy of your contract or receipt. The contract or receipt should be dated, show the name and address of the seller, and explain your right to cancel; these documents must be in the same language that is used in the sales presentation. The Cooling-Off Rule applies only to sales made in person at your home or at temporary facilities such as hotel rooms, convention centers, fairgrounds, or similar venues. It applies even if you invite the salesperson to come to your home.

The Rule does not apply to:

- Car sales, even at temporary locations, if the seller has a permanent place of business;
- purchases you make in a store;
- orders initiated and transacted entirely by mail or over the phone;
- purchases you need to meet an emergency; and
- arts and crafts sold at fairs, schools or civic centers (Source: United States Federal Trade Commission, "The Cooling-Off Rule," 1996).

Canceling a Contract

Should you decide to exercise your option to cancel a contract:

- Sign and date one of the two copies of the "Notice of Cancellation" form which you should have been given. You are under no obligation to state your reasons for the cancellation—they would be best left unsaid.
- Mail it to the address shown on the form by certified or registered mail so that you will have offcial proof of the date of mailing.
- Assure that the letter is postmarked on or before midnight of the third business day following the date of the contract. Saturday is considered a business day.
- Retain your copy of the cancellation form for your records. Attach it to your copy of the contract and include the record of mailing.
- If you did not receive the requisite cancellation forms, prepare a formal letter. By not providing the forms, the vendor has violated the law, in effect granting you additional time to cancel. However, you are still required to provide written notice of your intent as soon as you can possibly do so. Do not delay! It could cost you.

After You Have Cancelled

Once you have provided formal notification of cancellation as discussed here, the other party to the contract has ten business days to provide a refund of any deposit or payments you may have made and to return any promissory note you may have executed regarding any financing that may have been involved. Within ten days, the vendor is also required to advise you that any merchandise or products you have already received will be retrieved, or that you are not required to return the items in your possession. You are under no obligation to send the items back at your expense.

For Additional Information

The Federal Trade Commission has an extensive array of consumer information including how to protect yourself from fraudulent door-to-door salespersons. The FTC website can be found at: http://www.ftc.gov. The National Consumer Law Center website discusses the ways consumers can be defrauded by fraudulent door-to-door sales. The NCLC website can be accessed at http://www.consumer-law.org/initiatives/seniors_initiative/information.shtml.

Funerals

The Funeral Industry

Even the dead can be victims of fraud. "The multibillion dollar death-care industry has been transformed from a simple agreement with a local funeral home and cemetery to aggressively marketed plans sold by multinational corporations. Funeral arrangements are now being sold over the phone, on the Internet, through the mail, and door to door. The most alarming situation is that final arrangements are being sold as ardently as 'boiler-room' investments over the phone and through the mail. We caution you to spend wisely and know how every emotional lever is being pulled in an effort to separate you from your money—and best intentions" (Wasik, "Fraud in the Funeral Industry," 1995).

Like any industry, the funeral industry has many caring professionals. But, like any industry, it has operators who are not so caring,
and older Americans are frequent targets of these opportunists. Unfortunately, senior citizens often lack the resources, such as financial means
and good health, to fight back when they have been victimized by fraud
at a most vulnerable time.

The Federal Trade Commission advises: "Most funeral providers
are professionals who strive to serve their clients' needs and best interests. But some aren't. They may take advantage of their clients through
inflated prices, overcharges, double charges, or unnecessary services.
Fortunately, there's a federal law that makes it easier for you to choose
only those goods and services you want or need and to pay only for those
you select, whether you are making arrangements preneed or at need"
(United States Federal Trade Commission, "Funerals," 2000).

Preneed Plans

"Preneed" is a term coined by the funeral industry to describe the
arrangement of, and possibly the payment for, memorial rites and or
internment procedures prior to an individual's death. "Prearrangement"
is another term for preneed.

In the publication *Prepaying Your Funeral: Benefits and Dangers*, the
Funeral Consumers Alliance warns that "The marketing of preneed
plans for funeral services and merchandise is increasingly prevalent.
Everyone connected with the funeral industry is promoting preneed
purchases. Various companies, including insurance companies, 'for-
profit cremation societies,' and 'preneed associations' flood the mail
with advertising which touts the benefits of their preneed plans. There
are a number of pitfalls, as well as options, about which consumers
should be well-informed. Therefore, we say: 'Let the buyer beware'" (The
Funeral Consumers Alliance).

"Although funeral and cemetery professionals are by and large
skilled, honest and compassionate, a growing problem has been
identified in the financing of funerals. The funeral industry markets over
1 million 'preneed' contracts a year—to not only lock in your future business, but your money as well.... If you haven't been approached already,
you'll hear a lot more about preneed funeral plans. Such plans comprise the most powerful and profitable marketing tool in the 'death-care'

industry. Preneed is a priority with the corporate funeral-service chains that are buying up small and independent funeral homes from England to America to Australia" (Wasik, "Fraud in the Funeral Industry," 1995).

Most consumer complaints made against funeral homes relate to the total cost of the goods and services selected. "Often decisions and selections are made when the consumer is burdened with grief and is anxious to show love by 'selecting the best' for the deceased. This can lead to overspending, especially when the overall total is calculated. Sometimes consumers complain they are subjected to high-pressure salesmanship. In some situations this may occur. Another area of mis-understanding sometimes arises when the buyer does not clearly under-stand what is legally required and what is nice but not required. In reality, very few things are required" (Harrison, "Pyramids to Urns," 2000).

Your final arrangements are among the most expensive consumer purchases you will ever make. But there is no need to spend—or risk—thousands of dollars if you have the right information and plan ahead. Instead of waiting until grief strikes their survivors, before buying a funeral consumers should consider the expense in advance. Pre-plan-ning does not necessarily mean pre-paying. Plan ahead, but be careful about the financial obligations you make. Remember that a funeral can be an expensive undertaking. Anticipate the cost as you would with a house, home improvement, or new automobile. Plan ahead, shop around, compare prices and look for the best deal. The increasing trend toward pre-need planning suggests that many consumers want to com-pare prices and services so that ultimately, the funeral reflects a wise and well-informed purchasing decision, as well as a meaningful one.

Document your preferences—not in your will only, however, because a decedent's will often is not found or read until after the funeral. Avoid putting the only copy of the document in a safe deposit box, because your family and or executor may not be able to find the key or may have to wait until a business day to gain access to the box.

"There is at least $20 billion invested in preneed funeral and ceme-tery plans, but no way to tell how much of it is invested safely—or pro-tected at all. While the vast majority of funeral homes/cemeteries are honest, loopholes in state and federal laws practically invite theft by unsavory operators" (Wasik, "Fraud in the Funeral Industry," 1995). Pre-need agreements are among the least regulated products of the funeral industry. And to the extent pre-need trusts are regulated, more than one state office may regulate them; this leads to confusion and complexity for consumers and regulators. And that leads to fraud.

PRENEED FRAUD

The potential for abuse in preneed funeral planning is staggering. In 2003, there were about 23,000 funeral homes and 100,000 cemeteries of all types in the United States (public, private, military, municipal, and denominational) according to the International Cemetery and Funeral Association (ICFA), an organization composed of cemeteries, funeral homes, memorial designers, crematories, and related businesses worldwide (Source: International Cemetery and Funeral Association website).

The industry targets senior citizens with their aggressive preneed marketing because, quite understandably, the majority of deaths occur in persons 65 or older. "Badly managed or fraudulent preneed programs, however, are bilking tens of thousands of elderly citizens out of millions of dollars. The only federal law covering the industry—the Federal Trade Commission's Funeral Rule ... neither directly monitors preneed funding nor direct sales from cemeteries (only funeral homes or home/cemetery combinations are covered)" (Wasik, "Fraud in the Funeral Industry," 1995).

Prepaid Plans

You may wish to make decisions about your arrangements in advance, but not pay for them in advance. Keep in mind that over time, the cost of funerals may go up due to inflation; however, in some areas with increased competition, prices may go down over time. Millions of Americans—including many senior citizens—have entered into contracts to prearrange their funerals and prepay some or all of the expenses involved. Prepaying for one's funeral arrangements has two primary advantages:

1. You may ensure that adequate funds will be available for your funeral.
2. It provides some degree peace of mind in the event that you might no longer be able, or have no one to make suitable final arrangements on your behalf.

ADVICE ABOUT PREPAID PLANS

Laws of individual states govern the prepayment of funeral goods and services in an effort to ensure that these funds are available to pay for these expenses when they are needed. But protections vary widely from state to state, and some state laws offer little or no effective protection. Some require the funeral home or cemetery to place a percentage of the prepayment in a state-regulated trust or to purchase a life insurance policy with the death benefits assigned to the funeral home or cemetery.

If you are thinking about prepaying for your own funeral goods and services, it is important to consider these issues before putting down any money:

- Plan ahead, but be careful about the financial obligations you make. Will you be able to fulfill them? If death occurs prior to the time you complete payments, your agreement may not be honored in full.
- What are you are paying for? Are you buying only funerary goods, such as a casket and vault, or are you purchasing funeral services as well?
- Determine if the agreement is revocable. If it is, is there a charge for revocation? The plan should allow for a full refund with little or no penalty.
- Determine if your funeral agreement is portable. What happens if you move to a different area where you will then be interred? Some prepaid funeral plans can be transferred, but often at an added cost. In many states, you cannot transfer your arrangements to a new location or receive a refund unless you move out of that state.
- Ask for a guaranteed price plan. This protects you and your family from inordinate price increases in the future. Even with a such a plan there may be additional costs at the time of need, but they will be greatly reduced compared to what could occur with a non-guaranteed plan.
- Assure that the funds you are committing will be adequate to cover anticipated future costs. Inadequate funding could require unintended substitutions in your original choices, dis-

tributions from your estate, or cash contributions from caring but reluctant survivors and heirs.

- Funds you lock in for funeral arrangements may be needed in the event of an emergency. Will all or any part be accessible?
- What happens to the funds you have prepaid? States have different requirements for handling such funds. Confirm the understanding that any amount remaining will be paid to your estate; otherwise, the balance could revert to the funeral director.
- What happens to the interest income on money that is prepaid and put into a trust account? In many states part or all of the interest earned on your account may be withdrawn each year by the plan administrator as part of "administrative fees."
- Are you protected if the provider you dealt with goes out of business? The seller of today's funeral services may no longer be there at the time of your death. A successor might not elect to assume the responsibility.
- Be sure to inform your family and executor about any prepayment plans you have made. If you have not provided them with copies of the agreement, let them know where the documents are filed. If family members or executors do not know that you have prepaid the funeral costs, they could end up paying again for the same arrangements.

PREPAID PLAN FRAUD

Unfortunately for the elderly consumer, prepaid funeral fraud is particularly attractive to con artists for several reasons:

- First, more than 60 percent of the purchasers are over 60 years of age. This older population is more vulnerable to high-pressure sales tactics.
- Second, con artists can fairly easily acquire an appearance of legitimacy through affiliation with, or ownership of, established, reputable cemeteries and funeral homes. Consumers then assume the con artists are a part of the reputable establishment and buy prepaid contracts without questioning the integrity of the seller or realizing that con men may have taken over the reputable business.

• The third and last attraction for swindlers is the fact that prepaid contracts are usually purchased and held for years before they are needed. Purchasers of these contracts (or their survivors) do not know that they have been victimized until years later when they need the prepaid services and learn that the company is out of business or the contract is not valid (Source: Harrison, "Pyramids to Urns," 2000).

Tips on Preventing Funeral Fraud

Many people do not realize that they are not legally required to use a funeral home to plan and conduct a funeral. However, because they have little or no experience with the many details and legal requirements involved, and may be emotionally distraught when it is time to make the plans, they find the services of a professional funeral home to be a comfort and convenience. To avoid being victimized at these times you are advised to follow these tips.

• Do not be pressured by high-priced pitches from funeral industry vendors. Resist any pressure to buy goods and services you don't really want or need.
• Avoid emotional overspending. It is not necessary to have the fanciest casket or the most elaborate funeral to properly honor a loved one.
• Shop around. Compare prices from at least two funeral homes. Remember that you can supply your own casket or urn— bought on the Internet.
• Insist that all proposed plans and agreements be put in writing. (It is a requirement of the FTC's Funeral Rule.)
• Determine if the agreements you sign can be voided, taken back or transferred.
• Know and demand your rights. Laws regarding funerals and burials vary from state to state. As an educated consumer, you are advised to know which goods or services the applicable law requires you to purchase and which are optional.

Organizations that can offer advice on end of life services and plans include The Funeral Consumers Alliance that "exists to assist FCA and member affiliates in fulfilling their educational, informational, service, and consumer support mission. FCA recognizes that the dissemination of individual experiences, the reporting of public information, and linking to other websites on the Internet may contribute to the fulfillment of this same mission." The FCA website has several very informative consumer alert pages related to fraud in the funeral industry. Included are links to such online publications as:

- *Are You Wondering if the Funeral Home You Used Was an Ethical One?*
- *Prepaying Your Funeral: Benefits and Dangers*
- *Understanding the Tricks of the Funeral Trade: Self-defense for Consumers*
- *Monumental Manipulation: Written by an Insider*

These and other consumer information can be found online at the FCA website: http://www.funerals.org/alert/index.htm.

The Funeral Rule

Funeral practices in the United States are regulated under 16 CFR Part 453—"Funeral Industry Practices," as embodied in the Federal Trade Commission's "Funeral Rule." The goal of these regulations is to ensure that consumers have accurate information upon which to base their decisions. (The full text of the provisions of 16 CFR Part 453 can be found online at: http://www.access.gpo.gov/nara/cfr/waisidx_00/16cfr453_00.html.)

The Funeral Rule, enforced by the FTC, requires funeral homes to provide general price lists that contain the cost of each funeral item and service offered. The list must also include information about embalming, caskets for cremation, cemetery vaults, and required items. These lists allow you to pick and choose those services you want. You do not have to purchase any goods or services you do not want or that are not required. The Rule requires that the price of individual items and services be available over the telephone as well as provided in written form at the place of business. The Rule does not require any specific format for this information. Funeral providers may include it in any document they give you during your discussion of funeral arrangements.

Many funeral providers offer various packages of commonly selected items and services that are involved in a typical funeral. But when you arrange for a funeral, you have the right to buy individual funereal goods and services. That is, you do not have to accept a package that may include items or services you do not want. The Funeral Rule also requires that accurate information be given regarding what is legally required and what is optional and prohibits funeral providers from making false claims.

The FTC's Funeral Rule does not cover cemeteries and mausoleums unless they sell both funeral goods and funeral services, so be cautious in making your purchase to ensure that you receive all pertinent price and other information, and that you're being dealt with fairly.

Obituary Scams

Although not a funeral scam per se, con artists, known as "funeral chasers," routinely glean obituaries in newspapers to target widows (particularly) and widowers during their time of mourning, hoping they will be less vigilant against scams. In these situations, these sharks contact the survivors of a recently deceased individual, claiming that the decedent had ordered a service or item which is scheduled for delivery, but there's a "balance due."

They mention specific facts about the decedent designed to assure the family that the claimant—and the "order"—is legitimate. However, such facts are easily found in obituary columns and elsewhere. In such stressful circumstances, family members may be easy to convince, and the alleged balance due is often paid. Try not to make quick decisions under emotional or stressful conditions. Insist on documented proof that the decedent did, in fact, place the order as the person maintains; ask to see a receipt or a copy of the order that had been signed by the deceased. Should any doubts remain, refuse to pay and instruct the person to cancel the service or delivery; under the law, you may have no liability.

An excellent article entitled "10 Things Funeral Directors Don't Want You to Know," by Ellen Goldstein of Bankrate.com, is online at the URL shown in the sources. Although it does not address fraud in the funeral industry per se, it provides comprehensive guidelines that may help you become a better informed consumer and avoid the pitfalls.

Health

Health Fraud

Whether they are looking for a shortcut to losing weight or a cure for a serious ailment, American consumers may be spending billions of dollars a year on unproven, fraudulently marketed, often useless health-related products and treatments. Why? Because health fraud trades on false hope; it exploits desperation and desire; it promises quick cures and easy solutions to a variety of problems. But consumers who fall for fraudulent "cure-all" products do not find cures or improvements. Instead, they find themselves cheated out of their money, their valuable time, their well-being, and even their lives.

Fraudulently marketed health products can keep people from seeking and getting therapeutic treatment for serious illnesses from health care professionals. Most of these products are relatively expensive, and health insurance rarely covers unapproved treatments. Whether health fraud is packaged as exotic pills and potions, phony cures, or "miracle" remedies, it thrives on wishful thinking, naiveté, gullibility, or hopelessness.

Health Fraud and the Elderly

On September 10, 2001, at a hearing on health fraud and the elderly before the Senate Special Committee on Aging, a Federal Trade Commission official advised the panel that "Despite federal and state enforcement action, unfounded or exaggerated health claims remain common in the marketplace, and combating health fraud remains one of the Commission's top priorities" (United States Federal Trade Commission, "Health Fraud and the Elderly," 2001).

Health fraud poses a direct and immediate threat of both economic and physical injury to persons already suffering from serious conditions and diseases, with the elderly being particularly vulnerable because of the high incidence of health-related problems in this age group. According to the FTC official's testimony, a number of factors, including lack of information and false beliefs about health and the causes of disease, contribute to consumers' susceptibility to health fraud. He affirmed that "Although aggressive law enforcement is crucial, the best consumer protection comes from preventing consumers from being deceived in the first instance" (United States Federal Trade Commission, "Health Fraud and the Elderly," 2001).

Every day, millions of senior citizens face questions about health-related products and services they see in the marketplace, read about in the newspaper, hear about on radio and television, and which are proffered in the mail. Senior citizens are special targets of the quacks and hoaxters who are out to sell such worthless products. Unfortunately, it can be difficult for consumers to tell the difference between fact and fiction when it comes to selecting a health care product or service.

Their claims are invariably highly deceptive and usually promise miracles. The pills, lotions, and creams peddled by these charlatans make exaggerated claims such as "instant cure for arthritis," "lose weight without effort," "grow hair overnight," or "look years younger." They claim that their product will cure AIDS, cancer, heart disease, impotency, multiple sclerosis, obesity, Parkinson's disease, and a host of other diseases and illnesses. Despite their claims, hardly any of these products have ever been scientifically tested and proven to be curative.

These medically ineffective or dangerous products are sold by professional con men who have no medical training, and who will use every ruse to get consumers to buy their products. Sales gimmicks include bogus testimonials from "satisfied patients," emotional sales pitches to play on one's problems, and outright lies regarding a product's effectiveness.

To avoid being taken by a worthless quack cure, remember that you should not trust your health to a layperson. Also:

- Do not believe claims that a product is available only by mail or from an "exclusive" supplier or contains a "special," "secret," "foreign," or "ancient" ingredient or formula that will provide the cure or relief you may desperately seek.
- Do not believe claims that a "miracle" drug or product will effectively treat a wide variety of illnesses or diseases.

- Be very skeptical if the product is advertised as an "amazing break-through," or a "revolutionary new product."
- If the promoter claims the product is "scientifically proven," check it out with your physician or on the Internet. Claims that "clinical studies" prove a product works are invariably false. Generally, claims of high success rates should raise suspicions.
- Do not accept "testimonials" or case histories from satisfied "patients" as the only evidence that the product actually works as claimed.
- If the product is promoted by a "medical organization," call your physician to check the credentials. Or check it online. Phony "clinics" and sham "institutes" are touting bogus cures for every medical problem imaginable.
- Do not believe claims that the medical establishment has "ignored" or "suppressed" the "scientific breakthrough" the promoter is hawking. Ignore their persecution complex.

If you have any doubts about a product someone is trying to sell you that promises the relief you have long been looking for, discuss it first with your family physician or other qualified health professional, e.g. a nurse practitioner. Research the product or service on the Internet. (However, you are advised to consider the following discussion.) And remember, money-back guarantees are often worthless, and a health care product that sounds too good to be true probably will not—or cannot—do what its promoters claim.

Health Information on the Internet

On July 16, 2003, the Pew Internet & American Life Project reported that only 22 percent of Americans over the age of 65 have Internet access. Of those, 70 percent have searched for health topics on the Web (Pew Internet & American Life Project, *Internet Health Resources*, 2003).

A number of recent studies have shown that the Internet is having both positive and negative effects on health care and medical practice. It is making it easier for patients to communicate with their physicians—enhancing such communication is the good news. However when patients use the Internet to usurp the physician's knowledge and experience—to play doctor—self-diagnosis and treatment is a pre-scription for danger. Linking to a website must never be a substitute for consulting a physician or other health care professional when medical diagnosis and intervention is urgently needed.

Much of the health information on the Web is available on web-sites that have paid advertising and or shopping options. One way to make sure you are not being sold a bill of goods is to check whether the informational content of a website is effectively separated from adver-tisements or shopping sites (the number of "pop-up" ads is a good guide). *Caveat lector* and *caveat emptor!*

In an undated online article entitled "Evaluating Health Infor-mation on the Internet: How Good Are Your Sources?" AARP advises:

> When it comes to health care, the Internet is a mixed blessing. We now have more health and medical information at our fingertips than anyone ever dreamed possible just a few short years ago. We can bone up on our maladies by gathering medical data from innumerable sources without ever entering a medical library. We can ferret out treat-ment options our health care providers might never have considered, and prepare ourselves with sophisticated questions to ask at our next doctor visit.... But the sheer breadth of information in cyberspace can be overwhelming. Separating reliable from questionable health infor-mation can be a significant challenge at times, even for an experienced eye. There are no rules policing the kind of health information that appears on the Internet or who puts it there. Therefore, as health care consumers, we must rely on common sense, sound judgment, and some guidelines we can use to help us evaluate the quality of informa-tion we find on health and medical Web sites. The bottom line: Be a smart shopper for online health care information—rely on common sense and evaluate carefully what you see on the Web [AARP, "Evaluat-ing Health Information on the Internet," no date].

In a 17-page guide (online) prepared as the result of the SPRY (Set-ting Priorities for Retirement Years) Foundation Conference, "Older Adults, Health Information and the World Wide Web," held at the National Institutes of Health on February 26–28, 2001, SPRY reported:

> The World Wide Web is becoming the source of health information for a growing number of older adults and their caregivers. With thou-sands of health-only web sites available, as well as thousands more sites with subsections on health topics, the choices are staggering....
> Any web user can become frustrated and confused when searching

for specific health information, but these feelings can be even worse for people who may not have much web searching experience [e.g. senior citizens].... Without [Internet] experience, it can be difficult to structure a search to find exactly the information you might want. And, even when you do an effective search, you may be confused about the nature of different health web sites.... With all this variety, how can you find accurate, timely, understandable information on a specific topic without spending hours online? Also, how can you feel confident about the quality of the information once you arrive at a promising site? [SPRY Foundation, "Evaluating Health Information on the World Wide Web," 2001].

Online "Pharmacies"

Elderly persons are increasingly turning to online "pharmacies" to obtain their medications—often at significant savings and significant risks. The Internet is a global resource and more and more patients who want to obtain medications which their own physicians cannot or will not prescribe are turning to the Web—often to obtain medications that are not yet available in the United States.

Most of these Internet pharmacies require that the individual complete and submit a "medical history" (an online questionnaire). However, the vendors have no way to verify the information submitted, or even the identity of the individual providing it. Their "safeguards" are virtually worthless. It is vitally important that a licensed pharmacist and the patient's physician monitor, and be directly involved in, prescribing and dispensing all such medications. It must be noted, however, physicians' prescriptions are not necessary to purchase medications from sources outside of the United States.

The Internet has created a very dangerous opportunity for patients to circumvent the safeguards established by the medical and pharmacological professions, and by the U.S Food and Drug Administration (FDA). This is an area that the Internet community, the professionals, and lawmakers at the state and federal levels must continue to examine closely.

Often the prices charged by online pharmacies are relatively high and may include hidden charges or excessive shipping and handling costs. Some sources may offer cheaper or generic drugs for the same illness or treatment. Additionally, many web sites require consumers to agree to a "waiver of liability" which asks them, in effect, to forego all of their legal rights. Consumers should *never* agree to such liability waivers to receive goods or services.

Finally, some sites may simply be scams. You may find yourself paying for something which you never receive or end up giving out credit card and other information only to be ripped off again. As with any online purchase, complete the transaction only on a "secure" site, using a credit card for added protection.

Imported Drugs

On July 25, 2003, at the time this book was being prepared, a coalition in the House of Representatives that spanned the ideological spectrum passed the Pharmaceutical Market Access Act of 2003 (HR 2427) that would allow individuals to save money by filling prescriptions with cheaper foreign drugs, even though the measure was opposed by GOP leadership and the pharmaceutical industry. The House bill authorizes the Secretary of Health and Human Services to write regulations to allow individuals to import FDA-approved prescription drugs from FDA-approved sources. The Senate had passed a narrower version of a drug importation measure earlier. When Congress was scheduled to return in the fall of 2003, the issue was likely to be incorporated in the larger debate over including prescription drug coverage in Medicare. If the bill is passed, Americans will be able to import prescription drugs lawfully from neighboring Canada and twenty-four other industrialized nations, where the same medications often sell at a fraction of their costs to consumers in the U.S. Backers of the bill said it would give American citizens—particularly the elderly—immediate financial relief from some of the highest drug prices in the world.

Opponents—including lobbyists for the pharmaceutical industry—assert that such imports will create serious safety hazards by facilitating the importation of counterfeit, adulterated, or otherwise ineffective medications. The FDA, the FTC, and a number of senior advocacy organizations share those concerns. On July 25, 2003, the bill was referred to the Senate Committee on Health, Education, Labor, and Pensions. As of January 2004, the bill was still in committee and there were no new actions regarding HR 2427.

Counterfeit Medications

Counterfeit drugs, a term encompassing outright fakes and legitimate medicines that have been tampered with—including adulteration—have long been an epidemic in parts of the world. Once a problem mainly in developing countries, counterfeit medications are increasingly turning up in the United States, prompting federal health officials to develop new methods to keep the nation's drugs safe. Any changes in U.S. law which would permit the importation of foreign medications will markedly compound the challenges for consumers and regulatory authorities.

There are no reliable data on how often counterfeits are marketed in America, where pharmaceutical regulation is the world's strictest. But experts say that while the vast majority of U.S. drugs are of the highest quality, the influx of foreign contraband and counterfeits does suggest a rising problem. A major factor is the lack of effective monitoring of Internet drug sales. Counterfeit medications purchased online have become another major concern for law enforcement officials. As many as 8 percent of all drugs imported into the U. S. have been deemed fake and present serious health risks associated with their use.

On July 9, 2002, the Senate Special Committee on Aging warned consumers of the dangers of counterfeit medicines imported from foreign countries: "Counterfeit prescription drugs endanger the lives of Americans every day. Without our domestic safety net to ensure the integrity of these pharmaceuticals, consumers simply do not know what medicine they are buying. Even worse, foregoing these U.S. drug protections leaves millions of seniors at risk of serious health problems and even death" (United States Senate Special Committee on Aging, "Buyer Beware: Public Health Concerns of Counterfeit Medicine," 2002).

Obtaining any prescription medicine from an unfamiliar source and then self-medicating can be extremely dangerous. Prescription drugs purchased online from unverifiable sources can originate from foreign, unregulated markets and may be more likely to be bogus, impure or adulterated. They can be lethal!

Health Quackery

"Quackery" refers to the practice or pretensions and methods of a "quack"—an individual who is unqualified or incompetent in the field to which his or her pretensions, misrepresentations, practices, and methods pertain, and who promotes medical remedies that do not work or have never been proven to work. It is the fraudulent misrepresentation of one's ability and experience in the diagnosis and treatment of illness or disease, or of the effects to be achieved by the treatment offered; the exaggeration of the effectiveness of a substance or device for the prevention or treatment of medical condition; and the act of promoting health products, services, or practices of questionable safety, effectiveness, or validity for an intended purpose. For many, quackery includes much of which its promoters call "alternative" or "complementary" medicine.

A quack is a charlatan who speaks pretentiously without sound knowledge of the subject discussed—a pretender to medical skill and one who claims an ability to diagnose and heal. The word comes from Dutch *quacksalver*, a "salve peddler." This derives from a now obsolete Dutch verb "quacken," which meant "to chatter or prattle" and "salf" the origin of the English word "salve." Quacksalvers were individuals who boasted about their salves, who bragged about the nostrums they concocted and proffered, claiming special benefits or cures from treatment with them.

We may think that the day of patent medicines salesmen is gone, but look around you and you will still see them in various guises. They appeal to our desire to believe that every disease is curable, or at least treatable. As authors William T. Jarvis, and Stephen Barrett observe:

> Modern health quacks are super salesmen. They play on fear. They cater to hope. And once they have you, they'll keep you coming back for more ... and more ... and more. Seldom do their victims realize how often or how skillfully they are cheated.
>
> Most people think that quackery is easy to spot. Often it is not. Its promoters wear the cloak of science. They use scientific terms and quote (or misquote) scientific references. Talk show hosts may refer to them as experts or as "scientists ahead of their time." The very word "quack" helps their camouflage by making us think of an outlandish character selling snake oil from the back of a covered wagon—and, of course, no intelligent people would buy snake oil nowadays, would they?
>
> The most important characteristic to which the success of quacks can be attributed is probably their ability to exude confidence. Even when they admit that a method is unproven, they can attempt to mini-

mize this by mentioning how difficult and expensive it is to get something proven to the satisfaction of the FDA these days. If they exude self-confidence and enthusiasm, it is likely to be contagious and spread to patients and their loved ones. Because people like the idea of making choices, quacks often refer to their methods as alternatives" [Jarvis and Barrett, "How Quackery Sells," 2000].

Quackery versus Fraud

Doctor Stephen Barrett (cited above), renowned author, editor, consumer advocate, and founder of the website Quackwatch, has attempted to distinguish between health fraud and quackery. Doctor Barrett states:

> These definitions suggest that the promotion of quackery involves deliberate deception, but many promoters sincerely believe in what they are doing. The FDA defines health fraud as "the promotion, for profit, of a medical remedy known to be false or unproven." This also can cause confusion because in ordinary usage—and in the courts—the word "fraud" connotes deliberate deception. Quackery's paramount characteristic is promotion ("Quacks quack!") rather than fraud, greed, or misinformation. Most people think of quackery as promoted by charlatans who deliberately exploit their victims. Actually, most promoters are unwitting victims who share misinformation and personal experiences with others.... Much quackery is involved in telling people something is bad for them (such as food additives) and selling a substitute (such as "organic" or "natural" food). Quackery is also involved in misleading advertising of dietary supplements, homeopathic products, and some nonprescription drugs. In many such instances no individual "quack" is involved—just deception by manufacturers and their advertising agencies. A practitioner may be scientific in many respects and only minimally involved in unscientific practices. Also, products can be useful for some purposes but worthless for others.... [Q]uackery could be broadly defined as "anything involving overpromotion in the field of health." This definition would include questionable ideas as well as questionable products and services, regardless of the sincerity of their promoters. In line with this definition, the word "fraud" would be reserved only for situations in which deliberate deception is involved. Unproven methods are not necessarily quackery. Those consistent with established scientific concepts may be considered experimental. Legitimate researchers and practitioners do not promote unproven procedures in the marketplace but engage in responsible, properly-designed

studies. Methods not compatible with established scientific concepts should be classified as nonsensical or disproven rather than experimental [Barrett, "Quackery: How Should It Be Defined?" no date].

Quacks have been around for centuries and found in every culture. "You may remember the 'snake oil' salesman who traveled from town to town putting on a show and making amazing claims about his 'fabulous' product. Today's quack is only a little more slick. Sometimes only money is wasted, but it can be a serious problem if quackery prevents you from seeking professional medical care" (National Institute on Aging, "Health Quackery," 1994).

Who Are the Victims?

When it comes to products that promise increased cognitive function, virility, physical conditioning, anti-aging, anti-cancer properties, and so on, older Americans make up the segment of the population most concerned about these issues, and, therefore, primary targets of, and particularly susceptible to, health fraud and quackery.

William Jarvis, citing "Quackery: A $10 Billion Scandal" (United States House of Representatives, Select Committee on Aging, Subcommittee on Health and Long-term Care. Washington, DC, 1984, U.S. Government Printing Office), notes that "In 1983 and 1984 respectively, the U.S. Senate and the House of Representatives independently concluded that medical quackery was the leading cause of harmful consumer fraud targeting the elderly in the U.S." (Jarvis, "Alternative Healthcare," 1998).

To the quack, people of all ages are fair game, but older people form the largest group of victims. In fact, a government study found that 60 percent of all victims of health care fraud are older people (Source: National Institute on Aging, "Health Quackery," 1994). And the promotion of dubious health practices is not limited to the elderly or sick. "Quackery has something for everyone because we all have wishes that exceed reality" (Barrett et al., 2002).

Most people who are taken in by a quack's worthless and often dangerous "treatments" are desperate for some offer of hope. Because older persons as a group have more chronic illnesses than younger persons, they are likely targets for fraud.

The Federal Bureau of Investigation has affirmed that

[They] are targeted for one simple reason. The con man knows that many of these individuals are desperate to find some reason to believe that a "miracle cure" exists. These people, many of whom are elderly but some who are not, are willing to pay whatever price is asked and subject themselves to whatever risk is required to gain an advantage over their disease. Regrettably, in most cases, it is the con man taking advantage of these individuals. In addition to the financial loss, these patients often lose valuable time away from conventional medical treatment which could have resulted in a higher quality of life and/or prolonged life [United States Federal Bureau of Investigation, "Fraud Against the Elderly," 2001].

Why Quackery Sells

The "cures" and "miracles" that quacks peddle to the elderly include:

• Anti-Aging products.

The normal processes of aging are a rich territory for medical quackery. In a youth-oriented society, quacks find it easy to promote a wide variety of rejuvenating products. They brazenly claim that their products can stop or reverse aging processes or relieve conditions associated with old age. While there are products that may temporarily reduce wrinkles or reverse baldness for some people, these products cannot slow the body's natural and inexorable aging process. However, a healthy lifestyle may help prevent or forestall some conditions that occur more often as individuals age.

• Arthritis remedies.

These are especially easy for the elderly to fall for because symptoms of arthritis tend to come and go. Persons with arthritis easily associate the remedy they are using with relief from symptoms. Arthritis sufferers have paid for bottled seawater, "extracts" from New Zealand green lipped mussels, and Chinese herbal medicines (which may contain no herbs but may contain components that can be dangerous). There is no cure for most forms of arthritis, but palliative treatments that can help reduce pain and enable greater movement are available. These include drugs, heat treatments, a balance of rest and exercise, and, in some cases, surgery.

• Cures for cancer.

Quacks prey on the older person's fear of cancer by offering "treatments" that have no proven value; for example, a diet dangerously low in protein or drugs such as Laetrile which was recently largely discredited as a fad. By using unproven methods, patients may lose valuable time and the chance to receive proven, effective therapy. This can reduce the chance for controlling the course of or possibly curing the disease.

How to Avoid Being Quacked

Quackopractors have polished their marketing skills in promoting their ostensible medical proficiency and knowledge. They claim to sell sure cures when in fact they sell false hopes during a time when the individual is desperate and most vulnerable. It is then that quacks are able to sway their victims—not with the quality and efficacy of their intervention but with the quantity and effrontery of their invention.

One way to protect yourself is to question treatment claims that appear in the media. With some exceptions, newspaper and magazine editors and producers of radio and television commercials do not routinely screen advertisements for the truth or accuracy of their claims—as is evident from frequent news reports describing FDA or FTC action taken against the promoter of one therapy or another—fraudulent weight loss programs and the controversy over ephedrine are a recent examples.

On the Quackwatch website Doctor Barnett suggests ten strategies to avoid being quacked:

1. Remember that the claims of a quack may not necessarily be outrageous or implausible. They may include impressive "proof" from "scientific studies" cited in obscure references which cannot be found and so corroborated.
2. Dismiss any claims that every disease or illness is caused by nutritional deficits of one kind or another and that the cure lies in correcting the deficit by taking the quack's supplement. When a dietary etiology has been identified, the cure likely lies in changing one's diet.
3. Be highly skeptical of testimonials or case histories from "satisfied patients." If someone claims to have been helped by an unorthodox remedy, ask yourself, and your physician,

whether there might be another explanation. Most single episodes of disease recover with the passage of time, and most chronic ailments have symptom-free periods. Most people who give testimonials about recovery from cancer have undergone effective treatment as well as unorthodox treatment, but give credit to the latter—they are getting paid for those. Some so-called testimonials are complete fabrications by compensated actors.

4. Be alert to balderdash. Quackery spiels typically include very impressive sounding medical jargon and scientific terminology or such cryptic claims to "detoxify," "correct the weakness," "balance," "restore harmony," or "release your natural energy"—or all of these. Such personal, spiritual, and mystical concepts are scientifically irreproducible.

5. Disregard the quack's paranoid accusations which involve claims that the medical and scientific communities, the pharmaceutical industry and, of course, the "*government*," are all in collusion in a massive effort to suppress the treatment or cure the quack has "discovered." No evidence to support such pervasive conspiracy theories has ever been presented. It also flies in the face of logic to believe that large numbers of individuals or organizations would oppose the development of treatment methods that might someday help them or their loved ones.

6. Ignore the claims of a "secret" discovery or "special formula." The scientific method demands that results be published and research findings be reproducible in any laboratory. Why would anyone be willing to divulge a "secret cure" that could bring him or her enormous wealth and fame? Quacks keep their methods and formulations secret to shield themselves and their products from scientific scrutiny and proof that they are worthless.

7. Be extremely cautious in embracing herbal remedies. These are always "ancient," and have their origins in folklore, shamanism, or superstition. Many of these herbal concoctions have been shown to contain potentially toxic substances which have never been scientifically studied. Always consult your physician or pharmacist before taking such potions.

8. There is absolutely no such thing as a "cure-all"—a magical rem-

edy for anything and everything that afflicts the human race or for a condition "that is not yet understood by medical science." Such claims of a panacea are fatuous at the least, fatal at their worst.

9. "Think for yourself!" Quacks strongly encourage this. Vanity is a persuasive incentive. "Do not follow the standard, accepted course of treatment; try a dramatically new approach. Even though it may not have proven effective in every case, it may cure you." Yes, think for yourself—but *think* first—about yourself.

10. In desperate hope, do not relinquish good judgment and common sense. If you have been told that there is no hope do not surrender—especially to quackery (Source: Barrett, "Ten Ways to Avoid Being Quacked," 1997).

Quackwatch[SM]

The most outstanding source of information on health quackery will be found on Doctor Stephen Barrett's website "Quackwatch: Your guide to health fraud, quackery, and intelligent decisions." (http:// www.quackwatch.org). The Quackwatch Mission Statement affirms: "Quackwatch, Inc., a member of Consumer Federation of America, is a nonprofit corporation whose purpose is to combat health-related frauds, myths, fads, and fallacies. Its primary focus is on quackery-related information that is difficult or impossible to get elsewhere" (Quackwatch).

The extensive and very informative Quackwatch site has several hundred pages including numerous hyperlinks to topics relating to health quackery, such as "Chirobase: A Skeptical Guide to Chiropractic History, Theories, and Current Practices"; "HomeoWatch, Your Skeptical Guide to Homeopathic History, Theories, and Current Practices"; and "NutriWatch, Your Guide to Sensible Nutrition."

Medical Discount Cards

Medical costs are rising—especially for senior citizens. So it is no wonder that fraudulent telemarketers have turned to promoting medical discount plans as a new way to bilk unsuspecting consumers.

Legitimate discount cards can offer savings on prescription drugs and visits to health care providers. However, the cards touted by tele-marketers, on the Internet, and in the media frequently exaggerate expected savings, fail to disclose various "administrative fees" and other costs or bury them in fine print, and or inflate the number of providers that will accept them.

Some issuers of bogus medical discount cards mislead buyers into thinking the cards are a substitute for or a supplement to health insur-ance. Patients who have been victimized are presenting them at hospi-tals or the offices of providers under the impression that they have adequate medical coverage. When he or she is rejected, the patient real-izes that he or she is liable for payment and often lacks the financial resources to do so.

The Federal Trade Commission wants consumers to know that promoters of bogus medical discount plans and cards are doing just what they always do: following the headlines to take advantage of con-sumer vulnerability. In this case, the FTC says, the fraudulent tele-marketers are perpetrating an "unauthorized billing" scam on people who are simply trying to save money. The FTC has filed suit against sev-eral companies that claim to offer consumers medical discount plans and cards and then bill their accounts for hundreds of dollars whether or not the consumer wants the plan or card.

How the Scam Works

According to the FTC, fraudulent telemarketers are offering con-sumers a healthcare discount plan that supposedly will generate savings on prescription drugs and dental, vision, hearing, chiropractic, and nursing services. As part of their pitch, they lead consumers to believe that they're affiliated with the consumer's insurance company, financial institution, or state government. The agency says seniors can often get these benefits on their own for free or at minimal cost.

The tip-off to the medical discount rip-off comes when the pro-moter asks the consumer to "confirm" some personal financial infor-mation, like a credit card or checking account number. The FTC says the promoters do this in an effort to convince the consumers that they're simply verifying information they already have. That's not the case. Indeed, says the FTC, once the fraudulent promoters have a consumer's account information, they use it to make money by placing an unau-thorized charge or debit on the consumer's account.

The FTC advises consumers not to give out personal information—including financial information like credit card or bank account numbers—on the phone or the Internet unless you're familiar with the business that's asking for it. Not only can scam artists use the information to bill your accounts without your permission, but they also can use it to commit identity theft and other types of fraud. You are advised to ask for all the details in writing before applying for a medical discount card. If the information is not forthcoming you have probably avoided a scam.

Home Improvement

Scope of the Problem

In a news broadcast on March 1, 2002, MSNBC correspondent Fred Francis reported that "The home repair scam is one of the oldest on the books, but it remains an enormous problem, especially for the elderly.... Home improvement is a $180 billion-a-year industry, but with that comes home improvement fraud and contractors who fail to live up to their end of the bargain" (MSNBC, "Home Improvement Scams," 2002).

Inevitably every home needs repairs or improvements to one extent or another. The vast majority of contractors are honest, competent professionals. However, although many reputable home improvement companies do good work, many do not. These are primarily interested in taking your money, and not repairing or improving your home. Unfortunately, many of them have targeted senior citizens because their gracious old homes are often in need of repairs or improvements and their gracious old owners often live in a state of seedy gentility. As *Consumer News* confirms, "Elderly homeowners are the most frequent targets of traveling handymen who appear unannounced, often with a vague story about doing other work in the neighborhood. They offer to perform such chores as gutter repair, driveway paving and landscaping" (*Consumer News*, "Home Improvement Scams Bloom in Spring," 2002). The National Consumer Law Center also confirms that "Many low-income elderly homeowners are targeted by scam artists who use high pressure tactics to sell un-needed and overpriced contracts for 'home improvements.' Often these scam artists charge more than their quoted prices or their work does not live up to their promises. When the senior refuses to pay for shoddy or incomplete work, the contractor or an affiliated lender threatens foreclosure on the senior's home" (National Consumer Law Center, "Home Improvement Scams Alert," 2000).

While con artists scam people of all ages, based on the number and nature of complaints filed with investigatory and law enforcement officials, they are more likely to mark the elderly. They seem to believe that the elderly are more susceptible—a seemingly valid premise—to their scams than younger people, and consequently are victimized more than any other age group. Therefore, if you are a senior citizen, you have to be more aware as a consumer so you do not become another victim.

Deceptive Sales Tactics

Because home repairs and improvements are expensive undertakings, con men and thieves have infiltrated the industry to rip consumers off. Consumer agencies warn that spring is the time of year when home improvement scams abound. When the weather gets warm the con artists blossom like dandelions and elderly homeowners must be wary. Be careful if someone approaches you or mails you a brochure offering to do an expensive repair or improvement job for an unusually low price. This is a favorite trick of dishonest contractors. Once you sign the contract, you learn why the price is so low—the contractor never even starts, let alone completes the work you may have paid for in advance.

Disreputable contractors use several methods of targeting seniors. A scam can start with a high-pressure telephone call, flyers posted or mailed, advertisements in the media, or a knock on the door by a total stranger offering to "help" with home repairs or improvements that they have determined you "need." (They have identified your need by walking by or around the outside of the house—the "curbside appraisal.") Unscrupulous contractors often employ one or more of the following sales tactics:

- Bait and switch—an offer of low prices for installation of windows or siding. The senior citizen is then told that the item is "out of stock" and only a substitute is available—at a higher price;

- related to bait and switch is the claim that the product is more expensive than advertised because it must be "custom made" for the senior's home;
- exaggeration of the urgency and need of a repair—"it *must* be done *now!*";
- the misrepresentation that the homeowner is receiving a "discount" because their home has been selected as a "model" or "display"; in reality, they will be paying the full price, or likely more;
- that energy savings, health benefits, and enhanced property value will result from the proposed repair or improvement; and
- misrepresentation of the terms on which financing is likely to be arranged (Source: National Consumer Law Center, "Home Improvement Scams Alert," 2000).

The Most Common Home Repair Rip-Offs

Repaving your driveway? Replacing your furnace? Repairing your roof? These sound like easy jobs, especially when a contractor comes knocking at your door. But take your time before you agree to have the work done. The FTC reports that complaints about unscrupulous home improvement and repair contractors rank second with consumer protection officials across the country.

The most common home repair scams involve chimneys, windows, roofing, siding, painting, gutter cleaning, electrical wiring, pest extermination, driveway paving, furnace cleaning, yardwork including landscaping and tree trimming, and walkways. What do these—and many others—have in common? They are all potential scams by con artists who will take your money and leave you with nothing, or at best an inferior job done with inferior materials.

The Scams in Operation

The scam typically begins with a stranger approaching the homeowner and stating: "I was just in the neighborhood and ... (then the pitch)." AARP cautions:

> Beware of a home improvement salesperson who comes to your door uninvited, saying he or she was in your neighborhood and noticed you need repairs to your roof, chimney, trees, driveway, windows, or what-

ever. Also beware of someone who wants to sell you a security system because of burglaries in the area or who wants to test your water and inspect your plumbing or furnace.

Don't let them in your house and don't do any business with them! This kind of sales approach is standard practice for scam artists, who prey particularly on older persons. The person who has just enough shingles left over from a job in the neighborhood to do your roof will, most likely, take your money and disappear, or do such a sloppy job you will wish he or she had never appeared [AARP, "Home Improvement Fraud," no date].

EXAMPLES OF HOME IMPROVEMENT SCAMS

- You are approached by someone who offers to perform a "free termite inspection." The "inspector" will always find exactly what he is looking for—he has brought the evidence in with him, dead termites in a container concealed on his person. The "exterminator" then proceeds with a perfunctory, but costly, spraying of an "insecticide" to rid you of the problem.
- The con man gives a low quote—typically "half price"—to install siding on your home. But he will require a deposit in advance for "expenses." When, and if, he is finished you may find he has applied only the siding but has not included needed work on the eaves, gutters, or window moldings, as any reputable contractor would. He then will attempt to charge you an additional and substantial amount to complete the job.
- In repairing a minor leak in the roof, the con man begins the work and then announces that the underlayment of the roof has deteriorated so badly that it must be replaced before the new roofing can be applied. He may even show you evidence in the form of decayed wood (which he has retrieved from his truck.)
- Reputable painters will agree to use a specific brand of high-quality paint. The con artist will do the same, then substitute a cheap, low-quality paint which has been put into cans labeled with quality brand names. (Drips around the rims or on the labels of "new" cans should be a clue.) The cans the painter brings to the job should be clean, unused, and tightly sealed. If they appear to have been opened, ask why. The reason given

will likely be that the paint had to be "stirred" before it could be used—something any hardware store can do without opening a can.

- In the case of paving schemes, a contractor may drop by and offer to resurface or reseal a driveway. He may demand payment in advance or a sizable deposit, and, having received payment, never return. Or he and his "helper" may spread a material on your driveway that looks like asphalt sealer, but in reality will wash away in the next rainstorm. Beware of the "asphalt gypsy"—the one who says he has asphalt "left over" from a nearby job and to get rid of it he is willing to seal your driveway for a very low price—e.g. $60 for a five-gallon bucket. When the job is finished, he will demand as much as ten times the amount quoted, claiming he had to use ten buckets. He will produce ten empty buckets—stacked in the back of his truck—where they were when he arrived. If the homeowner protests, he may settle for less, but he refuses to take a check and while he accompanies the homeowner/victim to the bank, the "helper" can be helping himself to the contents of the home.

- Free "inspections" by con men always discover expensive repairs you do not need. Some vagabond thieves may not even mail you an offer to do a repair job. They just show up at your front door and attempt to gain access by posing as utility repairmen or "inspectors" offering their services. They may quickly flash something that, at first glance, appears to be official credentials in an effort to convince you to let them enter your home. Often these shady operators will offer to do remedial work on the spot. However, when they leave, you may be left with a large bill and a faulty repair job.

- Beware of the door-to-door "furnace inspector" who offers a free inspection or a low price for cleaning and servicing. He may also claim to be a "fire inspector." Invariably he warns you that your furnace is in extremely dire need of repair—this after a cursory examination. Of course, he will always find a condition that is "extremely dangerous" and advise the homeowner that furnace must be replaced immediately before someone is harmed or killed. And, of course, he just happens to know someone who can replace that faulty furnace immediately. If you agree, the "new" furnace will likely be an old, used, refurbished unit; and your furnace—fully operational and safe—will be hauled off, cleaned up, and passed off to the next victim of the scam.

• A variation of the inspector scam is the "utility inspector." An individual—perhaps dressed in an official-looking uniform—appears and claims to have been sent by the local utility company to conduct a "routine" or "required" inspection of the gas meter, electric meter, or electrical system. Once admitted, this "inspector" determines that there is a "serious code violation" that requires immediate repairs or corrective measures. And they just happen to have a friend that can do the job on short notice at a reasonable price. Of course, there is absolutely nothing wrong with the wiring or utility equipment.

As a homeowner you are always cautioned to demand to see the credentials—including a photo identification—of any person who claims to be a representative of a utility company before you admit him. You are also advised to telephone the utility company directly to verify the credentials you are being shown and the legitimacy of the visit. Always use your telephone directory when making such a call rather than a number given to you by the "inspector." There could be an accomplice waiting to answer that number.

Home Improvement Scams:
Tips and Warning Signs

Do your homework and be prepared. Before you contact a home improvement company or start on a project determine how much you can afford to spend and make sure you know exactly what you want and really need. Make a list of those items. Assure yourself that the proposed repair or improvement is really necessary. It would be foolish to take the word of a total stranger who appears at your door or wanders into your yard. A little advance work now can save you a lot of headaches later.

The FTC warns: "Thinking about a home improvement? Don't get nailed." A new home repair scam is pulled off every minute. To protect yourself, deal only with licensed contractors that you have contacted personally. Misguided efforts to save money by hiring individuals unfamiliar to you can prove to be far more expensive in the long run than the fee a legitimate, reputable contractor may charge. Do not let an unknown contractor impose decisions on you. Read one of the many books on home repairs or improvements. Visit one of the many websites that discuss these topics and inform homeowners as to what is involved in a particular project. Many sites also provide advice on avoiding the scams.

Everyday common sense can often help you avoid the pitfalls of home repair swindlers and door-to-door thieves. But there is one rule you should follow before agreeing to any home repairs or door-to-door sales: *Shop around!* Getting more than one estimate is the only way to do it right. Remember, con artists want only one thing from you—your money. The best guarantee against getting ripped off is *information*. So ask many questions, and be slow to sign anything or to part with your money. A few simple precautions when undertaking home maintenance, repairs, and improvements can save you hundreds or even thousands of dollars. They may even save you from losing your home!

There is no certain way to avoid being a victim of home improvement scams. Even the most reputable and well-intentioned contractor or handyman can run into unforeseen problems that may escalate the cost of a project, but there are a few points to consider:

- Know your contractor. When you have decided to proceed with a repair or improvement project start looking for a reputable professional. Discuss your plans with friends, family, and neighbors. Ask for the names of contractors they may have used. They can be a ready source in finding someone who is honest, dependable, and who will do a good job.
- With or without a recommendation, however, take the time to obtain several bids or estimates on the work you want done. Get at least two or three *written* estimates. Confirm that each proposal exactly addresses the proposed project. Most reputable contractors provide free inspection services and written estimates.
- Remember that the lowest price is not always the best deal. Compare costs, materials, and methods suggested by different con-

tractors to decide on those that are best for you. Resist the impulse to grab a "bargain."

• Deal only with licensed contractors. Make sure that any contractor you are considering has a current license to operate in your state. Contractors who are required to be licensed often list their license number in their ads. Check out licensed contractors with the BBB and state and local consumer protection officials. They will be able to confirm if there are unresolved consumer complaints on file. One *caveat*: No record of complaints against a particular contractor does not necessarily mean no previous consumer problems. It may be that problems exist but have not been reported, or that the contractor has been doing business under several different names.

• Confirm that the contractor is bonded and insured. Ask to see the evidentiary documents. Avoid doing business with contractors who do not carry the appropriate insurance. Otherwise, you could be held liable for any injuries and damage due to the contractor's negligence that occur on your premises during the project.

• Confirm that the contractor has all the required permits to do the work. Be especially suspicious of the contractor who tries to assure you that you do not need a permit for a particular repair or improvement.

• Ask for references and then check them out. These should be from within your own community, not out of your immediate area, and certainly not out-of-state. When interviewing a contractor, get a written list of work they have done in your community. Then visit and inspect those projects or contact the previous customers.

• Insist on a written agreement stating what will be done and the cost and the quality of building materials to be used in the work under consideration. Ask if there is a guarantee or warranty. If so, insist it be in writing. If the contractor balks at this request, look for another one.

• Be especially careful in committing to repair jobs that are prone to problems, e.g. leaky windows, cracked asphalt driveways, or improperly installed roofing material. These are best left to the professionals.

- Do not rely on leaflets stuffed in mailboxes or posted on bulletin boards. An advertisement in the Yellow Pages is no guarantee that a contractor is licensed and reputable. Anyone can advertise in the Yellow Pages. A prominent and colorful ad should not be considered a testimony to the quality of a contractor's work.
- The individual who solicits door-to-door is a sure warning sign of a disreputable operator. The first alert should be when a stranger initiates the contact—he or she comes to your home uninvited and with no prior arrangement, or calls you on the telephone. Be extremely cautious of such home repairmen who were "just passing by." The best way to protect yourself is never to hire anyone who suddenly appears at your door or calls you on the telephone. If you have even the slightest suspicion that something is not right, get a second opinion before you sign any contract or give an oral agreement. As a general rule, do not deal with any itinerant handyman who comes to your door. If he become persistent, demand that he leave immediately. Do not allow him to enter your home under the pretext of "checking" it so he can give you an estimate. This is often an invitation to a scam, a burglary, or an incident that can be dangerous or possibly deadly. Insist that he leave; call the police if he refuses. Under no circumstances go outside to accompany the handyman as he "inspects" your property. The objective is to lure the resident outside and distract them while an accomplice enters to rob the home.
- The contractor pressures you for an immediate decision—insists that you need to make the proposed repairs "immediately." Typically he or she will speak rapidly (to confuse you) and pressure you to sign a contract proffered to you on the spot. High-pressure sales tactics are usually an indicator of unscrupulous operators. A reputable contractor will not pressure you to sign a contract, and accepts the fact that you need time to review it or consult a trusted friend or relative. Do not let anyone rush you or pressure you into making a decision or sign anything. Legitimate deals are usually available for a reasonable amount of time—certainly more than one day.
- There may be an offer of a reduced price for work using materials

"left over" from a previous job in your neighborhood. The "leftover" material (typically asphalt) may be stolen. The "hot" tar may be just that! Never agree to buy leftover asphalt. The so-called "black-top" is typically motor oil—*used* motor oil! A competent, reliable contractor can correctly estimate how much material will be needed for a particular job and will not likely have any significant excess.

• Be cautious with a contractor who does not list a business number in the local telephone directory or who provides only a post office box without a street address or phone number, or if a phone number is given it is just an answering service. Be dubious of the contractor who is always unavailable by phone except for an answering machine.

• A con man may tell you your job will be a "demonstration" or "model," and propose the use of your home as a "display" home. He or she will offer a discounted price or other incentives for referrals, but only if you accept the offer "today!" Be wary of offers of discounts for finding other customers. You could lose many friends this way.

• The contractor insists that you pay for the entire job in advance and will accept only cash. If a contractor needs money to purchase supplies, that is a sure sign of a problem. Often, the handyman receives payment for materials, then leaves, supposedly headed for the building supply dealer, never to return. A legitimate contractor will have adequate credit with his suppliers.

• Try to avoid paying any funds in advance, and do not pay any amount before you read, understand, and sign a contract. If you agree to make a down payment to cover costs of materials, the down payment should not be more than one-third of the total price. According to most state laws, only licensed contractors and salespeople can require and accept any payments before the job is completed. Pay the final payment only *after* the work is completed to your satisfaction. In many cases, a price is agreed upon but when the work is finished, the contractor presents a final bill that far exceeds the original quote. Intimidated or confused by the explanation for the higher charge, the homeowner pays the inflated bill. Any later efforts to dispute the bill and reclaim the overcharges are virtually always futile, since the scam operator has already moved on to another town and another victim.

- Typically, the shady contractor offers exceptionally long guarantees and warranties—all worthless, of course.

The "Travelers"

A discussion of home-improvement scams would not be complete without mention of the notorious "Travelers"—an infamous group that has attained an almost legendary status in this particular art of bamboozle. In the past, this nefarious group was generally referred to by the pejorative term "gypsies." This deprecatory stereotype is no longer politically correct and socially acceptable and considered offensive to the Rom who comprise a highly respectable segment of American society and of the world population.

The California Contractors State License Board has described this disreputable migratory group and the tactics they commonly use: "Travelers" are clans of seasonally itinerant door-to-door home repair contractors who commit painting, roofing, and paving repair scams against homeowners throughout the U.S. (Source: California Contractors State License Board, "Traveler Tip Sheet," no date). They frequently prey on elderly, widowed or single homeowners. They are known for door-to-door solicitation by individuals related by family who often use confusing inverted names. Their trademarks include brand new vehicles—usually flashy pickup trucks with an abundance of chrome trim and accessories and displaying out-of-state license plates—usually all from the same state where they live in enclaves.

Identity Theft

Identity Theft and Fraud

Good name in man and woman, dear my lord,
Is the immediate jewel of their souls:
 Who steals my purse steals trash; 'tis something, nothing;
'Twas mine, 'tis his, and has been slave to thousands;

But he that filches from me my good name
Robs me of that which not enriches him,
And makes me poor indeed.
—Shakespeare, *Othello*, act III, scene 3.

Identity theft occurs when someone deceptively and wrongfully appropriates another person's personal information without his or her knowledge and uses that information to commit crimes of fraud or theft for the thief's personal economic gain. The Identity Theft Resource Center has affirmed that

> Identity theft is an absolute epidemic.... It's certainly picked up in the last four or five years. It is nationwide. It affects everybody, and there is very little you can do to prevent it and ... the worst of all—you can't detect it until it's probably too late. Some law-enforcement authorities call identity theft "the fastest growing crime across the country right now." .... Most victims don't even know how the perpetrators got their identity numbers. In many states, identity theft is not against the law!! In identity-theft cases, the victim often has to prove his or her innocence. This shocks most identity-theft victims. They naturally expect the police ... and others in high places to help them. Maybe it should be that way ... but often it isn't [Identity Theft Resource Center, "Identity Theft Prevention and Survival," 2003].

Unlike your fingerprints, which are unique to you and cannot be given to someone else for his use, your personal data—especially your Social Security number, bank account or credit card number, and other valuable identifying data—can be used, if they fall into the wrong hands, to personally profit a total stranger at your expense. Virtually all of this information can be purchased from a number of sites on the Internet for as little as $30 for a SSN to $300 for a bank account number. In the United States and Canada, for example, many people have reported that unauthorized persons have taken funds out of their bank or other financial accounts, or, in the worst cases, taken over their identities altogether, running up vast debts and committing crimes while using the victim's name.

With sufficient identifying information about a person, a criminal can assume an unsuspecting individual's persona and conduct a wide range of unlawful activities. These often include false applications for loans and credit cards, fraudulent withdrawals from financial accounts, fraudulent use of telephone calling cards, or obtaining other goods or privileges which the criminal would be denied if he were to use his or her real name.

If the criminal takes steps to ensure that bills for the falsely obtained credit cards, or bank statements showing the unauthorized transactions, are sent to an address other than the victim's, the victim may not become aware of what is happening until the criminal has already inflicted substantial damage on his or her assets, credit, and reputation.

The U.S. Department of Justice (DOJ) has advised: "To victims of identity theft and fraud, the task of correcting incorrect information about their financial or personal status, and trying to restore their good names and reputations, may seem as daunting as trying to solve a puzzle in which some of the pieces are missing and other pieces no longer fit as they once did. Unfortunately, the damage that criminals do in stealing another person's identity and using it to commit fraud often takes far longer to undo than it took the criminal to commit the crimes" (United States Department of Justice, "Identity Theft and Fraud," 2002).

The Extent of Identity Theft and Fraud

On September 3, 2003, the Federal Trade Commission released a survey showing that 27.3 million Americans have been victims of identity theft in the last five years, including 9.9 million people in the preceding year alone. According to the survey, in 2002 identity theft losses to businesses and financial institutions totaled nearly $48 billion and consumer victims reported $5 billion in out-of-pocket expenses. "For several years we have been seeing anecdotal evidence that identity theft is a significant problem that is on the rise. Now we know. It is affecting millions of consumers and costing billions of dollars. This information can serve to galvanize federal, state, and local law enforcers, the business community, and consumers to work together to combat this menace" (United States Federal Trade Commission, "FTC Releases Survey of Identity Theft in the U.S.," 2003).

On January 22, 2004, the FTC released its annual report detailing consumer complaints about identity theft and listing the top 10 fraud complaint categories reported by consumers in 2003. For the fourth year in a row, identity theft topped the list, accounting for 42 percent of the complaints lodged in the FTC's Consumer Sentinel database. The FTC received more than half a million complaints in 2003, up from 404,000 in 2002, and Internet-related complaints accounted for 55 percent of all fraud reports, up from 45 percent in 2002. The full text of the FTC report is online (Source: United States Federal Trade Commission, "Top 10 Consumer Complaint Categories in 2003," 2004).

Recent Federal Law to Fight Identity Theft

The Fair and Accurate Credit Transactions Act of 2003 (FACT Act, PL 108-15) was signed into law by President Bush on December 4, 2003. The Act, which amends the Fair Credit Reporting Act, will provide new measures for consumers, companies, consumer reporting agencies, and regulators with important new tools that expand access to credit and other financial services for all Americans, enhance the accuracy of consumers' financial information, and help fight identity theft.

The Scope of the Problem for Senior Citizens

On July 18, 2002, an official of the Federal Trade Commission advised the U.S. Senate Special Committee on Aging that in 2001, the FTC received 117,000 consumer contacts from both victims of identity theft and others concerned about identity theft. Of the 117,000 contacts, 75 percent, or 86,000, reported that they were actually victims of identity theft. About 10 percent of those consumers who called were age 60 years or older (Source: United States Federal Trade Commission, "FTC Testifies on Identity Theft and the Impact on Seniors," 2002). The Director of the FTC's Bureau of Consumer Protection advised the panel that although there are some differences in what senior identity theft victims were reporting to the agency, overall, their experiences were similar to those of other consumers.

How Identity Thieves Obtain and Use Your Personal Information

How a thief ends up with the victim's identity is often a mystery. The FTC reports that about 80 percent of victims don't know how their personal information ended up in the hands of a thief. But the results are far from mysterious. In many cases, a victim's losses may include not only out-of-pocket financial losses, but substantial additional financial costs associated with trying to restore his or her reputation in the community and correcting erroneous information for which the criminal is responsible.

In the course of a busy day, you may be involved in many personal financial transactions. Chances are you don't give these everyday transactions a second thought. But someone else may—a potential thief may be most interested; identity thieves' stock in trade are your everyday transactions. Many transactions require you to divulge certain personal information such as your bank and credit card account numbers, your income, your Social Security number, and your name, address, and phone number. An identity thief can appropriate some small but significant piece of this personal information without your knowledge and use it to fabricate an extensive structure of fraud or theft (Source: United States Federal Trade Commission, *ID Theft*, 2002).

Despite your best efforts to manage the flow of your personal information or to keep it to yourself, skilled identity thieves may use a variety of methods—low-tech and hi-tech—to gain access to your data. Many people do not realize how easily criminals can invade our privacy without invading our premises. In public places, such as malls for example, criminals may engage in "shoulder surfing"—watching you from a nearby location as you punch in your credit card number or eavesdropping unnoticed as you recite the number or other personal information over the telephone.

Even the area outside of your home or office may not be secure. Some criminals engage in "dumpster diving"—going through trash cans or a communal trash bin—to obtain copies of checks, credit card or bank statements, or other records that, in addition to account numbers, also typically bear your name, address, and telephone number. These types of records make it easy for criminals to take control over accounts in your name and assume your identity.

If you receive applications for "preapproved" credit cards in the mail but discard them without tearing up the enclosed materials, criminals may retrieve them and try to activate the cards for their use without your knowledge. (Some credit card companies, when sending such credit cards, have adopted security measures that allow a card recipient to activate the card only from his or her home telephone number but this is not yet a universal practice.) Also, if your mail is delivered to a place where others might have ready access to it, criminals may simply intercept and redirect your mail to another address—theirs.

In recent years, the Internet has become an appealing place for criminals to obtain identifying data, such as passwords or even banking information. In their haste to explore the exciting features of the Internet, many people respond to "spam"—unsolicited e-mail—that promises them some benefit but requests identifying data, without realizing that in many cases, the requestor has no intention of keeping his or her promise. In some cases, criminals reportedly have used computer technology to obtain large amounts of personal data.

One of the most recent scams has been the account "update" or "billing" ruse. In July 2003, the Federal Trade Commission issued this consumer alert:

> Internet scammers casting about for people's financial information have a new way to lure unsuspecting victims: They go "phishing." Phishing, also called "carding," is a high-tech scam that uses spam to deceive consumers into disclosing their credit card numbers, bank account information, Social Security numbers, passwords, and other sensitive information. The e-mails pretend to be from businesses the potential victims deal with—for example, their Internet service provider (ISP), online payment service or bank. The fraudsters tell recipients that they need to "update" or "validate" their billing information to keep their accounts active, and direct them to a "look-alike" Web site of the legitimate business, further tricking consumers into thinking they are responding to a bona fide request. Unknowingly, consumers submit their financial information—not to the businesses— but the scammers, who use it to order goods and services and obtain credit [United States Federal Trade Commission," How Not to Get Hooked by a 'Phishing' Scam," 2003].

These phishing enthusiasts may also troll by telephone. To avoid getting caught by one of these scams, the FTC offers this guidance: "If you get an e-mail that warns you, with little or no notice, that an account of yours will be shut down unless you reconfirm your billing information, do not reply or click on the link in the e-mail. Instead, contact the company cited in the e-mail using a telephone number or Web site address you know to be genuine. Avoid e-mailing personal and financial information. Before submitting financial information through a Web site, look for the 'lock' icon on the browser's status bar. It signals that your information is secure during transmission" (United States Federal Trade Commission, "How Not to Get Hooked," 2003).

How to Protect Yourself

Can you completely prevent identity theft from occurring? Probably not, especially if the potential thief is determined to commit the crime. But you can minimize your risk by managing your personal information wisely, cautiously, and with heightened sensitivity. The biggest problem that you as a victim may face: You may not know your identity has been stolen until you notice that something is amiss; you may get bills for a credit card account you never opened; your credit report may include debts you never knew you had; a billing cycle may pass without your receiving a statement; or you may see charges on your bills that you didn't sign for, didn't authorize, and know nothing about.

While you probably cannot absolutely prevent identity theft, there are a number things that you can do to reduce or minimize your risk of falling prey to identity thieves, but most officials admit that a determined thief can find a way into your personal information. That doesn't mean that anything you do to protect yourself may be futile. You can make it more difficult for criminals by following a few simple rules and taking some basic steps. For starters, just remember the word "scam," and as a general rule, be very reluctant about giving out your personal information to others unless you have a valid reason to trust them and an absolute need to so.

At Home

- Start by adopting a "need to know" approach to your personal data. Your credit card company may need to know your mother's maiden name so that it can verify your identity when you call to inquire about your account. A person who calls you and says he or she is from your bank does not need to know information that is already on file with the bank. The only purpose of such a call is to acquire that information for the caller's personal benefit. Also, the more information that you have printed on your personal bank checks the more personal data you are routinely handing out to people who may not need that information. Only your name is sufficient.

- Do not give out personal information on the phone, through the mail or over the Internet unless you have initiated the contact or know with whom you are dealing. Legitimate organizations with whom you regularly do business should have all of the information they require and will not have to ask for it.
- Before you reveal any personal information, find out how it will be used and whether it will be shared with others. Ask if you have a choice about the use of your information; can you choose to have it kept confidential?
- Senior citizens are cautioned to be very careful guarding their Social Security number. It is one of the most important pieces of personal identity information you have. Memorize it and do not routinely carry your card with you, because if you lose it, it could become very valuable to anyone who finds it. Leave it at home in a safe place—it is rare that you actually have to produce it anyway. As a general rule, for your protection give your SSN only when absolutely necessary. Many people are far too free in disclosing their SSN.
- Stolen mail is one of the easiest ways to get someone's personal information. Monitor your mail carefully; guard it from theft. Theft of your mail may indicate that you are a potential victim of theft of your identity. Deposit outgoing mail in post office collection boxes or at your local post office. Retrieve mail from your mailbox as quickly as possible, or have someone do it for you, so thieves don't get there before you. Don't let mail accumulate in your box—especially if you go away. If you're planning to be away from home and can't arrange to have your mail picked up, call the your local post office to request a vacation hold. The post office will retain your mail until you return and can pick it up. Invest in a lockable mailbox that meets U.S. Postal Service standards.
- Maintain careful records of your banking and other financial accounts. Check these regularly and carefully; look for what should be there and what shouldn't. If you find that your statements are being sent to an address that you haven't authorized, tell the financial institution or credit card representative immediately that you did not authorize the change of address and that someone may be improperly using your accounts. If

someone has gotten your financial data and made unauthorized debits or charges against your financial accounts, checking your monthly statements carefully may be the quickest way for you to find out.

- Be cautious about where you leave personal information in your home, especially if you have frequent visitors, tenants, employ outside help, or have services provided in your home. Keep documents with personal information on them in a secure, discrete place.
- Cut up old or expired debit and credit cards. Do not simply discard them.
- If appropriate, consider investing in an inexpensive paper shredder and use it to shred every unneeded financial statement, old bill and preapproved credit solicitation before you toss it into the trash. This leaves the "dumpster divers" with only useless confetti.

AWAY FROM HOME

- Minimize the identification information and the number of credit cards you carry to those that you'll actually need. Carry only that information with you that you may absolutely need for day-to-day dealings.
- Keep a watchful eye on your credit cards during all purchases.
- Make sure that no one can see or overhear your PIN when using an ATM, public phone, or making a point of sale purchase.
- Always take your ATM or credit card receipts. Never leave receipts behind at ATM machines, in public trash bins, or at gasoline pumps.
- If you have to telephone someone while you're traveling, and need to pass on personal financial information to the person you're calling, don't do it at an open telephone booth where passersby can overhear what you're saying; use a telephone booth where you can close the door, or wait until you're at a less public location to call. Always be aware of your surroundings and the persons near you.

What to Do If Your Identity Is Stolen

Sometimes an identity thief can strike even if you've been very careful about keeping your personal information to yourself. If you suspect that your personal information has been hijacked and misappropriated to commit fraud or theft, take action immediately to minimize the damage to your personal funds and financial accounts, as well as your reputation. In doing so, keep detailed records of your conversations and correspondence. Exactly which steps you should take to protect yourself depends on your circumstances and how your identity has been misused. However, certain basic actions are appropriate in almost every case.

FIRST THINGS FIRST

If someone has stolen your identity, the Federal Trade Commission recommends that you take three actions immediately.

- First, contact the fraud departments of each of the three major credit bureaus. Advise them that you're an identity theft victim. Request that a fraud alert and a victim's impact report be placed on you account. Prepare a statement asking that creditors call you before opening any new accounts or changing your existing accounts. This can help prevent an identity thief from opening additional accounts in your name.
- Second, contact all creditors with whom your name or identifying data have been fraudulently used and regarding any accounts that have been, or could be, tampered with or opened fraudulently; include credit card companies, phone companies and other utilities, and banks and other lenders.
- Third, file a report with your local police or the police in the community where the identity theft took place. Get a copy of the police report in case the bank, credit card company or others need proof of the crime. Even if the police can't catch the identity thief in your case, having a copy of the police report can help you when dealing with creditors.

NEXT: TAKE CONTROL

Although identity thieves can wreak havoc on your personal

finances, there are some things you can do to take control of the situation. Here's how to handle some of the most common forms of identity theft.

- Social Security Number: Immediately report suspected or actual identity theft to the Social Security Administration. Ask the SSA to help you by issuing a new number and flagging your old number to thwart possible fraudulent use.
- Stolen mail: If an identity thief has stolen your mail or has falsified change-of-address forms, notify the postal authorities immediately.
- Credit card accounts: If you discover that someone has changed the billing address on an existing credit card account, close the account. When you open a new account, ask that a password be used before any inquiries or changes can be made on the account.
- Bank accounts: If you have reason to believe that someone has accessed and tampered with your bank accounts or ATM card, you may need to close those accounts immediately.

  If your checks have been stolen or misused, place stop-payment orders on any outstanding checks that may not have cleared. While no federal law limits your losses if someone steals your checks and forges your signature, state laws should protect you. Most states hold the bank responsible for losses from a forged check. At the same time, however, most states require you to take reasonable care of your account. For example, you may be held responsible for the forgery if you fail to notify the bank in a timely manner that checks were lost or stolen. If your ATM card has been lost, stolen, or otherwise compromised, cancel the card and get another with a new PIN.
- Investments: If you believe that an identity thief has tampered with your securities investments or a brokerage account, immediately report it to your broker or account manager and to the Securities and Exchange Commission (SEC).
- Phone service: If someone has established new phone service in your name or is making unauthorized calls, contact your service provider immediately to cancel the account.

• Criminal records: In rare instances, an identity thief could create a criminal record using your name. For example, the impostor may give your name when being cited or arrested. If this happens to you, you may need to hire an attorney to help resolve the problem. The procedures for clearing your name vary by jurisdiction (Source: United States Federal Trade Commission, *ID Theft*, 2002).

Investments

The Scope of the Problem

According to recent news reports, investment fraud is increasingly targeting the elderly (CNN, "Investment Scams Targeting the Elderly," 2000). On April 12, 2002, an MSNBC report stated:

> If you're over 50 years of age, you're twice as likely to be on the list of fraudulent solicitors. That, coupled with two years of shrinking portfolios, and the fear of not having enough to live on, can put retirees in a fragile position. More than half the people on the lists of unscrupulous telemarketers are age 50 or older, and many of these solicitors try to induce recently retired people to invest their retirement savings in phony investment schemes with claims of large profits in a short time period. The result of all of this is that safe investments may be turned worthless by promises that can't be met or are misunderstood [MSNBC, "Investment Fraud Against the Retired," 2002].

It has been estimated that the American public loses $40 billion a year to fraudulent schemes and scams involving everything from sham sweepstakes, fake magazine subscriptions, phony charities, to securities fraud. State securities regulators estimate that the latter costs Americans as much as $10 billion each year (Source: Seniors.gov, "The Top Ten Investment Scams," 2001).

Certainly many investment plans are sound. Those that are not take many forms. Typical investments sold by fraudulent operators have included fine art, rare coins, gemstones, oil and gas leases, interests in oil wells, cellular telephone licenses, precious metals such as gold and silver, or strategic metals used in defense and high-tech industries.

Most consumers invest in traditional offerings—stocks, bonds, and commodities—that are regulated by the Securities and Exchange Commission, the Commodities Futures Trading Commission (CFTC), and state securities regulators. However, many consumers also invest large sums in less traditional offerings that either are outside SEC and CFTC jurisdiction or are subject to shared jurisdiction with the Federal Trade Commission. And it is in these that fraud prevails.

The operators often choose to sell investments that may fluctuate substantially in response to world events. For example, they may offer an investment based on the scarcity of a foreign metal after news of a trade embargo, or they might offer an investment in a new, widely publicized high-tech product. Their goal is to make it difficult for consumers to scrutinize their overinflated value claims.

Fraudulent investment promoters typically use aggressive marketing tools such as infomercials and telemarketing to reach consumers. They also flout state and federal securities registration laws using ways which make their promotional materials—including profit projections, use of proceeds, and risk disclosures—not subject to routine regulatory scrutiny. Consumers may believe that a scheme's slick promotional materials, with risk disclosures in fine-print, fully set forth the investment's profit potential and risks. Instead, the SEC warns that "investors must be aware that their first line of defense against telecommunications technology and other securities fraud is their own diligence and skepticism in evaluating a proposed investment—especially one not registered with the [Securities and Exchange] Commission" (Federal Trade Commission, *Fighting Consumer Fraud*, 1997).

These hawkers fill specious security offerings with "investment opportunities" that mimic legitimate investments. The history of investment fraud demonstrates that the promoters look to the mainstream marketplace for ideas to imitate and for ways to induce consumers to invest. Law enforcement officials and consumers need to follow the headlines to forecast likely fraudulent investment schemes. And based on recent news stories, fraud watchers can expect to see a general increase in "too good to be true" pitches regarding Internet business investments and partnerships to build our new "information superhighway" communications systems.

If you invest in what turns out to be a fraudulent scheme, the likelihood of getting any or all of your investment back is very remote. Even in cases where investment funds are recovered, consumers usually receive less than ten cents of every dollar they have expended. The reason is that promoters usually operate a particular scam for a short time, quickly spend the money they take in, and close down before they can be detected. Then they move on, resume operations under a new name, and start selling another investment scam.

Why Senior Citizens Are Targets of Investment Fraud

Senior Citizens have become prime targets for fraudulent investment schemes. AARP has affirmed: "Anybody can be taken in, experts say. The fact of the matter is that victims come in all shapes and sizes, older Americans may be especially vulnerable" (AARP, "Stock Frauds on the Rise," 2000). This population tends to have more assets, including retirement savings and investments than the younger population who usually do not have the holdings that attract the con artists.

This fact, and the prevailing fear among senior citizens that they could outlive their retirement funds, or lose them entirely in the event a health catastrophe, compounds the implications of investment fraud. The young person is far more able to recoup such a loss than the retiree whose income may depend substantially on their investments. If a large sum of money has been received by the retiree, an unscrupulous salesman may try to induce him or her to invest it all in highly risky investments. Most promise either a large increase in the value of your investment or higher-than-market interest on your capital or both. The FTC has said that: "Investment fraud, like telemarketing fraud in general, often targets older people, who may be least able to afford the hit to their savings accounts.... [B]ecause their prime earning years have passed and the sources of extraordinary income may be one-time life events, older Americans are less able to repair the damage when they are the victims of fraud" (Federal Trade Commission, *Fighting Consumer Fraud*, 1997).

Compounding the senior citizen's financial loss may be imposed restrictions on, or loss of, their rights to manage their own affairs—particularly their financial affairs. Over-zealous members of their family may react by petitioning a court to have the elderly relative declared incompetent. This can have devastating effects on an individual who has managed their own assets adequately and responsibly throughout a long life. It can be especially difficult for the senior citizen who has worked very hard and saved very carefully for retirement only to find that he is now obliged to depend on someone else to manage their life in its last years. They can lose money, control, pride, and dignity—all to an insidious scheme.

Investment Scams

Our volatile stock markets have investors, particularly older Americans dependent on predictable interest income, looking for safe havens. So scammers are pitching their investments as low risk and high return. That is an impossible combination. The higher the return, the higher the risk.

While the list of scams includes repeat offenders, such as broadly marketed promissory notes, bogus prime bank schemes, and risky viatical settlements, the people selling them are moving out of the boiler room and onto Main Street. What is new is that scammers are targeting independent life insurance agents to act as sellers. While the vast majority of agents are doing what they should and looking out for their clients, a growing minority, lured by high commissions, are relying solely on marketing dubious investments and making claims about them that are misleading or downright false.

Tips to Identify and Avoid Investment Scams

Identifying fraud before you become a victim is the only sure way to avoid it. "Fraud is always a possibility, even with secured, regulated investments. Before investing, ask tough questions, both of yourself and those who are soliciting your investments. If the answer to any of these questions is 'no'—or if the answers are vague or complicated—more than likely the investment being pitched is a fraud" (United States Federal Trade Commission, "Investment Risks," 1997).

Because it is highly unlikely that you will ever recover funds you have given to fraudulent stock promoters, the wisest approach you can take is not to give them any money in the first place. Therefore, if you are contacted by a stranger offering you an investment opportunity, remember the following general cautions.

- Understand what you are investing in. It is difficult to invest and profit when you do not know what you are doing. It is reckless to invest in a proposal that you do not understand, or have not investigated and verified. You should be especially cautious of any investment in which you are expected to depend solely on the seller's representation of its value and merits.
- Do your homework! Research all of the available information about the proposed investment from various authoritative, independent, sources. Get expert advice. Carefully examine any prospectus which, by law, you must be given.
- Any reluctance or resistance on the part of the seller in response to your inquiries for detailed information and financial data should be suspect. If the seller is forthcoming with such information, that is not a guarantee that it is reliable.
- Should you have any unresolved questions or lingering doubts, do not proceed with the investment.
- How can you be certain a promoter is not lying to you? Scam artists lie! Their success depends on having a plausible answer for everything. They have well-rehearsed rebuttals prepared for any possible excuses a reluctant prospect may offer (Source: United States Federal Trade Commission, "Investment Risks," 1997).

These promoters create the illusion of authenticity and prosperity by surrounding themselves with the trappings of success—they incorporate, lease posh office space, employ support staff including investment "counselors," and present slick, professionally designed color brochures describing their operation.

It is easy to make a new venture sound like a sure-fire money-maker, especially if the press is writing about successful legitimate companies in similar industries. But while scam artists claim to offer investments in exciting businesses or sell lucrative stocks and bonds, they deliver only empty promises. They inflate the costs and value of worthless investments. They promise profits years down the road so you will not discover that your investment is a scam until long after they have disappeared with your money. In the interim victims remain unaware that they have invested in something of little or no value until their money is long-gone. These schemes are fraught with danger. In most cases, you will never again see the funds you invested.

Red Flags

A growing number of senior citizens are investing their hard-earned savings in hopes of getting more favorable returns. While there are many legitimate and worthwhile opportunities available, investments have also become fertile ground for scam artists who present messages mixed with truth and lies. How will you know if the offer is too good to be true? Whether the initial contact comes from a telemarketer, over the Internet, at a seminar, or by direct mail, most investment frauds share certain characteristics and, although investment scams come in many different packages, there are some common red flags to help you spot the schemes and scams.

- The "special" deal to "special" clients. "You are going to be let in on a 'ground floor opportunity.'" "You have been specially selected to participate in an unusual investment opportunity." "It is a special deal for a select few." Every potential victim is "select" and is "special."
- "There is no risk." These schemes invariably offer investors an irresistible and virtually "risk-free way to get rich quick" and guarantees of high returns. Does the salesperson make the proposal sound as though you "cannot lose?" Be very dubious of claims of high profits with practically no risk; there really is no such thing. Every potentially high profit investment is high risk. Investing is an inherently risky business. The FTC has confirmed in numerous reports that consumers lose millions of dollars each year in an array of get-rich-quick schemes that promise high returns with little or no risk.
- "Chance of a lifetime." "You must act now to capitalize on this opportunity!" "*Carpe diem*! You must buy now or forever lose your chance to profit!" Are you being pressured to make a decision immediately or within a short period of time because new investment units "are selling fast" or "because the market is moving"? Be very wary of these "now-or-never" or "limited time" offers. Using carefully crafted sales scripts, scam artists

create the impression that only a few shares of a stock are left. They try to convince you that you will miss out on a big opportunity if you do not send them thousands of dollars by overnight courier or wire transfer. Such high-pressure sales tactics are typical of all fraudulent operators. Do not allow yourself to be pressured into buying. If you are, simply hang up the telephone. Remember: Reputable investment firms rarely if ever operate exclusively by telephone solicitation, and—by law—must provide written information in the form of a prospectus, and sufficient time for a client to consider an investment proposal.

• Playing on fear: Fear can cloud one's judgment. The scam artists know that many senior citizens worry that they will either outlive their savings or see them dissipated as a result of a catastrophic event, such as a costly hospitalization or nursing home care. Do not give in to fear or scare tactics.

• Glowing testimonials: Beware of glowing testimonials. Fraudulent operators can easily hire "references"—"satisfied customers" to claim that an investment they purchased brought them quick and easy wealth. Be very skeptical of "testimonials"; the source may be a shill (Source: United States Federal Trade Commission, "Investment Risks," 1997).

Telemarketing Investment Fraud

Off the Hook, an AARP Foundation study funded by the U. S. Justice Department that was released in July 2003, confirmed that the crime of telemarketing fraud is grossly underreported among older victims. In one portion of the study, AARP researchers found that 73 percent of *known* investment fraud victims interviewed would not acknowledge having lost money although they had previously been in contact with law enforcement authorities to file complaints. The complete text of the AARP publication *Off the Hook* can be found at: http://research.aarp.org/consume/d17812_fraud.html.

Investment frauds come in many guises. The FTC reports that three-fourths of the investment scams reported to the Commission involve telemarketers operating from boiler rooms and utilizing the "pump and dump" tactics described in the following section. There has been a dramatic increase in this mode of fraud because of the ease of setting up such operations and the prevalence of telephone sales for innumerable products and services. Every senior citizen with a telephone is a potential victim. Your own common sense is your first and best line of defense against telemarketing investment fraud. If you hear any of the red flags listed here, hang up!

The "Pump and Dump" Scam

In this investment scheme the "brokers" push stock of little-known or moribund companies—typically those whose shares trade over-the-counter at less than $5. Insiders hire these spurious brokers to tout a stock and build a market to hike the price. When the shares peak, the insiders get out taking large profits. The gullible investors who had been lured into the scheme by the boiler room operators are left holding the bag.

The Boiler Room

A sizable portion of the telemarketing calls received by Americans, old and young alike, come from these shadowy, little-known "boiler rooms." Boiler rooms are not new. The descriptive term comes from the traditionally windowless, smoke-filled basement offices (next to the boiler room) where the telemarketing investment scam operation would install extensive telephone banks and employ mercenaries who spend abject hours randomly and relentlessly calling hundreds of prospects all around the country, and, using high-pressure, well coached sales tactics, glibly push products or services of any kind.

With today's sophisticated communications technology and computerized dialing software, a boiler room can function with only one or two persons on telephones, and is likely to be situated—if only temporarily, and one step ahead of the law—on an upper floor in a modern and comfortable suburban office building. As AARP reports: "Salespersons in boiler room operations often spend years going from fraud to fraud. Their years of selling experience and natural sales talent make them very good at what they do. They use persuasive sales pitches that weave together facts and half-truths in ways that are likely to deceive all but the most experienced investor. Their sales pitches are directed to the universal desire to get great financial return for very little risk" (AARP, "Online Fraud on the Rise," 2003).

You are likely to be called if you have ever responded to an advertisement or filled out a card asking for more information about a product or service of any kind, not just an investment. Or you might receive a cold call. Fraudulent operators also mark investors who have been victims of previous scams; they then become prime targets for the "recovery room" or "reloading" scam (discussed in detail in a chapter to follow) in which a con artist offers to help victims get back some of the money they lost in an earlier fraud—knowing that individuals who have been deceived once can be vulnerable because they hope to recoup their previous losses. These rogue promoters know whom to call for either of these schemes because they purchase mooch lists from other brokers and telemarketers. These are lists of names of people who have fallen, or are apt to fall, for investment scams. They can be compiled from numerous sources such as catalog sales, magazine subscriptions, warranty forms, registration for prizes, and online transactions. The more you purchase from certain sources or express an interest in their products, the more valuable your name is—and the more likely it is to appear on several mooch lists in circulation.

TACTICS BOILER ROOM CALLERS USE

The tactics these operators are coached to use include:

- Softening up the customer by making him or her feel part of an elite group getting "special service" or a "special deal."
- Creating a sense of urgency.
- Using the "don't just watch your friends get rich" pitch.
- Aggressivness, always pushing to close the sale. "There's no such thing as a no-sale call." "Either you sell the prospect some stock, or he sells you on a reason he cannot buy." (The only question is who is going to close, you or the stock hawker.)
"Do not take 'no' for answer." They have rebuttals ready for any conceivable excuse not to buy.

In addition to being very glib, these operators are highly resourceful. They use a wide variety of reasons why their investment opportunity is a "sure thing." In their sales pitch, they may say, for example, that they have high-level financial "connections" or that they are privy to "inside information" about a company or product that will soon send the stock price soaring. It is always false and designed to get persons to invest when they otherwise would not. In any event, trading on inside information can be a violation of the law, as recent news reports confirm. They will "guarantee" the investment (whatever that may mean) or promise to repurchase it after a certain time period. To close a sale these hucksters will present a confusing array of skewed statistics, misrepresent the significance of a current event, or stress the unique quality of their offering—anything to deter the prospect from verifying the numbers or facts they expound.

Cyberspace: New Medium, Same Old Scams

The Internet serves as an excellent tool for investors, allowing them to easily and inexpensively research innumerable legitimate investment opportunities. But the Internet is also an excellent tool for shysters. That is why you should always think twice before you invest your money in any opportunity you learn about through the Web.

If you want to invest wisely and steer clear of frauds, you must get the facts. *Never* make an investment based solely on what you read in an online newsletter or bulletin board posting, especially if the investment involves a small, thinly-traded company that is not well known. And do not even think about investing on your own in small companies that do not file regular reports with the SEC, unless you are willing to investigate each company thoroughly and to check the truth of every bit of data about it. For instance, you will need to get financial statements from the company and be able to analyze them and verify the claims about new product developments or lucrative contracts. Are you able to do this? Do you know anyone who can? (Source: Securities and Exchange Commission, "Internet Fraud," 2001).

The types of investment fraud seen online mirror the frauds perpetrated over the phone or through the mail. Remember that fraudulent investment promoters can use a variety of Internet tools to spread false information. The Internet allows individuals or companies to communicate with a large audience without spending a great deal of time, effort, or money. Anyone can reach millions of online users by building a flashy and highly sophisticated website, posting messages on online bulletin boards, publishing online newsletters, entering discussions in live "chat" rooms, or sending mass e-mails (spam)—a favorite method. All of these tools cost very little money and can be easily placed at the fingertips of fraudsters—literally at their fingertips, on a keyboard. It is easy for these operators to make their messages look real and credible. And it can be virtually impossible for novice investors to tell the difference between fact and fiction.

Living Trusts

Definition of a Living Trust

A living trust—created while the grantor lives—is a legal instrument that allows the grantor to control the distribution of his or her property after he or she is deceased. The term "living" refers to the fact that such trusts take effect while the grantor is still alive, and only when he or she has transferred assets into (funded) the trust. You can serve as the trustee, or you can select a person or an institution to be the trustee. If you are the trustee, you will have to name a successor trustee to distribute the assets in the event of your death. Under most living trust arrangements, grantors, while still competent, are free to change the terms of the trust. A living trust should not be confused with a living will; these are two entirely different concepts.

Living Trusts: Are They Trust-Worthy?

In your long lifetime you have worked hard for your money, and made every attempt to be a conscientious saver. So it is only natural that you want some control over what happens to your assets—your estate—in the event of your death. At the very least, you want to minimize or avoid potential problems for your heirs, particularly those involved in probate. You must plan your estate. Even if you are a person of modest means, you have an estate—and you also have several options to choose from to assure that the assets that comprise it are distributed as you wish and in a timely and fiscally effective way. The right strategies depend on your individual circumstances. What is best for a friend or neighbor might not be appropriate for you.

Con artists are ready to play on the elderly's fears of the unknown. These provide the perfect opportunity for scammers who have created a veritable industry out of older persons' fears—that after their deaths, their life savings and assets will be drained away by the government or by predatory probate attorneys; that their estates could be eaten up by costs; or that the distribution of their assets could be delayed for an inordinately long period. These operators disseminate or exploit such misinformation and misunderstanding. They use high-pressure tactics and deceptive claims to coerce vulnerable seniors into setting up a living trust—a fiscal instrument that many of them do not need and cannot afford. It is true that for some people, a living trust can be a useful and practical tool, but for many others, it can be a waste of money and time. A simple will would be quite adequate for them.

Often a living trust can be a more efficient and less costly alternative to a will. But scam artists are using living trusts to fleece the trusting. In doing so they will rely on what for some laypersons may be unfamiliar terms such as "probate" and "executor" to convince elderly consumers that a living trust is right for them even though many of the complex rules and fees that can complicate estate distributions may never be applicable to them, or do not exist in their state of jurisdiction. Elderly consumers are bombarded with advertisements, approached directly, or solicited by phone or mail to attend seminars or to call for in-home appointments to learn whether a living trust is right for them—invariably it will be! The scam artist will make it right for them.

In these encounters, living trusts are frequently marketed through high-pressure sales pitches which prey on the fear that assets will be tied up indefinitely or that estates are prone to heavy taxes and fees if a living trust is not in place. Slick promotional materials and presentations will claim that thousands of dollars in probate costs and taxes can be saved simply by purchasing a living trust. These sales representatives typically indicate that the consumer "must act quickly," often the same day, in order to take advantage of the offer. It is common for the salesperson to exaggerate the benefits or the suitability of the living trust and claim—falsely—"licensed attorneys" will prepare the trust documents.

The advantage of a living trust? Properly drafted and executed, it can mitigate some effects of probate because the trust owns the assets, not the deceased grantor. The downside? Poorly drawn or unfunded trusts can cost you money and obviate your best intentions. Seniors who decide they want to go ahead with a living trust should be advised that the process could be relatively expensive. It can take a great deal of time to set one up, and to do so an attorney may charge five or six times the cost of preparing a will. Depending on the size of the estate, the costs of a living trust may be much higher than the costs of probate. This depends on the individual's situation. Drafting the legal document is not enough. The trust will not be valid until property is transferred from the individual's name to the trust—"funding the trust." Seniors should also be counseled that even if they decide to set up a living trust, it is still a good idea to have a will that has been prepared by an attorney.

Consumer education and legal assistance are critical to help senior citizens understand their estate planning options and avoid the traps of unscrupulous living trust purveyors. Such education is important for seniors of all income levels. Concern about property distribution after death is an issue that crosses socioeconomic and class lines. The amount of anxiety generated does not necessarily correspond to the size of the estate. However, the stakes are higher in most cases for low-income seniors who are too often persuaded to dip into limited funds in order to purchase a product that does not meet their needs and which they cannot afford.

For many seniors, education and advice about living trusts will come too late. They will have already made a purchase, often from a so-called "living trust mill." In some instances, the product may be legitimate, but grossly overpriced. In others, problems arise because of false or misleading claims and advertisements. The FTC advises you to proceed with caution. Because state laws and requirements vary, "cookie-cutter" approaches to estate planning are not always the most efficient way to handle your financial affairs. Before you sign any documents to create a will, a living trust, or any other kind of trust, explore all your options with an experienced and licensed estate planning attorney or financial advisor. As a general rule, state laws require that an *attorney* draft the instrument of trust. And avoid high-pressure sales tactics and glib sales pitches by anyone who is selling estate planning tools or arrangements such as "kits" or "packages" (Source: United States Federal Trade Commission, "Living Trust Offers," 2000).

Living Trust Kits or Packages

Fraudulent living trust promoters advertise and sell "self-help living trust kits," or living trust "packages." These worthless products may cost several thousand dollars—which is usually much more than an experienced attorney would charge to prepare a living trust that complies with all statutory requirements.

Consumers who pay exorbitant amounts for these do-it-yourself products receive nothing of any real value in return. The kits usually include basic information about wills and living trusts, and, in many cases, an assortment of legal forms for the consumer to fill out. These are nothing more than standard forms (readily available on the Internet for free) that may or may not have legal force in a particular jurisdiction—another major consideration. These documents may not have been drafted by attorneys, or are written by attorneys who are not licensed to practice in the consumer's state of residence. These "legal" documents may not comply with the statutes, rules, and regulations that vary from state to state. These kits are usually not a good idea because they are not tailored to a grantor's individual needs and intentions; they generally do not provide many options. Beware of the cookie-cutter legal documents presented in these kits; they could be just so much worthless paper.

Sellers of these packages often greatly exaggerate the complexity and cost of probating a will and falsely claim that creditors will never be able to reach assets placed in a living trust. There are a few high quality products available, but very many are rip-offs. The basic lesson for senior citizens is to be cautious and ask many questions before buying such a kit or package.

Living Trust Scams

On March 20, 1996, the Nightly Business Report, in a segment entitled "When It Comes to Living Trusts, You Can't Always 'Trust' What You Hear," noted: "Every few years, living trust seminars are intensively marketed in the media throughout the country. Once you attend, you'll receive coffee and cookies to be swallowed along with a powerful sales pitch touting the money-saving advantages of living trusts. Used as an alternative to a will, a living trust is another method of transferring assets to loved ones when you die. Advocates maintain that living trusts avoid the so-called high costs of probate, cost less than wills, and some even imply that there are taxes to be saved. But most of these supposed advantages simply don't ring true" (Nightly Business Report, "When It Comes to Living Trusts," 1996). Potential victims are persuaded to reveal everything about their finances in a questionnaire known among the scammers as a "smoke sheet" because its purpose is to smoke out the funds these elderly victims have in their retirement plans, savings accounts, investment portfolios, and anywhere else that can be discovered.

FALSE CLAIMS

Common exaggerated or false claims regarding living trusts include:

- Living trusts ensure privacy. Indeed, while probate proceedings are matters of public record, the likelihood of a stranger making an effort to find out about your will is remote.
- Exaggerated claims about the probate process—including an overstatement of the length, headaches, and costs.
- Misrepresentation of the tax advantages of living trusts. The truth is that a simple living trust (as opposed to a more complicated, hence more expensive, tax-saving living trust) has no appreciable effect on taxes. You will not save a significant amount in taxes by using a living trust. Everyone can be liable for estate taxes, and income taxes are not avoided by putting assets in trusts.
- Misrepresentations about the legal requirements of setting up a living trust. There are none; the choice is at the consumer's discretion.
- The sales representatives are "licensed" and qualified "attorneys." Typically they are not. If someone is trying to sell you a living trust, ask if he or she is an attorney. Some states require that only attorneys are permitted to set up living trusts. In any case, it is illegal if the seller is not an attorney but represents him or herself as such. That is fraud.
- Claims regarding the expense involved in setting up a living trust. The preparation of a living trust can require a great deal of an attorney's billable time. Drafting the trust instrument is not

enough. The trust will not be legally valid until the trust is funded.

- You do not need a will if you have a living trust. Should you decide to establish a living trust, it is still wise have a will as a backup.
- Creditors cannot go after assets that have been transferred to a living trust The truth: Property in a living trust is not automatically sheltered from creditors.
- Misrepresentations as to endorsements or approval of their products or services by national organizations or associations. These operators have commonly misrepresented that they are connected to AARP (see "The Name Game," following). Others have falsely claimed endorsements by state Attorneys General.

THE NAME GAME

Living trust scam promoters have commonly misrepresented that they are connected with or endorsed by AARP. Beware of companies that use names that sound like legitimate organizations. The scam promoters will often try to use nationally recognized names in an attempt convince a potential buyer that their operation is affiliated with or endorsed by such seniors advocacy groups. Especially avoid those sales representatives who attempt to create the impression that AARP is actually marketing, promoting, or somehow endorsing their product line. AARP does not sell or endorse any living trust product or service, and does not work cooperatively with any organization that promotes or sells such products—including kits or packages. The AARP website (http://www.aarp.org) does have a wealth of information on living trusts and many other topics of interest to senior citizens—including fraud.

Tips to Avoid Living Trust Scams

To avoid being taken advantage of by these con artists, keep the following tips in mind:

- *Always* consult an attorney regarding your need for and the creation of a living trust. Confirm that he or she has experience and expertise in estate planning matters. It is also important to ask how a living trust may affect your eligibility for future Medicaid nursing home benefits.

• Shop around. Check out offers with a trusted attorney or estate planner.

• Confirm that a living trust is your best option given your financial situation.

• Never sign anything containing options or legal terminology you do not understand. Ask the attorney to define and explain.

• Beware of anyone portraying living trusts as being a general solution to estate planning. There is no "one size fits all" option.

• Verify any averred affiliation with or endorsement by any government agency or reputable organization.

• Learn as much as you can about the company or individual promoting the trust.

• Always thoroughly check out offers from telephone solicitors or door-to-door sales people. Remember the FTC Cooling Off Rule.

• Consumers should be wary of entrepreneurially inclined lawyers and so-called "estate planners" who are attempting to sell them a living trust that they do not want or need. Here is a simple tip—ask if he or she has one.

• Avoid readily revealing private financial information. Many "estate planning," "financial advisory" services, insurance agents, and other promoters who sell trust packages will use the proposal of a living trust as an excuse to gain access to the consumer's financial information and then attempt to push other financial products, such as life insurance or annuities. Any or all of which may not be appropriate for that individual.

• If considering a living trust, be careful whom you trust.

Loss Recovery

The Scam

Loss recovery scams are also known as "recovery," "recovery room," "reloading," or "double-scamming" because they are designed to take a victim's money not just once, but repeatedly. The life-blood of these swindlers are lead lists (mooch or sucker lists) of people who have been defrauded in the past and are seen to be particularly vulnerable to being scammed again. The victims have become increasingly desperate in their attempts to recover a portion of their losses, and increasingly concerned about the embarrassment that they would feel if they had to report the true extent of their losses to law enforcement officials or to their families.

These schemes are often extensions of one or more of the many other telemarketing scams designed to gradually deprive victims of most of their funds, and they have been characterized as a particularly ruthless and egregious form of fraud in which the operator falsely promises to help the victim "recover" prizes promised or money they have already lost in an earlier scam—for a substantial up-front fee, of course. The FTC has consistently found such claims to be false. After paying the fee (or sending a donation to a specified "charity") the consumer never hears from the recovery scammer again. They learn that they have been re-victimized—no refund, no prize, just the loss of more money. In some cases, the recovery scam operation was committed by the very same individuals or their associates who had previously defrauded the consumer!

Recovery scams have plagued the elderly. In testimony before the U.S. Senate Special Committee on Aging on August 10, 2000, an official of the FTC confirmed that in its investigations, Commission staff determined that of the total number of individuals victimized by recovery room scams, 81 percent were at least 65 years of age; 47 percent were at least 75; and 23 percent were at least 80. Losses per consumer victimized by recovery rooms ranged from a few hundred dollars to thousands of dollars (Source: United States Federal Trade Commission, "Fraud Against Seniors," 2000).

How the Scam Works

If you've taken the bait and lost money to a telemarketer in the past, expect that the same, or another, telemarketer will try to hook you again. The double scammers, or "reloaders," use a variety of misrepresentations to add credibility to their pitches and their attempts to repeatedly victimize consumers. You are likely to receive a call from someone claiming to work for a government agency, private company, a law firm, or consumer organization. Some scam operators have falsely imper-sonated FBI, IRS, and U. S. Customs agents, while others use more neb-ulous language to suggest a connection to a government agency.

Some say they are "holding" money that they have already recov-ered for you. (How they became aware of your situation or how they may have accomplished this recovery is never explained.) Others offer to file the necessary documents to register your complaint with the appropriate government agencies. Still others claim they can move your name up on a list of victims due reimbursements. The fact is that recov-ery room scam operators never file any complaints. But they will demand an exorbitant fee for providing addresses of various seemingly relevant government agencies—addresses that nonprofit consumer protection agencies may offer free of charge or at a low cost, or which are available on the Internet, or even in a telephone directory.

The victims are told that they must send the fee in advance so that their reimbursement funds can be released by a "a court-appointed cus-todian" and forwarded to them. This allows the scam artist to bilk vic-tims of even more money, while at the same time encouraging them to believe that steps are being taken to protect their interests. This effectively causes the victims to postpone the filing of complaints with genuine law enforcement or regulatory authorities. If you pay the recov-ery fee, you have been double-scammed. It is very difficult—impossi-ble—to get your money back; the fraudulent telemarketer who contacted you initially is likely to have absconded. In whatever guise they adopt they will make basically the same pitch. The catch is that the second caller is as phony as the first, and may even be, or work in collusion with, the operator that scammed you the first time.

How Do They Know the Details of Your Previous Experience?

Because these operators may have perpetrated the scheme that had previously defrauded the victims, they are well-equipped to disclose information about the amounts and other details of victims' past losses. This in turn gives the loss recovery operator additional credibility with the victims, who assume that only a legitimate law enforcement or con-sumer protection agency could have access to such information.

They have access to the information because the consumer's name had been placed on a sucker list, a database of people who have lost money to scams. These data include names, addresses, phone numbers, and detailed descriptive information on any previous successful cons. These lists are considered invaluable and are bought and sold by unscrupulous promoters who know that consumers who have been deceived once become highly susceptible to repeat scams.

A Variation of the Reloading Scam

Another reloading scam uses prize incentives to get you to continue to buy merchandise. If you buy, you may get a second call claiming you're eligible to win an even more valuable prize. The second caller makes you think that buying more merchandise increases your chances of winning. If you take the bait, you may be called yet again with another sales pitch. The only difference is that the caller now claims that you're a "finalist" and, if you buy even more, you could win the "grand prize." Typically it takes at least several weeks to get your products and prizes. When, and if, you do receive them, you'll probably find that you've overpaid for shoddy goods and cheap trinkets and that you didn't win the "grand prize" at all. Unfortunately, your credit card has long since been debited or your check cashed. You discover that *you* were their grand prize!

How to Protect Yourself

Fortunately, there is a virtually foolproof way to tell whether the caller offering help in your loss recovery efforts is legitimate: If he or she requests payment of a fee in advance or "guarantees" to get your money back, it's a *fraud*. Hang up!!

Be advised that some federal and local government agencies and consumer organizations provide assistance to consumers who have lost money to fraudulent promoters. They never charge a fee, or guarantee to get back even a portion of the money you have lost.

To avoid being victimized by a recovery room or reloading operation, consider the following precautions:

- Be skeptical of individuals claiming to represent companies, consumer organizations, or government agencies who offer to recover money, merchandise, or prizes, especially those who want their fee in advance. Legitimate organizations, such as national, state, and local consumer enforcement agencies and non-profit organizations, like the National Fraud Information Center (NFIC) or Call For Action (CFA), do not charge for their services or guarantee results. Under the FTC's Telemarketing Sales Rule, it is illegal for a recovery room operator to request or receive payment until seven business days after you receive the recovered money or other item.

• Before you commit for any recovery services by phone ask the company representative to send you written materials about their operation. Ask what specific services they provide and the cost of each. Check out the company. This is not always foolproof but it is prudent.

• Be skeptical of promoters who repeatedly contact you, stating that if you purchase more of their merchandise, you have a better chance of winning valuable prizes. Wait until you receive and inspect your first order of merchandise or a prize before making additional purchases (Source: United States Federal Trade Commission, "Reloading Scams," 1998).

Magazine Sales

Increasingly, scams involving magazine subscriptions specifically target senior citizens. There have been instances of a relative or friend visiting an elderly person and finding the residence cluttered with unopened, unread magazines on topics that are of little or no interest to that person—and the dunning bills for these useless publications are usually piled nearby. Senior citizens are frequent victims of this scam and can incur large amounts in seemingly inexhaustible subscription charges for which they can be legally liable but cannot pay. Elderly consumers who have attempted to cancel such subscriptions or stop payment on their checks have been harassed and threatened by the telemarketers and door-to-door salespersons who victimized them in the first place.

In other scams, elderly consumers who never agreed to order magazines were threatened and badgered to collect inflated payments due for specious subscriptions. A magazine salesperson has violated federal law by affirming that a binding contract exists between themselves and consumers and that legal action will be taken to enforce that contract if the consumer does not pay for the subscription. There have been instances in which the telemarketers sent consumers bogus documents stating that the consumer had been sued to intimidate them into paying for subscriptions they did not want. "Buying magazine subscriptions from telephone or door-to-door salespeople, even those who seem to represent legitimate organizations, is risky business. These are some of the best scams there are! And take advantage of our innate need to 'help.' We hear stories of 'working' their way through college, selling for this charity or that 'good cause.' And automatically we reach for our wallets! It is for the betterment of something of someone right?" (2ScamU!, "Magazine Scams," no date). *Wrong!*

Every year many thousands of consumers purchase magazine subscriptions from legitimate marketers. However, according to the FTC many of them are scammed by unscrupulous salespeople into paying hundreds of dollars for multi-year subscriptions. These operators make presentations so well-rehearsed and slick that many consumers are unaware they have actually purchased magazines until they receive the first bill. Seniors are cautioned to avoid becoming entangled in magazine subscription contracts which they never intended, cannot afford, and which can be extremely difficult to escape.

How the Scam Begins

Most magazine subscription scams fit into one of three categories, depending on how the initial sales contact with the potential subscriber/victim is made:

1. Telemarketing
   Beware of telephone sales pitches for magazine subscription deals. An impulse purchase could leave you with years of monthly payments. In some states, once you orally agree to receive these magazines, you're legally obligated to pay for them. When buying magazines over the phone, you do not have the advantage or protection of first seeing the written terms of the sales agreement.

2. Field Sales

These are the door-to-door sales where the consumer is most likely to hear the "Can you help me?" pitch—the sob story.

3. Direct Mail

You may receive a postcard or other mailing piece that says nothing about magazine subscriptions but strongly encourages you to call a telephone number about a contest, prize, or sweepstakes entry. If you call, you may get information about contest prizes or drawing dates—you will definitely get a sales pitch for magazine subscriptions. The problem: Offers for "free," "prepaid," or "special" magazine subscription deals can leave you with years of monthly payments for magazines you may not want, never read, or could buy for less elsewhere. These are deals you can do without.

Telemarketing

Through its enforcement of the Telemarketing Sales Rule, the FTC regulates the telephone sale of consumer products, including magazine subscriptions. The FTC and the Magazine Publishers of America have collaborated to write *Guidelines for Managers of Telemarketing Enterprises Who Sell Magazine Subscriptions*. Under these guidelines, telemarketing professionals who sell such subscriptions are notified that "communications with prospective magazine subscription purchasers must be clear and courteous, and that their sales solicitations must be accurate, truthful, and complete, ... it's the law." Although prepared for telemarketers, selected portions of these guidelines, are included here because they can serve the consumer as a script for how to listen to such sales pitches—as a primer on fraud prevention.

Guidelines for Managers of Telemarketing Enterprises Who Sell Magazine Subscriptions

Initial Contact: After You've Said Hello

When you [the telemarketer] are making an outbound call, you must disclose clearly and promptly, prior to the consumer's purchase, and in a way that is unlikely to mislead the consumer:

• That the purpose of your call is to sell magazine subscriptions.
• Who is selling the magazine subscriptions.

- A description of the magazine subscriptions you are selling.
- You must not misrepresent the reasons why the consumer was chosen for the call. You may not suggest that the consumer was "specially" selected because he or she is a "good customer," a contest winner, or a survey participant—unless that is true.

Prize Promotions: You Never Have to Pay to Play

If you are offering a prize promotion in connection with an outbound call solicitation, you must state clearly and promptly, and prior to purchase, that no purchase is necessary to play or to win. You also must disclose:

- A description of any prize you offer in the sales promotion and a statement of its value.
- The "no purchase/no payment" way consumers can participate in the prize promotion with instructions on how to participate, or an address or toll-free telephone number where consumers can get instructions on how to participate.
- The odds of winning the prize in the promotion or the factors used to calculate the odds.
- Any material costs, restrictions, limitations, or conditions on receiving, redeeming or using a prize that you offer in the promotion.

Sympathy Appeals and Enticements: No Lies Allowed

The law does not allow you to make false statements to encourage a purchase. Specifically, you must not falsely state that:

- You are affiliated with an educational, charitable, social, or governmental organization or cause, that you are selling subscriptions on their behalf, or that they will receive part of the sales proceeds.
- The consumer's subscriptions will be distributed as gifts to educational, charitable, social, or governmental organizations or causes.
- The consumer's relatives or friends will receive free gift subscriptions.
- You are working your way through school or competing for a scholarship or in a contest. That is, you must not make false statements to create a sympathy appeal about yourself—including claiming illness, disease, disability, or low-income or student status.

- Consumers will receive free gifts, goods, or services with the purchase of magazine subscriptions unless the subscription costs the same as or less than the regular subscription price (or "basic" subscription price published in the magazine).
- The subscription is available at a special or reduced rate unless the cost of the subscription is less than the regular subscription price (or 'basic' subscription price published in the magazine) and less than the price that similar subscriptions have been sold in substantial quantities to similar consumers.
- The subscription is being offered free unless the cost of any other subscription(s) or other products that the consumer must purchase to get the free subscription is no more than the cost the consumer must pay to buy the other subscription(s) or other products without receiving the free subscription.
- The subscription is available at a reduced rate because the consumer will be charged only for postage or for shipping and handling.

Payment and Subscription Terms: Just the Facts

Before the consumer buys any subscription, you must clearly state:

- The total costs of the subscription(s); if you state the price of installment payments, you must give the amount of each installment and the total number of installment payments.
- The name and duration of each magazine subscription in your solicitation, including the number of issues or frequency of each subscription.
- A description of all material restrictions on the subscriptions, including the amount of any down payment that is required or the form of payment that is required.

Consumer Authorization for Payment: Getting the Okay

If you ask consumers for their bank account numbers to facilitate payment through "phone checks" or "demand drafts," you must get the consumer's advance "express [sic] verifiable authorization." You can do this in one of three ways:

- By getting advance written authorization;
- by tape recording the consumer giving express [sic] oral verification; or
- by sending written confirmation of the transaction to the consumer before you submit the draft for payment.

At the same time, you must not:

- Bill a consumer's credit card without their express [sic] authorization;
- mislead a consumer about the reason you are asking for account information; or
- invoice the consumer for the subscription orders unless the consumer has expressly ordered the subscription.

Cancellation and Refund Rights: The Fine Print

You must not misrepresent the consumer's right to cancel. Before the purchase, you must clearly and truthfully disclose:

- Any "no refund" or "no cancellation" policy, if you have such a policy.

Abusive Telemarketing Practices:

Regarding restrictions on phone calls and abusive practices you must not:

- Threaten, intimidate, or use obscene language when you make sales calls;
- cause a phone to ring or engage consumers in phone conversations, repeatedly or continuously, to annoy, abuse, or harass the person who answers the phone;
- call consumers who have previously said they do not wish to get calls from you or the seller of the magazine subscriptions that you are selling; or
- call consumers' homes earlier than 8 AM or later than 9 PM local time—unless you have their permission in advance [United States Federal Trade Commission, Guidelines, 2000].

Tips and Cautions

There are several cautionary points the consumer should keep in mind.

- Be careful of what you say on the phone to the seller. Some marketers may advise you (as required by federal law) that they will tape your telephone conversation, saying "it is for your protection." In reality, they may ultimately try to use this recording to prove that you agreed to buy the magazines; approved of the terms and method of payment; and fully understood all the terms of the purchase agreement. Remember, your oral agreement to purchase may constitute a legal contract in some states. You could be obligated to pay.

- If you don't want a subscription, and you don't want to be called again, tell the caller to put you on the company's do not call list, or list your name on the national registry and on your state's registry, if it has one. If the company calls again, hang up. It is breaking the law.
- If you ordered magazines over the phone once, you will likely be called again. Although you may think the call is about customer satisfaction, chances are it's about future renewals or to push additional subscriptions.
- Be alert for impostors. Scam artists may pretend to be calling on behalf of well-known magazine publishers and request payment to renew your subscriptions—which they will attempt to "confirm" and have you list—when they have absolutely no connection with any publisher and will simply pocket your money if you fall for the scam.
- Scam operators have sent phony invoices or renewal notices. These are designed to appear to be legitimate but somewhere in the fine print it states that it is actually a subscription offer. The payment due on the "invoice" or notice usually requires half of the total amount due. If in fact you already subscribe to the magazine, check the expiration date on the mailing label. Also check the statement carefully to see if it came from the publisher. If you're not a subscriber and you never ordered the magazine, you're certainly not obligated to make payment on such an invoice or notice.

Canceling Magazine Subscriptions

Do not agree to buy magazines on the assumption that you can easily cancel later. Once you agree to buy magazine subscriptions over the phone, you cannot simply call the company to cancel your order if you change your mind. Magazine subscription companies typically do not honor oral cancellations. Where cancellation notices are honored, they must be in writing and occur within a limited time period.

Magazine sellers can be among the most persistent, annoying, and infuriating individuals. Their methods are invariably high-pressure. They will try to manipulate your emotions. Be aware. And don't give in to their high-pressure or intimidation tactics.

Nigerian Letter

History of the Scam

The so-called "Nigerian Letter" is another variation of advance-fee fraud (AFF). This particular scam has been around for quite awhile. It is also known as the "419" scam after the section of the Nigerian penal law that deals with this type of fraud. It began with letters sent by regular mail—historically from Nigeria—sent mostly to business owners. Although small businesses, churches, and non-profit organizations have been the primary targets in the past, individual consumers are reporting that these types of letters are now showing up in their mailboxes. Regulatory authorities have begun to see the scam expand recently to other countries. Lately it appears to have reached pandemic proportions.

This particular confidence scheme appears to be one of the largest, and longest running, scams in the world. It is rather elaborate and sophisticated. It can also be very dangerous. Though basically a nonviolent crime, it has resulted in the kidnapping or death of a number of foreign victims who were lured to Nigeria or to other countries. Although these scams may target American senior citizens, they are designed to snare persons of all ages in illegal activity, resulting in extortion or bodily harm—even murder. Your trip to Nigeria or any other foreign country in response to the scheme may be one-way!

The Scam

In the best known variation, the initial contact can come in the form of a very official looking letter, fax, or e-mail from Nigeria. If you respond to the communication, you will then receive numerous "official" documents with stamps, seals, and other logos testifying to their genuineness and that of the proposal. Victims are often convinced of the authenticity of these schemes by the forged or false documents on official-looking government letterhead, bearing apparently authentic seals. They frequently invoke the authority of one or more ministries or offices of the Nigerian government and many attest to the support of a Nigerian government "official" whom they may cite by name. The use in some scams of actual government stationery, seals, and offices has been grounds for concern that some individual Nigerian officials may actually be involved in these activities. The sender usually affects an impressive title such as "doctor," "chief," "attorney," or even "prince"! The missive is invariably marked "urgent" or "confidential." There is always an aura of confidentiality, conspiracy, and covertness surrounding the proposal.

For the next week to ten days, the perpetrators establish a level of trust with the intended victim. This is accomplished by sending the them more "official" documentation to persuade them that the deal and the people involved are bona fide. The criminals will correspond with the victim via fax and courier mail because these may be more difficult to trace.

Although each scam letter may contain a slightly different pitch, it will state that a large sum of money is available, and proposes that the recipient agree to help transfer the funds out of Nigeria—Iraq, Afghanistan, or whatever world hotspot is in the news. In exchange for the recipient's cooperation, he or she will receive a percentage of the transferred funds. The promised payoff is typically in the millions of dollars. The intent is to bilk whatever amount they can out of those who respond. Those gullible enough to do so end up sending their money to the operators running the confidence game, or to their accomplices in the United States.

To effect the transfer, the scam artist proposes depositing the contraband funds in the victim's personal or business bank account in the United States. The victim's cooperation will be essential and involves providing their account number. Using that bit of information, the con artist can then quickly clean out the victim's account.

Or, employing a different tactic, they may try to get money directly. What happens next is the most crucial point in the fraud and can take a number of directions. The person who has fallen for the scam will be advised that all of the arrangements to transfer the money are near completion, however, a "problem" has arisen. These sequential "emergencies" predictably come up requiring further payments (always in advance) of funds to cover unforeseen transaction or transfer fees, travel expenses, various taxes, or attorney's fees, or an unnamed official has demanded a bribe to expedite the transfer process. These will have to be paid before the money can be released and the transaction can occur, and to avoid delay in the transfer of funds—and payment of your very generous share. If the requisite payment is made, the criminals will come up with yet another problem that, to be resolved, will require yet another payment. Each "problem" may be supported by more documentation.

The victim is assured that each fee will be the last one required. Invariably, "oversights" and "errors" are encountered necessitating additional payments and allowing the scheme to be stretched out interminably. The criminals can run this ruse for months or even years, depending on the gullibility of the victim or his or her desperation to recoup funds they have already committed. "The goal of the criminal is to delude the target into thinking that he is being drawn into a very lucrative, albeit questionable, arrangement. The intended victim must be reassured and confident of the potential success of the deal. He will become the primary supporter of the scheme and willingly contribute a large amount of money when the deal is threatened ... to save the venture" (United States Secret Service, "Advance-Fee Fraud Advisory," no date).

Some consumers have told the Federal Trade Commission they are receiving dozens of offers a day from supposed Nigerians politely promising big profits in exchange for help moving large sums of money out of their country. And apparently, many compassionate consumers are continuing to fall for the convincing sob stories, the unfailingly polite language, and the unequivocal promises of money. These AFF letters are scams, and according to the FTC, the scam artists are playing each and every consumer for a fool (Source: United States Federal Trade Commission, "The 'Nigerian' Scam," 2002).

Once a targeted victim forwards money and or items of value (usually jewelry) to Nigeria in one of these schemes, it is difficult, if not impossible, to recoup losses. Revictimization will be perpetrated either by the original criminals, or sold to another AFF team to operate.

In a news release dated October 3, 2003, Reuters reported that West African fraudsters, long known worldwide for mass-mailings that lure the gullible with get-rich-quick schemes, now appear to be rolling out updated tactics—tapping email networks and posing as major London banks.

A bogus email was recently sent out across the UK and abroad, purportedly from a top executive of Barclays Plc., one of Britain's largest banks, from an email address that appeared to belong to the bank itself. Barclays is not the only British bank targeted by cyber fraudsters; banks have also been hit in the U.S. and Australia. They have become a target because of their high profile and the trust they evoke.

The "email spoofing" requested permission for the bank to park $30 million temporarily in the recipient's bank account in return for a large share of the money. Once victims are hooked, they are then asked to put up hefty sums for air fares or other pretences. Intended victims are usually asked to enter bank account and credit card details.

British authorities said it was unclear who was behind the email scam but it bore the hallmarks of West African fraudsters, especially Nigerians who decades ago pioneered schemes using traditional mail and counterfeit letter-head stationery.

An official at Barclay's stated, "Funnily enough, a lot of very, very rich people fall for this type of scheme—very high net-worth individuals who are usually self-made," he said. "These people are accustomed to taking the sort of risk that you or I are not prepared to take" (Bendeich and Warner, "Fraudsters Pose as UK Bankers in New E-mail Scam," 2003).

The Scope of Nigerian Letter Fraud

The United States Secret Service Financial Crimes Division has confirmed that it receives as many as 100 calls a day from Americans approached and or defrauded by AFF criminals. The Secret Service has confirmed that "Nigerian organized crime rings running fraud schemes through the mail and phone lines are now so large, they represent a serious financial threat to the American citizens.... Indications are that advance-fee fraud grosses hundreds of millions of dollars annually and the losses are continuing to escalate" (United States Secret Service, "Advance-Fee Fraud Advisory," no date). Actual monetary losses to these scams are hard to obtain. In all likelihood, many victims are reluctant to come forward and report their losses because of fear or embarrassment. (The Service has a website on advance-fee fraud: www.secretservice.gov/alert419.shtml.)

A May 25, 2003, MSNBC story relating to The National Consumers League release of its report on the ten top bogus e-mail offers stated:

> The National Consumers League and AT&T WorldNet just released a survey of the top 10 e-mail scams running around—and 12 percent of respondents said they've been begged over e-mail to help route money out of the African nation [Nigeria].... [The] study conducted earlier this year ... indicated a 900 percent jump in the number of people receiving the Nigerian scam last year—making it the fastest growing e-mail scam, according the group. The Nigerian scam placed third, behind faked online auctions and merchandise offered on Web sites that's never delivered.
>
> But even the elaborate Nigerian money scheme, which has circulated around via snail mail, fax, and now e-mail for 20 years some say, has roped in victims. Internet Fraud Complaint Center says 16 people fell for the scheme last year, losing an average of $5,500 [Sullivan, "Nigerian Scam Spam on the Rise," 2003].

A year earlier, on May 26, 2002, the *Philadelphia Inquirer* reported that "According to an FBI report, about 2,600 Americans said they were victims of [AFF] scams in 2001. Sixteen reported losses totaling $345,000; two individuals lost more than $70,000 each. The Secret Service gets about 13,000 advance-fee-scam letters forwarded to its office every month" (Hopper, "An Old Scam Takes a New Form: E-Mail," 2002).

An article by Porus P. Cooper discussing the Nigerian scam, which appeared in the *Philadelphia Inquirer* shortly after on October 8, 2002, confirmed, "Americans are cheated out of an estimated $100 million a year this way.... Hundreds of millions of dollars are stolen worldwide ..." (Cooper, "Officials Again Warn of Money-Transfer Scam," 2002). Efforts to contain the scam have reported limited national and international success so far. This has been attributed to the fact that it has been difficult to get the cooperation of Nigerian law-enforcement authorities.

An Old Scam Takes a New Form

Recent scam letters refer to deaths from the September 11, 2001, terrorist attacks, and describe hoards of unclaimed cash, precious metals, or gems found in the rubble of the World Trade Center, or allude to substantial death benefits of personnel who were killed in the attack on the Pentagon. The Secret Service says these are some of the latest incarnations of a fraud scheme that targets hundreds of people each day.

In late 2002, the news media reported that the old Nigerian scam was being run with different face; the old con game that plays off a victim's greed has a new twist. The U.S. Secret Service warned about an e-mail circulating on the Internet which purports to be from an American "special-forces commando" located in Afghanistan who "found" several millions of dollars of Taliban drug money which he is hiding. The e-mail asks the recipient for help moving the fortune out of Afghanistan. Of course, the "commando" is willing to share the booty. The e-mail pitch from "Brandon Curtis" states: "We will thus send you the shipment waybill, so that you can help claim this luggage on behalf of me and my colleagues. Needless to say the trust [placed] in you at this junction is enormous. We are willing to offer you an agreeable percentage of [these] funds" (Hopper, "An Old Scam," 2002).

In the summer of 2003, the "special forces commando" had moved to Iraq and had come into possession of millions of dollars in American currency, gold, gems, or other loot, which had been stolen and hidden by the Saddam Hussein regime. The pitch: Help get the loot out of Iraq and you will profit handsomely! Nigeria, Afghanistan, Iraq—where do we go next?! Scam artists never rest, it seems. Their efforts evolve with technology and current events, and the Internet provides the least expensive way to find victims. Online scams are here to stay.

If You Receive a Nigerian Letter

If you're tempted to respond to any offer as described here, the FTC suggests you stop and ask yourself two important questions: Why would a complete stranger pick you to share such a fortune, and why would you share your bank account numbers with a complete stranger? Consumers who receive these types of letters are advised not to provide any personal or banking information to these con artists. "The best thing to do is not to respond at all" (Better Business Bureau, "Consumers Now Target of Nigerian Letter Scams," 2002; United States Federal Trade Commission, "The 'Nigerian' Scam," 2002).

Online Auctions

Online Auctions: Deal or Steal?

In April 2003, the FTC reported that online auction fraud is the single largest category of Internet related complaints in the FTC's Consumer Sentinel database, which logged more than 51,000 auction complaints in 2002. Many of the cases involved straightforward scams where consumers allegedly "won" the bid for merchandise through an Internet auction Website, sent in their money, but never received the item(s) (Source: Federal Trade Commission, "Internet Auction Fraud Targeted by Law Enforcers," 2003). The complaints suggest that con artists are monitoring reputable auction sites for victims—buyers and sellers—to lure away and trick into turning over their money or merchandise.

Online auctions have experienced incredible growth within the past few years; they have become a very big business. Since they began in 1995, Internet auctions have become perhaps the hottest phenomenon on the Web. A major reason for this growth is that such auctions make it very easy for persons all around the globe to find exceptional deals on merchandise and collectibles—or to get bilked.

They offer buyers a "virtual" bazaar from which to choose an endless array of merchandise, and they provide sellers a worldwide storefront from which to market their wares. "Every day more and more people go to Internet auction sites to buy everything from out-of-print books to vacation packages to luxury cars. These online auction houses act as huge international flea markets and allow shoppers to find a wide range of new and old merchandise from the comfort of their homes, often at bargain prices" (AARP, "Online Auctions: Bidder Beware," 2002). But online auctions can be a risky business. The excitement they engender also makes them prime hunting grounds for scam artists, ready to play on the desire many auction bidders have for that "unbelievable deal." And the sellers aren't the only ones committing fraud; buyers can be just as duplicitous.

The Extent of Online Auction Fraud

Internet fraud is now the number two consumer complaint, after identity theft. The FTC and other law enforcement and consumer organizations received 102,517 consumer complaints about Internet scams in 2002, nearly twice as many as in 2001. Half the complaints that were filed concerned online auctions (AARP 2003). California, New York, Florida, Texas, and Illinois have been identified as the top five states (in that order) for victims of Internet crime. In cases where the perpetrator has been identified, nearly four in five were male and over half resided in these states and in Pennsylvania (Source: United States Federal Bureau of Investigation, "Internet Fraud Complaint Center," 2003).

Online Auctions in Action

For the reader who may be interested in adventuring into the world of online auctions, eBay (which bills itself as "the world's largest online community of buyers and sellers") has a number of useful hyperlinks on its website, including help in registering, searching, buying, bidding, and a glossary of terms. The site also includes a "Getting Started Tutorial," and a "Safe Buying Guide" which advises the novice that "Learning more about your seller helps you make informed choices about your purchases" (eBay, "Help: Buying," 2003 and, "Help: Safe Trading," 2003).

For the uninitiated, the FTC's booklet *Internet Auctions: A Guide for Buyers and Sellers* provides a wealth of information and advice. This publication describes online auctions:

> Internet auctions are online bazaars. Some are the scenes of business-to-person activity, where a Web site operator physically controls the merchandise for sale and accepts payment for the goods. But most specialize in person-to-person activity where individual sellers or small businesses auction their items directly to consumers.
>
> In these auctions, the seller—not the site—has the merchandise. The person-to-person sites require sellers to register and obtain a "user account name" (or "screen name") before they can place items for bid. Sellers also must agree to pay a fee every time they conduct an auction.
>
> Many sellers set a time limit on bidding and, in some cases, a "reserve price"—the lowest price they will accept for an item. When the bidding closes at the scheduled time, the highest bidder "wins." If no one bids at or above the reserve price, the auction closes without a "winner." At the end of a successful person-to-person auction, the buyer and seller communicate—usually by e-mail—to arrange for payment and delivery [United States Federal Trade Commission, Internet Auctions, 2003].

Payment Options

Most of the large online auction sites accommodate a range of payment options, which are made either to the auction house or directly to the seller. These include personal checks, credit cards, money orders, cashiers checks, and payments through billing or escrow services. AARP advises, "The bottom line: Pay with a credit card or use an escrow service for online auction purchases" (AARP, "Online Auctions," 2002). However, it is in these latter two options that fraud prevails (Source: United States Federal Trade Commission, "Going, Going, Gone," 2003).

ONLINE PAYMENT SERVICES

Online payment or billing services are popular with both buyers and sellers. They allow buyers to use a credit card or electronic bank transfer to pay sellers who may not be set up to accept credit cards or electronic bank transactions. They also may protect buyers from unlawful use of their credit cards or bank accounts because the online payment service, not the seller, holds the account information. Many sellers prefer online payment services because payment services tend to provide more security than personal checks.

ONLINE ESCROW SERVICES

If you should have reservations and concerns regarding payment, consider using an escrow service. AARP advises anyone venturing into the world of online auctions to "use a reputable escrow service for expensive items. Although some honest sellers may not want to use a middleman who might slow down a sale, many are willing to do so. This is especially true if the buyer agrees to pay the [escrow service] fee. If a seller refuses to use an escrow service, think twice before making that purchase"(AARP 2002).

Unfortunately, these services have become another vehicle for Internet scams. "Con artists are now pretending to be escrow services and pocketing money from consumers who thought that they were choosing and using escrow services. It's especially important for consumers to make sure they're dealing with a service that is licensed and bonded" (National Consumers League, "Online Auctions Dominant Consumer Fraud," 2003).

Bob Sullivan of MSNBC has advised: "Worried about getting

scammed on an Internet auction? 'Just use an escrow service,' is the customary advice. Not so fast. The latest auction scam is an elaborate swindle involving creation of fake escrow services, complete with convincing Web sites.... Auction watchdogs are trying to shut the Web sites down as soon as they pop up, but several victims have already been bilked out of thousands of dollars" (Sullivan, "Fake Escrow Sites Lure Auction Users," 2002).

Types of Fraud in Online Auctions

Most people who file complaints about Internet auction fraud report problems with sellers who:

- Fail to deliver the merchandise;
- fail to deliver in a timely manner;
- send something of lesser value than advertised; or
- fail to disclose all relevant information about a product or terms of the sale.

AARP has said that "Although online auctions can be fun and convenient, buying things you cannot see from strangers can be risky. In fact, online auctions are one of the top consumer complaints in the country.... Most of these complaints were about items that were never received, arrived damaged, or were worth far less than advertised" (AARP, "Online Auctions," 2002).

But some buyers and sellers experience other problems, including:

- "Shilling" or "shill bidding": Artificially inflating the price of an item by the use of fake bids submitted by the seller's accomplices—their shills—with the object of aggressively driving up the price.
- "Bid shielding": When fraudulent buyers submit very high bids to run up the price in an effort to discourage other bidders from submitting competing bids for the same item. The shielding bidder then retracts his or her artificial bids, effectively providing them, or their friends, an opportunity for getting the item at a much lower price.
- "Bid siphoning": When con artists lure bidders away from legit-

imate auction sites by offering to sell the "same" item at a lower price. Their intent is to trick consumers into sending money for, but not delivering, the "same" item. Buyers lose any protections the reputable site may have provided, such as insurance, feedback forums, or guarantees.

- "Shell Auctions": No actual merchandise exists. The sole purpose of the offer at auction is to defraud buyers of funds or obtain credit card numbers to perpetrate additional fraud.
- Misrepresentation: One of the oldest tricks in business. The item the buyer eventually receives is not remotely as it was described. Its market value, condition, or authenticity had been greatly exaggerated (Source: Lanford, "Online Auctions" 2001 and United States Federal Trade Commission, *Internet Auctions*," 2003).

Tips for Online Auctions

Don't defraud yourself!! Despite complaints of fraud, online auctions can be an enjoyable, efficient, and relatively safe way to do business—if you approach them with common sense. What can you do to protect yourself, short of simply not venturing near them? You can do a great deal. The most important thing is to do your homework beforehand. Learn the ropes. The eBay site and the FTC publication *Internet Auctions: A Guide for Buyers and Sellers* are the places to learn the ropes.

"Pigeon Drop"

The "pigeon drop" is also known as the "found money" scam because it usually involves the "finding" of a what appears to be a large sum of cash. It is one of the most prevalent, insidious, frustrating—and simple—scams aimed at the elderly. It is most often seen during the spring and summer months when people are out walking and more likely to stop when approached by a seemingly friendly stranger who pretends to be seeking directions. The scam most often plays out in malls or shopping complex parking lots. It may also occur on downtown streets in small cities.

"Pigeon drop" is the generic name for a variety of scams, usually perpetrated on senior citizens of both genders (but mainly women) in an attempt to get them to withdraw money from their bank accounts and give it to the scammers. These operators may work solo but are most often a team—usually young females or a male and female. They often work in groups and will change players in an effort to hinder police investigations.

The pigeon drop scam preys on trust, greed, and sometimes fear. Les Henderson of Azilda, Ontario, Canada, in his online publication *Crimes of Persuasion*, states:

> It should be noted that strangers would not likely confide in other strangers regarding found money or offer to share their good fortune with you. There are various reasons why this works when it is targeted against elderly women:
>
> • Their vision may be blurred by hopes of getting something for nothing;
> • victims become concerned that resistance will result in physical violence;
> • they often carelessly carry larger sums of ready cash. This crime proliferates because victims, who fear being labeled incompetent, fail to report it. The cons know what to say and who to say it to, as they target as many victims as possible in a short period of time [Henderson, *Crimes of Passion*, 2002].

The Scam

The website *Mr. Kenyada's Neighborhood* posts several webpages relating to fraud against senior citizens. In discussing the pigeon drop scam he notes:

> The elderly are a favorite target for this one. In the pigeon drop scam, swindlers work in pairs or in teams. One befriends an unsuspecting consumer, the pigeon, while the other approaches them with money or valuables he claims to have just found. After some rehearsed conversation, the con artists agree to split the money three ways with you and arrange to meet at a lawyer's office or somewhere else of their choosing. But can they trust you, they ask. To get your share, you'll need to put up some "good faith" money, which they will return to you after the goods are divided. To prove yourself trustworthy, you turn over a large sum of money to them and, later, go to meet them at the designated spot. Soon after arriving, you realize the pair is long gone—and so is your money [*Mr. Kenyada's Neighborhood*, no date].

The Lawyer's Office Variation

In this scenario the operators actually accompany—even drive—the victim to the site of the fleecing—a bogus attorney's office—rather than agreeing to meet at a designated place at a designated time and simply not showing up.

This charade begins when a young, well-dressed woman approaches the "pigeon," the "mark," the potential victim. Initially she may attempt to engage the prospective victim in a friendly conversation. After a short interval, a third party (an accomplice) appears (on cue) purporting to be looking for the owner of a purse, wallet, briefcase, bag, or other receptacle they have "just found" and inquires politely if either of them may have lost it. One of the two "strangers" suggests looking inside the bag or case for possible identification of the owner. There will be none. What they will find is what appears to be a large amount of currency. There will also be a cryptic note that suggests that the money came from some form of illegal activity, perhaps gambling or drug dealing. One of the con artists will assert that the money represents the proceeds of criminal activities and therefore there is little likelihood that the criminals will risk returning to claim it, so it is "ours to keep." The game's afoot!

First, as the pigeon listens, the other two will talk excitedly about how much money there is and what he or she will do with their share. Because they appear so genuinely interested in finding the owner, and in sharing the money equally if the money is not claimed, and if they can do so legally—and playing on human greed—the potential victim is cleverly drawn into the scheme; he or she is convinced that the money has really been found and all three of them are going to share it. The pigeon is snared! The discussion then turns to what should be done first. The conspirators ask the mark for his or her opinion on how to handle the cash. All three must decide what do to next. Divide the money? Turn it in to the police?

It is agreed that they need the advice of "someone who can be trusted." That trusted third party is most likely to be a "lawyer friend" of one of the swindlers. One of the strangers will claim that he or she knows, or perhaps is employed by, an attorney (always located in a nearby office) whom they can trust to give them legal advice on what to do and the legal process for finding the owner or for ultimately claiming the money—all the while confirming that the pigeon is now a "partner" in the windfall by including him or her in the conversation and decisions.

One of the two conspirators will be leave to contact the "attorney" and seek "legal advice." He or she returns shortly thereafter and tells the other two that this is their "lucky day." Because the money is "probably illegal" the legitimate owners are not likely to attempt to recover it, so they will almost certainly be able to split it three ways.

The fictitious lawyer has advised that if ultimately they intend to share the booty, each will have to demonstrate that they can provide their share of the funds required for the attorney's fees in attempting to determine the true owner—"as required by law." (In all of this, the possibility that the police, if they should become involved, could seize the money as evidence of possible criminal activity is blithely ignored.) And if they are to share the wealth equally, to ensure that all those in the group are going to live up to the bargain, each party should be required to put up a designated amount in cash in order to show their "good faith" until the distribution can be effected properly. He also advises that their good faith deposits should be placed in a safe deposit box, trust, bank account, or the lawyer's safe hands for a certain amount of time—thirty to ninety days, again "as required by law"—until the legitimate owner can be found. If unclaimed at the end of the time period, they can each reclaim their good faith deposit and their share of the windfall.

All agree to withdraw a substantial amount of cash from their respective bank accounts as a gesture of good faith to the others. The con artists will persuade the victim to make cash advances on their credit cards or make a withdrawal at their local bank—they usually offer to drive the victim there. Or they will agree to accompany him or her to their home to retrieve the victim's deposit (cash only). The con artists then place what appears to be a large amount of their own money— some of it may be real—with the "found" cash. The victim duplicates this act of good faith with their own money, which is real. The trap has been sprung!

DROPPING THE PIGEON

The next step in this variation of the scam is to drop the pigeon that has been snared. Rather than simply not showing up at an appointed time or place, several diversionary tactics may be employed in dumping the victim. The team member who has claimed to have spoken to the attorney will state that the attorney must "check" the found money to verify its authenticity and confirm the good faith deposits of all parties and perhaps have them sign certain "legal documents."

It is agreed that all three will go to the attorney's office together. To avoid any suspicion, the victim is entrusted to take the package which he or she has been led to believe contains all of the money. The con artists will drive the victim there, drop him or her off, and wait in the car while the pigeon goes into the large and imposing office building. Or they will accompany the victim into the building. Once inside, one or both of the team suddenly must find a telephone or bathroom—they won't be back. If they had remained outside, when the victim eventually returns to the parking lot, not having found the nonexistent attorney's office, the other two are long gone. They disappear leaving the victim holding the bag—literally!

With the con artists gone, the victim discovers that the package that has been entrusted to them contains nothing but blank paper with a few genuine bills in the smallest denominations or even play money wrapped around it. At some moment during the trip, the package had been switched for one of equal weight and identical appearance containing blank paper cut to the size of dollar bills. This is the one that has been presented to the victim in the parking lot or inside the building. He or she has become another victim of the pigeon drop. They have lost the promise of quick riches, but also whatever good faith funds they have put up to secure that hope.

AARP advises, "Don't believe any story about sharing found money. This is almost certainly a swindle. These are criminals whose looks, manner of speaking, and story appear to be perfectly innocent. That's why this scheme has worked for years to swindle countless victims" (AARP, "The Pigeon Drop," no date).

What to Do if You Are Approached

If you're approached by one or more complete strangers who offer to share found money, or anything else of value such as jewelry or a winning lottery ticket, with you, tell him firmly that you are not interested. Say that you know the legal way to handle such situations, and direct the person to the nearest police station or offer to call the police.

In all likelihood he will disappear immediately. Try to remember an accurate description of the swindlers, their car, and the license number. Report the incident immediately to your police or sheriff's department. They will attempt to apprehend the con artists before they attempt to defraud another senior citizen.

Predatory Lending

Predatory Lending Defined

The media, regulatory agencies, and law enforcement officials have been reporting that something is robbing elderly homeowners and putting many of them at risk of losing their homes. It is a problem known as "predatory" lending. There is no clear-cut definition of a predatory loan, but many experts agree that it involves a lender misleading, deceiving, and sometimes coercing someone to take out a loan (typically a home equity loan or mortgage refinancing) at excessive costs and without regard to the borrower's ability to repay. Victims who have trouble repaying such a loan often face harassing collection tactics or are encouraged to refinance the loan at even higher fees.

Reports indicate that predatory lenders target any consumers they believe to be in need of cash or are otherwise vulnerable. They include older people who are likely to need money for medical bills or home repairs; moderate- and middle-income consumers who need to pay off credit card bills or consolidate other debts; and lower-income or minority communities where there may be limited competition from more reputable lenders.

For senior citizens particularly, both home equity loans and reverse mortgages can be forms of predatory lending. Either involves a mortgage lien against the elderly person's residence. More than 80 percent of Americans 50 and older are homeowners, and this population of our citizens is becoming increasingly victimized by such loans.

AARP has advised, "Frequently, older homeowners are ensnared in abusive loans because they are persuaded to borrow funds for home repairs, to cover health costs or to consolidate debts. There is an outrageous downside to the rosy scenarios offered by unscrupulous lenders.... There is ample evidence ... that [elderly] people—victims of abusive lenders—are sold loans as a miracle financial cure. Many homeowners are then stunned to find out that they cannot afford to pay off those loans and they may lose their homes" (Source: FirstGov for Seniors, "AARP Launches Drive Against Unscrupulous Mortgage Lenders," no date). This scenario involves the elderly in disproportionate numbers since they frequently have substantial equity built up over a long period of time but have insufficient income to repay these loans.

Home Equity Loan Scams: Borrowers Beware!

Do you own your home? If so, it is likely to be your greatest single asset. As is the case with many senior citizens, the equity you have amassed in your home may be your primary asset. Many elderly homeowners on fixed or limited incomes are equity-rich but cash poor and often need access to credit to meet financial needs. Unfortunately, if they agree to a loan that is based on that equity they may be putting their most valuable asset at risk and could lose their home if they borrow from unscrupulous lenders.

Predatory lenders seek to capitalize on seniors' financial needs by offering "easy" credit and persuading them to utilize their equity as collateral. They fail to advise them that these loans are packed with high interest rates, hidden payments, excessive fees and costs, credit insurance, balloon payments, and other disadvantageous and outrageous terms that could lead to the ultimate forfeiture of their home.

Many elderly homeowners who have been victimized and have sought legal recourse have stated that they did not fully understand the terms of the loan agreement they signed—that the terms were not fully explained to them. Before you commit to a loan, discuss the matter with an attorney, financial advisor or someone you trust if you do not understand the terms of the loan offered to you.

Frequently, home improvement companies act as brokers for many of these predatory mortgage loans. They will use high-pressure tactics or engage in other behavior to misrepresent the terms of the loan or hide its true cost. When elderly persons commit for loans that they are not able to repay, they quickly fall into arrears, and eventually face foreclosure on their property.

If you are considering using your home as collateral for a loan, be careful. The lure of extra money or the chance to consolidate debt and reduce monthly payments can be very costly in the long run. High interest rates and other credit costs could get you in over your head (Source: United States Federal Trade Commission, "Avoiding Home Equity Scams," 1998).

The Warning Signs of a Predatory Lender

Predatory lending has been described by federal agencies as involving one or all of these three elements:

1. Providing unaffordable loans based on the borrower's assets, rather than on ability to pay;
2. inducing a borrower to repeatedly refinance in order to charge high fees or points;
3. engaging in fraud or deception to hide some of the cost features of a loan.

Among a number of signs that are most often associated predatory loans are:

- Refinancing unsecured debt.
  Lenders encourage homeowners to finance or consolidate unsecured debt. Homeowners are told it is a way to lower monthly payments and increase their tax deduction. Lenders do not mention that the higher home-secured debt burden increases the risk of foreclosure when the elderly person faces financial distress.
- "Balloon" payments.
  Avoid loans with a balloon payment, a large lump sum of money due at the end of the term of the loan. Predatory lenders use balloon payments to make a loan appear affordable by highlighting the low monthly payments instead of the entire cost of the loan. The payments may be lower because the lender is offering a loan on which you repay only the interest each month. At the end of the loan term, the principal— that is, the entire amount that you originally borrowed—is due in one lump sum—the balloon payment. If the borrower

is not able to pay this substantial amount he may face foreclosure.

- "Equity stripping."

    Equity stripping is basically making loans to elderly home-
    owners that they simply cannot afford to repay. These loans
    are made based solely on the amount of equity in their prop-
    erty, and are made to individuals in financial need but who
    do not have adequate income to repay the loan. The lender
    may be out to strip you of your equity.

- "Loan flipping."

    In the scheme of loan flipping—also referred to as "multiple
    refinancing"—the lender encourages the borrower to repeat-
    edly refinance the loan and, often, to borrow more money
    each time. A loan may be flipped several times in this man-
    ner. Each time the consumer's debt is increased as each new
    loan has a higher principal balance and a new set of closing
    costs and fees based on that higher balance. This effects a
    depletion in the equity in the property with little or no ulti-
    mate benefit to the homeowner.

- Bait and switch.

    The lender offers one set of loan terms when you apply, then
    pressures you to accept higher charges when you sign to com-
    plete the transaction. The desperate sign. The predators count
    on it! (Sources: Federal Consumer Information Center, "High
    Cost 'Predatory' Home Loans," 2002; National Consumer Law
    Center, "Helping Elderly Home Owners," no date; United
    States Federal Trade Commission, "Avoiding Home Equity
    Scams," 1998).

The "Home Improvement" Loan

The variations of home improvement scams themselves are discussed in detail in the appropriate sections of this book. As confirmed
in those sections, senior citizens, commonly victims, are advised to
beware of home improvement scams. They must also beware of home
improvement loan scams should they be required to borrow funds to
make the necessary improvements.

An individual or firm contacts you and offers to install a new roof or remodel your kitchen at a price that sounds reasonable. You say that you are interested, but cannot afford it. The individual assures you that is "no problem"—he can arrange financing through a lender he "deals" with. You agree to the project, and the contractor begins work. At some point after the contractor begins, you are asked to sign a number of documents. Some of these may be blank or the lender may rush you to sign before you have time to read what has been presented to you. The contractor threatens to leave the job unfinished if you do not sign. You sign. Only later do you realize that the papers you signed are a home equity loan. The interest rate, points, and fees are very high. To make matters worse, the work on your home is not done right or has not been completed, and the contractor, who may have been paid by the lender, has little interest in completing the work to your satisfaction.

Do not let a home improvement company or contractor arrange a loan on your behalf; unscrupulous home improvement contractors frequently steer elderly homeowners to predatory lenders under the guise of arranging financing. The contractor has likely received a kickback for acting as an agent or broker for the loan. Deceptive lending practices, including those attributable to home improvement scams, are among the most frequent problems experienced by financially distressed elderly Americans. This is especially true of those homeowners who lack access to traditional banking services and rely disproportionately on finance companies or other lending institutions that may not be closely regulated.

Your Rights

Know your rights as a consumer in dealing with predatory lenders. Certain lending practices violate federal credit laws dealing with disclosures about loan terms, discrimination based on age, gender, marital status, race, or national origin, and debt collection. You also may have additional rights under state law that would allow you to bring a civil law suit.

Predatory lenders are aggressive and may try to pressure you into signing for a loan you do not want. If you do sign a loan agreement, whether it is a home equity loan, refinancing loan, or second mortgage, remember, federal law gives you three business days to change your mind for any reason. You have the right to:

- Have all your questions answered about the loan;
- examine each and every document; and
- say no to any loan you do not want (even if you are at closing).

Reverse Mortgages

Until recently, there were two principal ways to derive cash from the equity in your home. You could either sell the property and move, or borrow against it and then repay the loan in monthly installments. Now, for homeowners over the age of 62, there is a third way, a reverse mortgage (RM) which is a type of loan against your home that does not require any repayment of principal, interest, or servicing fees for as long as you live in your home. You receive payments *from* the lender.

A reverse mortgage may be a feasible option for the house-rich and cash-poor senior citizen who desires a better style of living or to be more financially independent. It can help seniors live out their lives in their own homes as long as they are physically able to do so. As people get older and need money to live on, reverse mortgages and the tax-free funds derived from them are becoming more popular. If you are age 62 or older, an RM may be an option to help increase your income.

A reverse mortgage is exactly what it sounds like: a traditional, "forward" mortgage—only in reverse. It is a type of loan that allows you to convert some of the equity in your property into cash flow while you retain ownership, as you do when you have a forward mortgage. Funds obtained from an RM may be used for any purpose, including meeting housing expenses such as taxes, insurance, fuel, and maintenance costs. Because you retain the title to your home, you remain fully responsible for these costs; any failure in this could nullify the terms of the mortgage. The home generally must be your "principal residence," which means you must live in it more than six months out of the year. Reverse mortgage programs usually do not lend on cooperative apartments or mobile homes. Some manufactured homes may qualify if they are built on a permanent foundation and are classed and taxed as real estate.

In a regular mortgage, you pay money to the lender and at the end of the mortgage term you own your home. In a reverse mortgage, the lender (usually a bank) pays money to you in a lump sum, in regular monthly advances, or on a schedule and in amounts that you select.

The amount of money you can obtain will depend on the specific reverse mortgage plan or program you select; the schedule and amounts of cash advances you choose; your age; and the market value of your home. The older you are, and the more your home is worth, the more cash you can get. The specific dollar amount that will be made available to you may also depend on interest rates and closing costs on home loans in your area. Some reverse mortgages cost considerably more than others, and this reduces the amount of the funds you can derive from them. Fees for a reverse mortgage are generally higher than those for a regular mortgage, primarily because the lender cannot know when the mortgage will come due.

Depending on your plan, the RM becomes due with interest when you move, sell or permanently leave your home, reach the end of the pre-determined loan term, or die. You or your heirs must then repay the total of the cash advances plus interest. The debt is usually repaid by refinancing the loan into a forward mortgage (if the heirs are eligible), or by using the proceeds derived from the sale of the property. The lender does not take title to your home when you die. Reputable lenders do not want your house; they want repayment of the mortgage (Sources: AARP, "Reverse Mortgage: Basic Loan Features," 2003; United States Federal Trade Commission, *Reverse Mortgages*, 1993).

The laws that went into effect a few years ago mandate that a counselor talk to the potential borrower and the heirs to make sure everyone understands the process. Both HUD and AARP offer extensive information for seniors about reverse mortgages. This can be found on their respective websites: www.hud.gov/buying/rvrsmort.cfm and www.aarp.org/revmort/.

Reverse Mortgage Scams

Reverse mortgage scams involve charging senior citizens thousands of dollars for reverse mortgage *information*. Promoters contact senior citizens with offers of assistance in getting reverse mortgages—for a fee. Unfortunately, many seniors have paid large sums to "estate planning" firms providing information services regarding reverse mortgages. In reality, these high-pressure promoters provide information that the Department of Housing and Urban Development (HUD) provides to anyone free of charge simply by contacting HUD. No one needs these "estate planning" services to apply for and obtain a reverse mortgage. Seniors are cautioned not to fall victim to these scam artists.

Remember, if anyone calls or writes representing himself as an estate planner and offers his services to help you obtain extra money for your daily expenses by getting you a reverse mortgage, a red flag should go up immediately. All these flim-flam artists will do is refer you to a reverse mortgage lender and charge you an exorbitant sum for this "service"—which, as we have said, is yours free simply by contacting HUD or any reputable lending institution.

Many older Americans signing contracts with the these scam artists are unaware that the firms will charge a fee of up to 10 percent of the total amount borrowed through a reverse mortgage. This works out to a fee of $5,000 on a $50,000 reverse mortgage, or $10,000 on a $100,000 reverse mortgage.

In March 1997, then HUD Secretary Andrew Cuomo joined bipartisan members of the House and Senate to propose legislation "to stop reverse mortgage rip-offs that rob elderly homeowners and that bilk senior citizens of thousands of dollars." Cuomo and the lawmakers jointly proposed the Elderly Homeowners Loan Protection Act to put an end to unscrupulous practices by companies that prey on senior citizens receiving reverse mortgages.

Secretary Cuomo asserted, "We will not tolerate white-collar muggings of our parents and grandparents.... We will not allow elderly homeowners who've made mortgage payments for decades to be robbed of thousands of dollars in an instant by smooth-talking con artists.... For an older American living on a fixed income, struggling to meet daily expenses, the loss of thousands of dollars is a terrible financial blow." He went on to say, "Excessive reverse mortgage servicing fees are gouging low-income seniors, who are usually on fixed incomes. That is just plain wrong. Our legislation outlaws this despicably practice and protects our seniors from being preyed upon by sharp operators" (United States Department of Housing and Urban Development, "Stop Reverse Mortgage Rip-Offs," 1997).

Because your home is such a valuable asset, you should consult with an attorney or financial advisor before applying for a RM. Be sure that your advisor reads all of the documents before finalizing the mortgage. Confirm that you are dealing with a reputable lender. The scam artists disguise their organizational names with important sounding words like "national," "American," "financial services," and "trust." Knowing your rights and responsibilities as a borrower may help to minimize your financial risks and avoid any threat of foreclosure or loss of your home.

Home Equity Loans:
The Three-Day Cancellation Rule

Under federal law (the Truth in Lending Act), for certain loans secured by your home, you have the "right to rescind" or "right to cancel" the agreement up until midnight of the third business day after signing a loan contract. You can cancel for *any* reason and without penalty. Your right is guaranteed, but it applies only if you are using your principal residence—whether it is a condominium, mobile home, or boat—as collateral. Under the statute, it cannot be exercised if the property is a vacation or second home (Source: National Consumer Law Center, "Helping Elderly Homeowners," no date).

Prizes, Contests, Lotteries, Sweepstakes, and Inheritance

Advance-Fee Schemes

Prizes, contests, lotteries, sweepstakes, and inheritance scams are all variations of the advance-fee scheme which always involves the victim paying money to someone in anticipation of receiving something of greater value such as a prize, "gift," cash "reward," "bonus," or various other form of largesse. Having paid his or her money in advance, the victim receives little or nothing in return. The variety and sophistication of advance-fee schemes is limited only by the imagination of the con artists who create and operate them.

In a 1994 consumer report, the AARP advised:

> Sweepstakes and puzzle contests increasingly target older people in schemes that cost consumers billions of dollars a year. Many sweepstakes promoters, particularly those who make telephone pitches, target older adults because they are friendlier and open to strangers.... Americans are being ripped off every day.... They need to be better informed about how to identify scams and what to do if they believe they have been taken advantage of.

Legitimate prize promotions do not require a purchase or payment of fees to win. Consumers should be wary of promotions that require entry fees with the submission of answers to a series of increasingly difficult questions. Other "red flags" include being asked for a credit card number over the telephone and receiving multiple solicitations from the same company [AARP, "Elderly Become Target of Scams," 1994].

Some Tips to Avoid Advance-Fee Schemes

Be extremely skeptical of unsolicited offers that require up-front payments, that sound too good to be true, or otherwise do not make sense. The strongest advice is to avoid any type of "prize," "bonus," or "reward" of any kind that requires you to send money before you can claim it. Try to imagine any plausible and licit circumstances where a legitimate business would propose that you do that. There are none. It does *not* make sense!

Prize and Sweepstakes Scams in Operation

The advance-fee scam begins with the unsuspecting victim receiving a congratulatory letter, phone call, or e-mail telling him or her that he or she has won a prize or a large sum of money in a sweepstakes, contest, or lottery, or that he or she has inherited wealth due them. The contact advises the mark that in order to collect the "winnings" or the reward he or she must first advance an amount of cash to cover up-front costs for bonding, various "expenses," and taxes—U.S. or Canadian—if a "gift" is involved, shipping and handling fees. After these have been paid, the prize can be delivered. The mark sends the advance to whomever sent the announcement. He or she has been taken in by the advance-fee scam!

Deceptive Prize Promotions

If an individual had at one time signed up for a contest or prize drawing at a public event he or she may get far more than they bargained for—promotional material in the mail, telemarketing calls, and unsolicited e-mail or "spam." This is because many prize promoters sell the information they collect to advertisers. Contest entrants might subject themselves to a bogus prize promotion scam.

Prize promotion frauds are not conducted exclusively through the telephone. In many cases, direct mail is used to capture the attention of the consumer. Promotions arrive by mail as a letter or postcard that instructs the consumer to respond by return mail or telephone to enter a contest or collect a prize. Beware of any solicitations that say you have won something. Most of them are looking for potential victims. The mail or phone call may announce that you may have "already won a fabulous prize," but you'll need to pay, at the very least, for a 900-number call and "shipping and handling," before you can collect it. Discard any solicitation that asks for money up front. The problem: Sham solicitations describe the prize as being far more valuable than that which they're asking you to pay for. The FTC warns: "Claims that you have already won a prize can be a ploy to get you to buy a product, magazine, or provide money. These prizes sometimes come with a high price tag for shipping and handling. Often once you provide your credit card number to pay for shipping costs, you'll likely never receive your 'prize'" (United States Federal Trade Commission, "Catch the Bandit in Your Mailbox," 2000). The FTC's Telemarketing Sales Rule prohibits telemarketers from misrepresenting any of the facts of eligibility, as well as the nature or value of the prizes. It also requires telemarketers who call you to pitch a prize promotion to tell you before they describe the prize that you do not have to buy or pay anything to enter or win.

Commenting on the extent and effect of prize promotion fraud on the elderly, the FBI has stated:

> One type of telemarketing fraud in which the victims are disproportionately elderly is the deceptive prize promotion. Typically, the consumer receives a call enthusiastically congratulating him or her on having been selected to receive a valuable award—often described as thousands in cash, a car, a vacation, or jewelry.
>
> However, there is a "catch" that requires the consumer to send payment, often by an overnight courier service, in order to receive the prize. Then, although the consumer sends the payment as instructed, he or she does not receive the promised valuable prize. If the consumer receives any award at all, it is generally an item of little or no value, such as inexpensive costume jewelry or a travel certificate that requires huge outlays of cash to redeem [United States Federal Bureau of Investigation, "What Is an Advance-Fee Scheme?" no date].

Losses per consumer for telemarketed prize promotions generally range from a few hundred dollars to thousands of dollars. Unwitting elderly victims have spent hundreds of dollars to travel to distant places to claim a fantasy. The physical, emotional, and financial toll can be devastating. Some have lost their entire life savings to such scams. Prize promotion telemarketers often ask for only a small amount initially, but then, in the tactic referred to as "reloading," these crooks request ever increasing amounts from consumers, promising ever more valuable awards. Once marked as receptive to this type of scam, the target is often bombarded with similar fraudulent offers from a host of other scam artists using mooch lists.

The FTC and state and local consumer protection agencies have been receiving a growing number of complaints about promotions that use deceptively-advertised prizes. Such promotions remain one of the top five categories of complaints reported by the FTC's "Consumer Sentinel"—a multi-agency law enforcement investigative cyber tool.

Every day, consumers throughout the United States lose thousands of dollars to unscrupulous prize promoters. During 1999 alone, the Federal Trade Commission received more than 10,000 complaints from consumers about prize promotions, gifts, and sweepstakes. Many of these complaints concerned the deceitful way in which a mailing, or a telemarketer, described the prizes or awards. Consumers are always disappointed with the inferior quality and questionable utility of the product they were required to purchase in order to receive the prize. They soon learn that it usually costs far more than a similar product they can purchase at a local discount store (Source: United States Federal Trade Commission, "Fraud Against Seniors," 2000).

Sweepstakes and Contests: When "Winners" Lose

There's a big difference between legitimate sweepstakes and fraudulent ones. Prizes in legitimate sweepstakes are awarded solely by chance, and participants do not have to pay a fee or buy something to enter or to increase their already astronomical odds of winning. In fraudulent schemes, however, "winners" almost always have to dip into their pockets to enter their name or collect their "winnings."

Some older consumers may not understand the hype of sweepstakes offers or that they do not have to purchase something in order to win. They are frequently convinced by the glowing promises that they are already a winner and may not understand or be unable to read the fine print—the qualifying language—usually in *very* fine print!

In a paper entitled "The Truth About Elder Fraud" published in February 2002, Barbara Martin-Worley of Colorado State University reported:

> Millions of Americans—eight out of every 10 households—receive sweepstakes pronouncements several times a year through the mail or over the phone. While many toss these offers or simply refuse to talk to aggressive telemarketers, others play along for the fun of it, and some end up financial losers.
>
> Perhaps out of boredom or as a form of entertainment, older adults are particularly attracted to playing sweepstakes or games of chance. While many Americans are quick to recognize the ruse in glossy and official-looking sweepstakes documents, many seniors are not as discerning. They often are not aware of the level of sophistication of computer-generated mail that can be produced en masse. For many older adults with age-related vision loss, it is very difficult to read the fine print that indicates their odds of winning. ... Although it's true that the major sweepstakes companies do pay out the advertised amounts, chances of winning even in these contests, are remarkably slim, typically one in 3 million.
>
> As harmless as it seems, playing the sweepstakes can become a costly obsession. Tragically, those close to experiencing such losses may begin to enter contests out of desperation—they need to keep at it so they can recapture what they have lost. Often, fear and shame keep them from revealing the magnitude of their situation before intervention is possible.
>
> Others may never believe, or refuse to admit, they've been taken. Despite their recurring loss, habitual contestants actually believe that sweepstakes winnings offer the only real chance of financial prosperity and security.... What starts out as an innocent activity may lead players down an irreversible path. They are unable to stop playing, despite the fact that their efforts have not paid off [Martin-Worley, "The Truth About Elder Fraud," 2002].

PROTECTING YOURSELF FROM PRIZE AND SWEEPSTAKES SCAMS

To protect yourself from being duped, keep these tips in mind before mailing any sweepstakes or contest entry:

• No reputable sweepstakes or contest promoter will ask you for money in advance to enter or claim a prize.

• Never pay money to claim what you have "won." If you've really won, you should not have to pay anything for having done so.

• Sweepstakes promotions are typically cloaked offers of magazine subscriptions and "free" merchandise, both of which will require money up front.

• Many people mistakenly believe that buying more products gives them a better chance of winning. In an illegal means of deception these offers imply that the chances of winning are measurably improved by such purchases. They are not!

• Don't believe the hype. Bold statements such as "You have already won!" are at the core of fraud and deception. Watch out for such statements. They may get your attention, but don't let them get your money.

• Be suspicious of any announcements that say you have won a contest that you cannot remember ever having entered.

• It's important to read any written solicitation you receive carefully. It's highly unlikely that you've won a "big" prize if your notification was mailed by bulk rate. Check the postmark on the envelope or postcard. If looks like junk mail, it most likely is junk mail!

• Bona fide offers clearly disclose the terms and conditions of the promotion, including rules, entry procedures, and usually, the odds of winning in plain English. Most legitimate offers clearly disclose this information. Pay particularly close attention to the fine print. Remember the old adage that "the devil is in the details"—and he also lurks in the fine print.

• Sponsors of legitimate contests identify themselves prominently. Fraudulent promoters are more likely to attempt to hide their identities. Legitimate promoters also provide you with an address or toll-free phone numbers so you can call and check, or ask that your name be removed from their mailing or call list.

• You may be advised that you are required to attend a seminar to participate in the contest. Agreeing to attend such a seminar (sales meeting) in an effort to win an "expensive" prize is likely to subject you to a relentless high-pressure sales pitch. Think carefully before you agree to attend such sales meetings. Your chances of winning anything of real value are slim to zero.

- Do not be deceived by letters that look official or are marked "urgent." Promoters regularly use mailing pieces that look like checks made payable to the addressee even though they must be clearly marked "nonnegotiable."

- Watch out for companies trying to capitalize on an official sounding name or those that appear to be well-known organizations or legitimate businesses; the objective is to mislead consumers into thinking the scheme is affiliated with a government group or nationally recognized organization. Don't be deceived by these "look-alikes." It is illegal for a promoter to misrepresent an affiliation with, or an endorsement by, a government agency or other well-known organization.

- Avoid the temptation to participate in Internet lotteries, sweepstakes, or gambling. These are generally a way to get personal information from you and some are outright scams to get money and/or your credit card information. In almost every state, they are illegal.

- Disclosing your checking account or credit card account number over the phone in response to a sweepstakes or contest promotion is a sure-fire way to set yourself up to get scammed in the future.

- Think carefully before sending funds to a contest promoter. If they advise you to use a delivery system other than the U.S. Postal Service—such as overnight or courier services—they may be trying to avoid detection and prosecution by postal authorities. This is a favorite ploy for con artists because it lets them take your money fast, before you realize you've been cheated (Source: United States Federal Trade Commission, "Prize Offers: You Don't Have to Pay to Play," 2000).

PROTECTING OTHERS FROM PRIZE AND SWEEPSTAKES SCAMS

You may know or suspect that an elderly friend or family member has been making excess purchases in response to prize or sweepstakes promotions. AARP advises that there are some common signs of such an addiction to look for. These include:

- An inordinately large volume of sweepstakes or similar promotional material regularly mailed to the person from multiple companies and usually affirming that the recipient is a "guaranteed winner!"
- An excessive number of packages containing items that the elderly person never ordered, probably does not want or need, will likely never use, and may have never opened. Such merchandise is being delivered to the recipient on a regular basis.
- Stacks of magazines or books, frequently of inappropriate subject matter for the elderly person's interests. (These might even include books on how to enter and win contests and sweepstakes!)
- Explanations by the elderly person that the items were received as "gifts" or "rewards" rather than merchandise that he or she was induced to order and pay for.
- His or her financial records may show numerous checks payable to the same companies or duplicate payments for the same orders.
- There may be evidence of multiple contributions to the same charities or to several charities that do not seem to be of interest or relevancy to the contributor (Source: AARP, "Sweepstakes in Action," 2002).

If you see signs that an elderly friend or family member is making excess purchases or is uncomfortable about sweepstakes or contest promotions, you may need to address his or her concerns.

AARP suggests some guidelines for the conversation:

- Don't lecture, scold, or belittle the victim.
- Don't threaten to take drastic action that would impair his or her independence, or imply that he or she is no longer competent to manage personal affairs.
- Confirm his or her understanding that—by law—no purchase can be required as a prerequisite of winning anything.
- Discuss the odds of winning and remind him or her that every entry stands an equal chance at winning.
- Tactfully explore the reasons why he or she purchases merchandise so frequently, and if he or she is satisfied with these products.

- Suggest the individual compare the actual value of prizes he or she has won with the money he or she has expended on the contests.
- Discuss the difference between entering sweepstakes or contests as a diversion and expending such amounts that personal necessities are neglected.
- Tactfully offer to assist with balancing his or her checkbook and, without being intrusive, inquire about questionable entries or canceled checks.
- With the person's consent, review credit card statements and confirm that all purchases listed were authorized (Source: AARP, "Sweepstakes Action," 2002).

The Phony Inheritance Scam

In this swindle, the prize or reward is a promise of money that you have "inherited." Wouldn't it be nice if you came into an inheritance from a long-lost relative or friend? It does happen, but not very often. So if you receive a notification in the mail from an "estate locator" saying that there is an unclaimed inheritance waiting for you, beware. You could be the next target of a slick con artist.

These unscrupulous white collar criminals also call themselves "research specialists"—but they didn't find you by doing exhaustive research. You are one of thousands across the nation who are targeted in mass mailings; each person with the same name as yours—a list easily derived from any of several Internet search engines—receives notification that inheritance funds have been located in their names. Many of these recipients are lured into mailing in a fee—usually $25 or more—for an "estate report" which will purportedly explain where the inheritance is located and how it can be claimed. The promoter may also offer to "process your claim"—for a fee.

All the individuals on the mailing list receive the same information, so chances are almost zero that you are the actual heir. In the extremely unlikely instance that someone on the mailing list has the right to claim the funds, the amount is usually negligible because most such accounts are so small. They may actually be worth less than the fee you must pay to the promoter for information on claiming them.

You can protect yourself by checking other sources before sending funds in response to an estate locator solicitation. Checking with relatives about recent deaths in the family is one approach. All states maintain unclaimed property registries which can easily be checked online using a link on the state's home page. It can be a time-consuming process, but it may be where the scam operator found your name in the first place. If you can demonstrate the legitimacy of your claim, the state, as custodian, will gladly award you the unclaimed property at no expense.

Remember that legitimate law firms, executors of wills, and others who have been named to distribute estate funds to heirs should not request that you pay a fee to confirm and dispense your rightful share of the estate. Executors, by law, are entitled to reasonable and stipulated compensation for their services. If you have been the victim of a phony estate locator scheme, or if you have received a suspicious solicitation in the mail stating an unclaimed inheritance awaits you, report your experience to your local postmaster or nearest postal inspector.

Foreign Lotteries

Scam operators—increasingly based in Canada—are using the telephone, Internet, and direct mail to entice U.S. consumers to participate in high-stakes lotteries from all around the world. They all guarantee huge winnings—possibly as high as $1 billion! These lottery solicitations violate U.S. law which prohibits the cross-border sale or purchase of lottery tickets by phone or mail. Still, federal law enforcement authorities are intercepting millions of foreign lottery mailings sent or delivered by the truckload into the U.S. Consumers, lured by prospects of instant wealth, are responding to the solicitations that do get through—to the tune of $120 million a year, according to the USPIS (Source: United States Postal Inspection Service, "Sweepstakes and Lotteries," no date).

The FTC has warned that any promotions for foreign lotteries are likely to be phony. The potential victim may receive an "award notice" announcing that he or she has already won a very large amount of money. To receive your winnings, you first have to send them money for so-called handling fees—as much as 10 percent of the prize they claim you have won. Or you are encouraged to send funds to buy lottery tickets—which scam operators don't buy or if they do buy any tickets with your money, they keep any winnings for themselves.

The FTC has these words of caution for consumers who are thinking about responding to such lotteries:

- If you play a foreign lottery through the mail or over the telephone, you're violating federal law. It is illegal for any foreign lottery— legitimate or not—to use the U.S. mail to solicit entrants.
- There are no "secret" systems for winning foreign lotteries. Your chances of winning more than the cost of your tickets are slim to none.
- If you purchase one foreign lottery ticket, expect many more bogus offers for lottery or investment "opportunities." Your name will be placed on sucker lists of people who have already fallen for scams,—the mooch lists that fraudulent telemarketers buy, sell, or trade. In today's vernacular: Once they have your name, "you're toast!"
- And, as always, keep your credit card and bank account numbers to yourself.
- Disregard all mail and phone solicitations for foreign lottery promotions.
- However, the postal service advises consumers not to discard letters soliciting foreign lottery participation. They may provide a paper trail and advise that if you receive one, return it to the post office (Source: United States Federal Trade Commission, "Catch the Bandit in Your Mailbox," 2000).

Other Lottery Scams

There are a variety of other schemes and scams involving lotteries. These include:

- Winning Tickets
  People claiming to have winning lottery tickets to sell you are con artists. These are generally counterfeit tickets that have absolutely no intrinsic value. How do they know it will win? Why would anyone in their right mind sell a ticket that has won?!
- "Secret" Ways to Win
  You also may receive solicitations offering you secret ways or systems to make you a winner of lotteries. They are always

scams. Ask yourself two key questions: If there were a secret system, why would a complete stranger want to share it with you? Why are you hearing about it for the first time through an advertisement? There are no ways to improve your odds or guarantee you will win a true game of chance. There is always a handsome price tag to divulge these arcane systems.
- 900-Numbers

  Some lottery promoters use a toll-free 800-number that directs you to dial a pay-per-call 900-number. Those "scratch and win" tickets or postcards telling you to call a 900-number to find out the amount of the prize you have won should always be considered suspect as fraudulent.

The Extent of Lottery Fraud among Older Victims

Off the Hook: Reducing Participation in Telemarketing Fraud, an AARP Foundation study published in July 2003, found that the crime of telemarketing fraud in general is grossly underreported among older victims. In one portion of the study, the AARP found that only half of those lottery fraud victims interviewed would acknowledge having lost money although they had previously been in contact with law enforcement authorities (Source: AARP, *Off the Hook*, 2003).

Pyramids and Multilevel Marketing

The Pyramid Scheme

The pyramid is the basic concept of the schemes and scams discussed in this section. A pyramid is a scam which, unlike those of Egypt—monuments of stone resting on sand—is a monumental fraud built of sand, resting on sand. Participants are completely unaware of the dynamics in play, convinced that the promised handsome return on their investment will derive from the pyramid operator's acumen in matters of business, oblivious to the fact that any return will come—for a brief interlude—from suckers like them who are eagerly buying into the scheme with the same hopes, expectations, and cupidity.

A pyramid is a hierarchical organization created when individuals agree to join at a level below those who have joined previously. In doing so, they, in effect, agree to make payments to those above them in the hierarchy, convinced that they will move up in the ranks of participants—ultimately to the top of the pyramid—while receiving continually increasing payments from all new "downline" recruits who subsequently clamber onto the levels below them.

Such schemes are in violation of federal statutes and those of all states, as well as most other foreign countries. Under these various laws, pyramid schemes are considered a form of gambling or outright fraud. In May of 1998, the FTC reported that there is a growing international problem of these schemes. What is striking about them is that while they are very old forms of fraud, modern technology has vastly multiplied their potential for harming citizens—particularly elderly citizens. The Internet in particular offers pyramid builders a multi-lane highway to world-wide recruits instantaneously. The FTC has said

> In the U.S., probably nothing has contributed to the growth of pyramid schemes as much as Internet marketing. The introduction of electronic commerce has allowed con artists to quickly and cost-effectively target victims around the globe. After buying a computer and a modem, scam artists can establish and maintain a site on the World Wide Web for $30 a month or less, and solicit anyone in the world with Internet access.... In addition, through ... spam, pyramid operators can engage in cheap one-on-one marketing. Whereas it might cost hundreds or thousands of dollars to rent a mailing list and send post cards to potential recruits, it costs only a fraction of that to send out similar e-mail solicitations. On the Internet, you can acquire one million e-mail addresses for as little as $10 and spend nothing on postage [United States Federal Trade Commission, "Pyramid Schemes," 1998].

Pyramid schemes can be quite seductive because they may be able to deliver a high rate of return to a few early investors for a short period of time. They are illegal because they inevitably must fall apart. No such program can recruit new members forever. Every pyramid scheme collapses because, as we will see, it cannot expand beyond realistically attainable limits. When the scheme collapses, most investors find themselves at the bottom of the pile of rubble, unable to recoup their losses. The 'Lectric Law Library comments: "The tragic aspect of pyramid schemes is that they concentrate on and exploit people with limited means and limited knowledge of business—people who can ill afford to lose the investment they put into the program. Thousands of unsuspecting and trusting investors have lost millions of dollars by investing in pyramid schemes. Even worse, the schemes have robbed some retired persons of their life savings" ('Lectric Law Library, "Multi-Level Marketing, no date).

How a Pyramid Scheme Operates

Let us examine one of the many types of pyramid schemes, from the perspective of how it purports to operate. You are given a list of six names and instructed to send $1 to each name and, after removing the name at the top of the list, send the list on to others. Assume you are successful in getting ten persons to join, and each of them recruits ten persons and so on, and the pyramid grows exponentially. Here is what would happen:

- The first level below you has ten people. They each send you a dollar, so you collect $10.
- The next level has a hundred people. (Each of your first ten gets ten more.) You collect $100.
- The next level has a thousand people. You collect $1,000.
- The next level has 10,000 people. You collect $10,000.
- The next level has 100,000 people. You collect $100,000.
- The next level has 1,000,000 people. You collect $1,000,000.

At this point, your name drops off the list, and you collect nothing more. Bob Blaylock remarks:

It's very easy to understand how this kind of scheme should work. It all seems so simple and so obvious. It is, unfortunately, somewhat more difficult to understand why this kind of scheme does not work, and why it is unethical and dishonest, and, in most cases, very much illegal. The truth is, this scheme does not work, except for those who get in at the first few levels. The vast majority of participants in such a scheme will only lose their original investment, and make no profit at all.... [In] every instance where a person is induced to join such a scheme, based on the promise that he will make a profit by participating, a fraud has been committed [Blaylock, "Pyramid Schemes, Ponzi Schemes, and Related Frauds," no date].

In order to understand why pyramid schemes do not work, consider these two essential factors:

1. The pyramid must inevitably collapse because there is a finite number of potential participants who can be recruited.
2. There can be no new wealth created. Any gains made by any new participant is, in reality, wealth lost by all of the other participants.

How many levels could this scheme run before it failed for lack of new participants? In the previous example, which assumed that each person who joined would bring in ten new participants, consider the basic mathematics underlying the concept:

Level	No. of Persons
1.	1
2.	10
3.	100
4.	1,000
5.	10,000
6.	100,000
7.	1,000,000
8.	10,000,000
9.	100,000,000
10.	1,000,000,000

As shown, there are ten levels, counting the one person at the top who started it. By the time these ten levels are filled, there will be a total of 1,111,111,111 participants. The eleventh level would require 10,000,000,000 new participants. There aren't that many human beings on the planet!! On March 2004, the U.S. Bureau of the Census estimated the total population of the world at approximately 6,355,549,778. (For the reader who may be interested, a current estimate of the world's population can be found at: http://www.census.gov/cgi-bin/ipc/popclockw/.)

Chain Letters

A chain letter may be an innocuous piece of mail, an e-mail message, or some other form of communication which encourages the recipient to copy the missive and send it to other persons. The body of the letter may be a prayer, blessing, or political statement—often there are inherent elements of spirituality, numerology, superstition, or the occult. Following the sender's instructions to propagate the message may promise untold blessings and good luck. Failure to do so may invoke unimaginable maledictions—"Bad luck will plague you for the rest of your life!" In this form, chain letters are not illegal no matter how silly or annoying they may be, or how utterly wasteful of postage or bandwidth. Even if they're not illegal, chain letters of any kind are very irritating to most anyone who receives one. Many ISPs prohibit them. Most recipients ignore them and consign them to the trash.

Not all chain letters are pyramid schemes, and not all pyramid schemes are chain letters; however, the term "chain letter" is often used as a synonym for pyramid scheme. If a chain letter asks the recipient to send money to those persons through whom the letter has previously passed, with the promise that the recipient will receive money from those to whom they relay the letter, then this becomes a form of pyramid—and consequently illegal. In this context, chain letters are a form of gambling, and sending them through the U.S. mail, e-mail, fax, or delivering them in person is a federal crime in violation of Title 18, United States Code, Section 1302, the Postal Lottery Statute.

The U.S. Postal Service's official statement on chain letters describes illegal pyramid schemes:

> A chain letter is a "get rich quick" scheme that promises that your mail box will soon be stuffed full of cash if you decide to participate. You're told you can make thousands of dollars every month if you follow the detailed instructions in the letter. A typical chain letter includes names and addresses of several individuals whom you may or may not know. You are instructed to send a certain amount of money—usually $5—to the person at the top of the list, and then eliminate that name and add yours to the bottom. You are then instructed to mail copies of the letter to a few more individuals who will hopefully repeat the entire process.
>
> The letter promises that if they follow the same procedure, your name will gradually move to the top of the list and you'll receive money—lots of it. There's at least one problem with chain letters. They're illegal if they request money or other items of value and promise a substantial return to the participants.
>
> The main thing to remember is that a chain letter is simply a bad

investment. You certainly won't get rich. You will receive little or no money. The few dollars you may get will probably not be as much as you spend making and mailing copies of the chain letter.

Chain letters don't work because the promise that all participants in a chain letter will be winners is mathematically impossible. Also, many people participate, but do not send money to the person at the top of the list. Some others create a chain letter that lists their name numerous times—in various forms with different addresses. So, in reality, all the money in a chain is going to one person.... Participating in a chain letter is a losing proposition [United States Postal Inspection Service, "Chain Letters," no date]

The FTC confirms the USPIS warning: "Chain e-mails—they used to circulate by postal mail, but these days, they're also showing up via e-mail and Internet chat rooms.... But here's the scoop on chain mail: If it promises any kind of return—like money—it's fraudulent and illegal! If you start or forward one, you could face legal action.... You can help eliminate chain e-mails. Just break the chain" (United States Federal Trade Commission, "Break the Chain," no date).

Gifting Clubs

In these schemes, individuals pay to join a "gifting club." The money they pay to join is described as a "gift" and these schemes are billed in promotional materials as a private club with members eager to help new friends—often from within their own neighborhood or social group. Local senior citizens associations are fertile ground.

In reality, these clubs are illegal pyramid schemes. New members give cash "gifts" to the highest-ranking members, with titles such as "captains." They are promised that if they can persuade others to join the gifting club, they, too, will rise to become captains and receive money—far more than they initially paid to join—from these newer members and "friends." It is a most convivial scheme!

The problem is that, like all pyramid schemes, illegal gifting clubs must continually recruit ever-increasing numbers of members to survive. When they fail to attract enough new members, they predictably collapse. Most members who had paid to join the clubs never receive the financial "gifts" they expected, and lose everything they had paid to join.

The FTC advises, "Don't get on the receiving end of a gifting club

'Gotcha'" (United States Federal Trade Commission, "The Gifting Club 'Gotcha,'" 2000). Promises of quick, easy money can be a powerful lure—especially when it comes with the additional benefit of new friendships or social contacts. So if you're approached about joining such a club but you aren't sure if it's an illegal gifting club, the FTC advises you to

- Consider that a legitimate gift has no strings attached and is not an "investment."
- Be wary of success stories or testimonials of tremendous payoffs. Very few members of illegal gifting clubs or pyramid schemes ever receive any money.
- Take your time. Don't succumb to a high-pressure sales pitch that requires you to join immediately or risk losing out on the opportunity. Remember, solid opportunities—and solid friendships —aren't formed through such nerve-wracking tactics.
- Avoid being misled into thinking a gifting club is legitimate because the ads say that members consider their payments a gift and expect nothing in return. This is an attempt to make an illegal transaction look legal. And you *will* get nothing in return!
- Be particularly wary of any claims that any money you might receive from such a scheme is "not taxable, because the Internal Revenue Service does not impose a tax on gifts in amounts under $10,000." This is patently false. The IRS defines a gift as something of value given to another with no expectation of receiving anything of value in return. Ironically, while the majority of the victims of the gifting club scam ultimately never receive anything in return, their so-called "gifts" are certainly not given without the full expectation of a considerable return. Therefore the amounts of money they contribute cannot be considered gifts for income tax purposes. In addition to the legal implications of participating in a pyramid scheme, failure to report as income any monetary returns that might accrue to them from such a scheme could make the recipients subject to tax evasion charges as well (Source: United States Federal Trade Commission, "The Gifting Club 'Gotcha,'" 2000).

Multilevel Marketing

Multilevel marketing (MLM) plans, also known as "network" or "matrix" marketing, are a way of selling goods or services through a network of distributors. A variety of quality consumer products have always been sold by independent businessmen and women usually in customers' homes at competitive prices. Many of these quality products are not available in retail stores and are sold only through such reputable distributors. Such direct marketing plans are a well-established, legitimate form of the retailing business. Many entrepreneurs have built successful careers on this concept because the main focus of their activities is their product and product sales. Unfortunately, many others offer goods that are overpriced, have questionable quality, or are downright unsafe to use.

Multi-Level Marketing: Legitimate Business or Pyramid Scheme?

These plans typically promise that if you sign up as a distributor you will receive commissions—not only on your sales of the plan's goods or services, but also on the sales of each of the persons you recruit to become distributors. These recruits—usually extending through two or more levels—are known as the distributor's "downline."

Multi-level marketing pyramid schemes can resemble legitimate MLM plans. They have a similar structure to them but a completely different focus. They operate as a pyramid by claiming participants can earn a great deal of money by concentrating most, if not all, of their efforts on recruiting new distributors. They focus primarily on the profits to be earned by selling the right to recruit others as new distributors. The emphasis is on aggressively persuading others to join the program, rather than on selling a product or service—activities that are virtually ignored. Most of the product sales are made to the distributors—not to consumers in general. The underlying variety of goods and services serve only to make the schemes appear legitimate.

For each and every distributor, the success of the whole operation depends on their continuously getting additional people to join the plan. However, there is a practical limit to how many distributors can be found and to how many product units they can sell or use. Participants attempt to recoup their investments in products they have purchased from the operators by recruiting from the ever-decreasing number of potential investors in a defined geographic area. Their downline goes offline very quickly.

There are two tell-tale signs that a product is being used just to disguise a pyramid scheme: 1. inventory loading and 2. a lack of retail sales. Inventory loading occurs when a company's incentive program forces recruited distributors to buy more products than they could ever sell, often at inflated prices. If this occurs throughout the plan's distribution system, the people at the top of the pyramid reap substantial profits, even though few, if any, products actually move into the marketplace. The persons at the bottom make excessive payments for inventory that simply accumulates in their basements or garages.

A lack of retail sales is also a red flag that a pyramid exists. Many MLM plans will claim that their product is selling very briskly. However, on closer examination, the sales occur only between and among individuals inside the pyramid structure, or to new recruits joining the structure—not to consumers, not to the general public.

If a plan offers to pay commissions for recruiting new distributors, watch out! As was noted previously, all states outlaw pyramid schemes, and their statutes generally prescribe that a multilevel marketing plan should pay commissions only for retail sales of goods or services, not for recruiting new distributors. The FTC advises: "Steer clear of multilevel marketing plans that pay commissions for recruiting new distributors. They're actually illegal pyramid schemes. Why is pyramiding dangerous? Because plans that pay commissions for recruiting new distributors inevitably collapse when no new distributors can be recruited. When a plan collapses, most people—except perhaps those at the very top of the pyramid—lose their money" (United States Federal Trade Commission, "Lotions and Potions," 2000).

BEFORE MAKING THE DECISION ABOUT MLM

The FTC suggests that you use common sense, and consider these seven tips before you make a decision to become involved in any MLM plan:

1. Avoid any plan that includes commissions for recruiting additional distributors.

2. Beware of plans that ask new distributors to purchase expensive inventory.
3. Be cautious of plans that claim you will make money through continued growth of your "downline"—the commissions on sales made by new distributors you recruit—rather than through sales of products you yourself have generated.
4. Beware of plans that claim to sell miracle products or promise enormous earnings. Just because a promoter of a plan makes a claim doesn't mean it's true! Ask the promoter of the plan to substantiate the claims.
5. Beware of shills boasting about their fictional success in the plan.
6. Don't pay or sign any contracts in an "opportunity meeting" or any other high-pressure situation. Insist on taking time to think it over.
7. Do your homework! (Source: United States Federal Trade Commission, "Multilevel Marketing Plans," 1996).

YOUR LEGAL RESPONSIBILITIES IN MLM

If, after careful consideration, you do decide to become a MLM distributor, remember that you are legally responsible for the claims you make about the parent company, its products or services, and any business opportunities it offers. That applies even if you are simply parroting claims presented in a company brochure or advertisement. When you promote the qualities of a product or service, you are obligated to present those claims truthfully and to ensure there is enough solid evidence to back them up. You are advised to verify the research behind any claims about a product's performance before repeating those claims to a potential customer.

If you decide to solicit new distributors, be aware that you are responsible for any claims you may make about their earnings potential. Be sure to represent the opportunity honestly and to avoid making unrealistic promises. If those promises do not materialize, you could be held liable in a civil lawsuit—or perhaps guilty in criminal proceedings (Source: United States Federal Trade Commission, "Lotions and Potions," 2000).

Taxes

On April 11, 2002, in testimony before the Senate Finance Committee, Internal Revenue Service Commissioner Charles O. Rossotti stated: "Seek expert advice before you subscribe to any scheme that offers instant wealth or exemption from your obligation as a United States Citizen to pay taxes. Buying into a tax evasion scheme can be very costly" (United States Internal Revenue Service, "Types of Schemes: Testimony on Promoted Tax Schemes," 2002).

The "Dirty Dozen" Tax Scams

In an update of an annual consumer alert, on February 19, 2003, the IRS issued "IRS Updates the 'Dirty Dozen' for 2003," alerting taxpayers not to fall victim to one of the twelve most prevalent tax scams. (The full text of the consumer alert can be found on the IRS website: www.irs.gov.) These types of schemes surface each year as tax filing season begins. Con artists shamelessly take advantage of the taxpaying public, charging them fees for their illegal schemes. "With the tax season in full swing, we're seeing the traditional upswing in tax trickery," noted acting commissioner Bob Wenzel. "Year after year, con artists across the nation try pulling a fast one on honest taxpayers with different types of miracle tax solutions. Don't be fooled by the 'Dirty Dozen' and other misleading scams. There is no secret way to get out of paying taxes" (United States Internal Revenue Service, "IRS Updates," 2003). All of these patently false arguments have no legal basis whatsoever, and despite the courts having consistently rejected them, their promoters continue to expound and market them, particularly to unsuspecting taxpayers and small businesses. Taxpayers may even incur penalties for bringing frivolous cases into court or for filing frivolous tax returns. In the 1980s, Congress, concerned about taxpayers misusing the courts, enacted a law allowing the courts to impose a penalty of up to $25,000 when they deem a taxpayer's argument specious.

The IRS and other federal agencies are aggressively pursuing and successfully prosecuting promoters of these schemes—and many of their clients—for fraud and tax evasion. These IRS actions can result in imprisonment, fines, and repayment of taxes owed with interest and penalties. Even innocent taxpayers involved in these schemes can face a staggering amount of back interest and penalties. The IRS urges all American citizens to avoid all twelve of the tax scams; however, senior citizens are particularly cautioned not to fall victim to certain of the scams listed. These include:

- Social Security Tax Refund

  Senior citizens are particularly vulnerable to this scam which lures elderly taxpayers into believing that they can get a refund of the Social Security taxes paid during their lifetime. This scam works by convincing the victim to pay a "paperwork" or "processing" fee to file a refund claim (Form 1041) with the IRS. Of course, this is nothing more than a hoax designed to fleece the victims for the up-front fee. The tax code does *not* allow a refund of Social Security taxes paid. The IRS processing centers are alert to this hoax and have been intercepting the false claims.

- African-Americans Get a "Special Tax Refund"

  Thousands of elderly African-Americans have been misled by offers to file for tax credits or refunds related to reparations for slavery. There is *no* provision in the U.S. tax code that allows African-Americans to receive tax credits or refunds related to slavery reparations. These unscrupulous promoters have encouraged clients to pay them to prepare a claim for this spurious refund, and or are deceiving citizens into paying money for advice on how to file these claims. The claims are a waste of money. Promoters of reparations tax schemes have been convicted and imprisoned. And taxpayers who file could face a $500 penalty for filing such claims if they do not withdraw them.

  The IRS reports: "In early 2002, the slavery reparations scam ranked as the No. 1 scheme on the Dirty Dozen list. Following a sweeping public outreach campaign and assistance from members of the Congressional Black Caucus and other organizations, the number of reparation scam claims fell sharply. Tens of thousands of claims were received in 2001, but the claims fell to less than 50 per week in 2002" (United States Internal Revenue Service, "IRS Updates," 2003).

- Improper Home-Based Business Deductions

  This scheme purports to offer tax "relief" but in reality is illegal tax avoidance. The promoters of these schemes claim that individual taxpayers can deduct most or all of their personal expenses as business expenses by setting up a bogus home-based business. However, the tax code firmly establishes that a clear business purpose and profit motive must exist in order to generate and claim allowable business expenses.

- Pay the Tax, Then Get the Prize

    The caller announces excitedly that you have won a "prize" and all you have to do to receive it is pay the income tax due on it—to the caller. Do not believe it. If you really won such a prize (which is highly unlikely) you may need to make an estimated tax payment to cover the taxes that will be due at the end of the tax year. But the payment goes to the IRS, not the entity that awards the so-called prize. Whether you have won a legitimate prize of cash, a car, or a trip, the organization awarding the prize generally sends you and the IRS a Form 1099 indicating the total market value of the prize that must be reported on your tax return.

- "I Can Get You a Big Refund"

    These refund scheme operators may approach you wanting to "borrow" your Social Security Number or give you a bogus W-2 form so it appears that you qualify for a big refund. They may promise to split the refund with you, but the IRS catches most of these false refund claims before they are remitted. And when one does go out, the participant/victim usually winds up paying back the refund along with stiff penalties and interest. Two lessons to remember: 1. anyone who promises you a larger refund without knowing your tax situation could be misleading you; and 2. never sign a tax return without examining it carefully and attesting to the truth of it. Otherwise, you could be committing a criminal act of perjury.

- IRS "Agent" Comes to Your Home to Collect

    A special caution for the senior citizen is in order here. This simply is *not* done. The IRS does not make house calls—except to investigate or apprehend criminal suspects. The hapless average taxpayer is summoned to appear before their agents. Never admit anyone into your home unless he or she identifies him or herself to your complete satisfaction. All IRS special agents, field auditors, and collection officers carry official credentials, including photo identification. In routine tax matters, following IRS procedures and guidelines, they will normally contact you in advance of their visit; they will not arrive unannounced and without prior arrangements. If you think the person at your door is an impostor, refuse to admit him, lock your door, and call the police. To report suspect IRS impostors, call the Treasury Inspector General's Hotline at 1-800-366-4484.

Beyond the "Dirty Dozen

The IRS sees many more tax schemes. In April 2003, the media reported that a company called "Tax Ready" had merged with a company called National Audit Defense Network, and was then operating as "NADN" and promising to "custom design a tax plan based on your income level," that would result in an average of "about a 20 percent reduction in your taxes." They claimed that this guaranteed tax savings would be attained through instructional materials and counseling sessions with "former IRS agents." Those taken in by the scam purchased a product that did not exist. One victim paid $9,000; his taxes were not reduced, but his bank account surely was! The "counseling session" with the "IRS agent" was less than ten minutes in duration and the instructional materials they received could have been obtained free at any library or on the Web. As for their money back "guarantee," victims' calls and letters were ignored. A lawsuit was filed in Nevada on behalf of at least 700 victims who claimed they could not get their money back when they requested refunds. Others claim they had been given bad or useless tax advice or sustained large losses. The owner of NADN blamed the problems on "overzealous sales people" and "bad boy behavior" (CBS News, "Costly Tax Advice," 2003).

Another example of a tax scam is that of improper abusive trusts which promise that "you will never have to pay taxes again." Promoters of abusive trust schemes may charge $5,000 to $70,000 for "trust" packages. The fee enables taxpayers to have trust documents prepared, to utilize foreign and domestic trustees—suggested by the promoters—and to use foreign bank accounts and corporations. Although these schemes give the appearance of the separation of responsibility and control from the benefits of ownership, these bogus trusts are in fact controlled and directed by the taxpayer. A legitimate trust is a form of ownership that usually separates responsibility and control of assets placed in the trust from all of the benefits of ownership.

Advice for Taxpayers

The best advice for taxpayers is to remember the time-honored concept of "buyer beware." Think carefully before paying for financial services of any kind or signing important documents; and don't be fooled by outrageous tax claims. Seek expert advice before you subscribe to any scheme that offers instant wealth or exemption from your obligation as a United States Citizen. Buying into a tax evasion scheme can be very costly (Source: United States Internal Revenue Service, "Types of Schemes," 2002).

Telephone Billing

For many, advancing age may bring a decline in visual and mental acuity. The simple act of reading and understanding a telephone bill—and identifying errors or fraud—can present many challenges for the senior citizen. The National Consumers League advises

> Life's a lot more complicated than it used to be—and so is your phone bill! With more competition for telephone service and new services being developed every day, you have more choices for your communications needs than ever before. But understanding your options—and your phone bill—has become much harder.
>
> Many phone companies are redesigning their bills to make them easier to understand. However, the charges may still be confusing unless you know some basics about how telephone billing works. Looking at your phone bill carefully—and understanding what it says—will help you use phone services wisely and avoid fraud [National Consumers League, "Understanding Your Phone Bill," no date].

Truth-in-Billing Rules

The Federal Communications Commission (FCC) has seen a tremendous growth in consumer complaints directly or indirectly arising out of the failure of telephone bills to provide consumers with essential information in a clear and conspicuous manner. Consumer confusion over telephone bills has contributed significantly to the growth of fraud. In response, the FCC has established rules that require telephone companies to make their phone bills more consumer-friendly. These rules enable consumers, when reading their bills, to determine more easily what services have been provided, by whom, and the charges assessed for these services—and if all of these charges are legitimate. Telephone companies must also list a toll-free number on their bills for customers with billing inquiries. These rules are designed to assist consumers make informed choices when they shop around in the competitive telecommunications marketplace to find the best telephone service to meet their needs, and to empower them to protect themselves from the various types of telephone billing fraud.

Common Telephone Billing Frauds

Consumer Action publishes *You Can Help Fight Phone Fraud*, a very informative 16-page guide to help consumers avoid and detect phone fraud, including slamming, cramming, toll fraud, calling card fraud, identity theft and wireless (cell) phone fraud. The guide also lists resources for information as well as reporting phone fraud. Note that the last revision of the publication was in 1999. You are advised to use this information as a general guide only; consult with a local consumer group for laws specific to your state. The guide can be downloaded from Consumer Action's website.

The two primary types of billing fraud are "slamming" and "cramming."

- Slamming
    "Slamming" is the term used to describe any practice that changes a telephone subscriber's preferred telephone service provider to another company without the subscriber's knowledge or consent. When this happens, you've been "slammed." It can happen with long distance service and as competition increases for local and local toll for those services as well. Sometimes slamming results from a simple clerical error; for example, the wrong number being entered into the system. But

in many cases it's a deliberate attempt by one company to "steal" the customer from another. The slammer falsely claims that you have agreed to change your service provider and directs your local phone company to make the change.

• Cramming

"Cramming" is the term used to describe the practice of placing unauthorized, misleading, or deceptive charges on consumers' telephone bills. Entities that engage in these practices appear to rely heavily on consumer confusion, particularly elderly consumers, over telephone bills to mislead them into paying for services that were not authorized or even received.

You've been "crammed" when charges for miscellaneous services that you never agreed to subscribe to have been added to your phone bill. Some examples of these charges are phone-related services such as voice mail, paging, or personal 800-numbers. But you might also find charges for other types of services on your bill, such as Internet access, club memberships, and even dating services (perhaps a red flag for the average senior citizen).

The crammer arranges to bill you, usually through your local phone company, by falsely claiming that you authorized the new services. These charges might appear on your bill just once, or they might recur on every bill—a good reason to look closely at each bill before you pay it.

Cramming also occurs when a local or long distance company or another type of service provider does not clearly or accurately describe all of the relevant charges to the consumer when marketing the service. Although the consumer did authorize the service, the charge is still considered cramming because the consumer was misled.

In addition to providing local service, local telephone companies often bill their customers for long distance and other services that other companies provide. When the local company, the long distance telephone company, or another type of service provider either accidentally or intentionally sends inaccurate billing data to be included on the consumer's local telephone bill, cramming can occur (Source: AARP, "Phone Cramming," 2002).

CRAMMING CHARGES: WHAT THEY LOOK LIKE

Cramming comes in many forms and is often hard to detect unless you carefully examine your telephone bill. The following charges would be legitimate if a consumer had authorized them, but, if unauthorized, these charges could constitute cramming:

- Charges for services that are explained on a consumer's telephone bill in general terms—such as "service fee," "service charge," "other fees," "voice-mail," "mail server," "calling plan," "psychic," and "membership";
- charges that are added to a consumer's telephone bill every month without a clear explanation of the services provided—such as a "monthly fee" or "minimum monthly usage fee"; and
- other charges from a local or long distance company for a service that it provides, but, like the other examples, could be cramming if unauthorized (Source: United States Federal Communications Commission, "Cramming," 2002).

Pay-per-call 800- and 900-number Scams

Information and entertainment provided by pay-per-call services are accessed through 900-numbers, some 800-numbers, and even some international phone numbers. If you, as many others do, think that all 800-number telephone calls are gratis, it could be a costly mistake. Many 800-numbers which provide various categories of information or types of entertainment do so at a cost to the caller who is not told about this; callers are being charged for calls that are advertised as "free." The consumer calls an 800-number and later learns that the call had been shunted to an expensive entertainment service, an international telephone number, or a pricey 900-number. Consumers are being charged for these "free" calls—unlawfully.

In the past, swindlers used toll-free 800-numbers to carry out many of the scams they now promote via 900-numbers. The scams include phony free prize and free vacation offers, as well as deceptive credit card promotions. The scams often begin when the swindler sends you a notification in the mail claiming that you have won something, are entitled to a gift, have qualified for credit, or uses some other ploy. A call to the scammer's number will provide all the details of your good fortune. These swindlers may promise you a product or service, such as credit repair or a travel package, but what you actually receive will be quite disappointing. Those with bad credit hoping to receive a credit card by calling a 900-number might receive a list of banks to which they can apply for such a card. Those who are told to call because they're winners in a sweepstakes receive nothing at all. But you'll be even more unhappy with the charges that appear on your phone bill—as much as $30 or more for each call!

Frequently, when you call a 900-number, you will be required to listen to a long recorded sales pitch. Remember, the longer you are on the telephone, the higher the phone charges will be. To add insult to injury, at the end of the relentless spiel, you will often be directed to call *another* 900-number for additional information or to order the product or service. If you call the second 900-number you will then be billed for an additional 900-number telephone call.

How to Protect Yourself and Save Money

Carefully review your telephone bill every month. Treat your telephone service just as you would any other consumer purchase; examine your monthly telephone bills just as closely as you examine your monthly credit card and bank statements.

Ask yourself the following questions as you review your telephone bill:

- "Do I recognize the names of all of the companies listed on my bill?"
- "What services were provided by the listed companies?"
- "Does the bill include charges for calls I did not place or services I did not authorize?"
- "Are the rates charged by each company consistent with the rates that the company quoted to me?"

Keep in mind that you may sometimes be billed for a call you placed or a service you used, but the description listed on your telephone bill for the call or service may be unclear. If you do not know what service was provided for a charge listed on your bill, ask the company that billed the charge to explain the service provided before paying the bill. The cost of small, incorrect charges for telephone-related services adds up over time. Make sure you know what service was provided for such small charges. Crammers often try to go undetected by submitting $2.00 or $3.00 charges to many thousands of customers. Maintain a detailed record of the telephone services you have authorized and used—including calls placed to 900-numbers and other types of telephone information; these records can be helpful when billing descriptions are unclear.

Some Tip-offs to Potential Telephone Billing Scams

Many questionable telephone information services:

- Advertise on late-night television, in the tabloids, and in classified or personal advertisements. Remember that both legitimate services and those that violate the law may advertise in the same media.
- May include services for "adult" (pornographic) chat lines, dating, horoscope, or "psychic" readings.
- Provide telephone numbers that include international prefixes as shown in your telephone book.
- Assert that they are "not a 900-number" or "a premium does not apply." It is or it will!
- Be alert to the "dialer" trap that lurks on many Internet web-pages which surreptitiously shunt your browser to a long-distance toll call, often overseas, when they are accessed. You may not be aware of this scam until you receive your telephone bill.

Vacation and Travel

Many senior citizens are inveterate travelers. Most are inveterate bargain hunters. The combination can leave them vulnerable to vacation and travel scams. "Have you ever been tempted to sign up to win a 'free' trip at a fair, trade show, shopping mall or restaurant? What you are signing up for is a sales pitch. What follows will be a phone call, letter, unsolicited fax, e-mail or letter telling you that you've won a vacation. Be careful. It may be a 'trip trap.' The vacation that you've 'won' likely isn't free. And the 'bargain-priced' travel package you're offered over the telephone or Internet may not fit your idea of luxury" (United States Federal Trade Commission, "Traveler's Advisory," 2000).

Travel scams often combine phone and mail fraud. A phone call from a "travel club" announces that you are the "grand prize winner" of a contest. In all likelihood you never entered any such contest, but naturally you would be happy to win a prize—grand or otherwise. The catch: You are told that your prize can be claimed only if you first pay a fee in advance and before they can send you further details. If you pay the fee, you have fallen into the trip trap. Have you ever been tempted to buy one of those bargain-priced travel packages glowingly described in the media? Be careful. Your dream of adventure could become a dreadful and costly misadventure if you fall victim to a travel and vacation scam. AARP cautions: "Go to paradise rather than to the cleaners! Looking for travel bargains to your dream vacation spot? Do not turn your travel dream into a travel nightmare. It is good to look for travel bargains. But look closely at all offers and read the fine print. If the deal sounds too good to be true, be leery" (AARP, "Travel Fraud," no date).

Certainly, some travel opportunities sold over the phone or offered through the mail or on the Internet are legitimate; however, many of them are scam operations that are defrauding senior citizens and other consumers out of hundreds of millions of dollars each year. When you get such a phone call, or place a call in response to a letter, e-mail, or Internet ad, you will certainly be subject to a sales pitch for a supposedly luxurious trip—one that you could pay dearly for and one which, instead of sending you up a scenic river, could send you up the creek! The United States Postal Inspection Service warns: "When you get a postcard or letter in the mail (or an unexpected phone call from an unknown company) promising a complimentary vacation in an exotic spot, someone is probably trying to make you a victim of the free vacation scam. Don't fall for it" (United States Postal Inspection Service, "The Free Vacation Scam," no date).

In a newer approach, travel "certificates" verifying and congratulating you on "winning" a fabulous "free" vacation are among the scams arriving by e-mail. Usually they affirm that you are one-in-a-million who have been "specially selected" to receive a *spectacular luxury dream vacation!* offer. The truth: You're one of several million who have been "specially" selected. Most unsolicited commercial e-mail goes to millions of recipients at a time. The promoters couldn't possibly make good on the promises. If you are one of the fortunate few who actually receives a vacation, your "fabulous cruise ship" will be a freighter and you will most likely be booked into substandard accommodations. The "luxury" hotel will be derelict and shabby, and you usually have to pay for an upgrade—at an outrageous rate. Your airfare may be free, but your anticipated $50 hotel room can wind up costing seven or eight times that.

The Scam in Operation

As you see, this common scheme offers "free" vacation travel packages. A consumer pays hundreds of dollars or much more to receive a deal that includes round-trip airfare to, and lodging at, an "exciting" or "exotic" getaway. The catch? Frequently you must purchase a high-priced round-trip ticket from the fraudulent travel operation for a second person or you are required to pay for less-than-desirable accommodations in less-than-ideal destinations. In the end, you are likely to end up paying far more than what it would have cost had you initially made all of the arrangements through a reputable travel agency.

In the "down-payment downer" all you have to do is make a deposit with your credit card and select your preferred travel dates. The fraudulent promoter strings you along, citing various problems in accommodating the dates you selected until the offer expires or the promoter disappears—as do all chances of getting your deposit back.

If you fall for the trip trap here's what you can expect:

- To be eligible for a "free" vacation you will be required to pay a service charge or to purchase a "membership" in a travel club. This fee may be as little as $10 or as much as several hundred dollars.
- The travel packet describing your vacation will be filled with restrictions and qualifications—all negotiable—for a fee.
- If you protest, you may be offered an "upgrade." To receive the actual destinations, accommodations, means of travel, or dates you were initially promised, you will be obliged to pay additional fees.
- The travel dates you prefer will be "unavailable." Your schedule can always be accommodated—for a fee.
- To book and confirm your reservations, your requests must be accompanied by a "handling" fee.

• Some offers may require you to pay more for port charges, hotel taxes, or service fees.

Do you see a pattern developing? Additional fees and charges for your "free" vacation are being tacked on at every step of the way. Invariably you never get your "free" trip because for some reason or another your reservations cannot be confirmed, or you have failed to comply with elaborate, obtuse, or expensive "conditions." What started as a "free" vacation quickly becomes a "fee" vacation.

"Ultimately, as the law closes in, some vacation scam operators will close down, move on, and set up operations elsewhere and bilk other unsuspecting consumers of their money. You will be left without the promised vacation and stuck at home with a much smaller balance in your bank account" (United States Postal Inspection Service, "The Free Vacation Scam," no date).

Sales Tactics

If you are first contacted through the mail or in an e-mail, you may be instructed to call a toll-free 800-number (or a costly 900-number) to claim your vacation and receive all the details about the trip you have "won." Unable to resist the lure, you make the call. You then become victim to a relentless sales pitch for a deal that is in no way free. If you are first contacted by telephone, be aware that telemarketing travel scams, like investment scams aimed at the elderly, usually originate out of boiler rooms. Skilled, well-rehearsed, and glib salespeople, with years of experience selling dubious products and services over the phone, pitch travel packages that may sound exciting and legitimate, but usually are neither. (The excitement comes when the victim discovers that the grand offer was a grand con.)

These sales pitches usually include:

• Oral Misrepresentations
  Particular schemes vary, but all fraudulent telemarketers promise you a "deal you can't refuse"—and that they can't possibly deliver. Unfortunately, you won't know this until your money is gone.
• The Usual High Pressure or Time Pressure Tactics
  Scam operators assert that you must take advantage of the

offer *now*! because it is available only for a limited time, and will soon expire. He or she insists on an immediate decision and commitment, and typically brushes aside hesitancy, questions, or concerns with vague answers or glowing assurances.

• "Affordable" Offers

Unlike fraudulent telemarketers who try to persuade people to spend thousands of dollars on an investment scheme, fraudulent travel operators usually pitch club membership or vacation offers in a lower price range—usually several hundred dollars. Their offers sound reasonably priced and are designed to appeal to anyone with limited means who is looking for a relatively inexpensive vacation.

• Contradictory Follow-up Material

Some operators may agree to send you written confirmation of your travel deal. However, the literature you receive usually bears little or no resemblance to the offer that was described and which you accepted over the phone. The written materials often disclose an dizzying array of additional terms, conditions, and unanticipated costs (Source: Federal Trade Commission, "Traveler's Advisory," 2000).

Red Flags

Be alert to the following red flags in the colorful travel brochures or the telemarketer's pitch that may signal fraudulent vacation promotions:

• The use of excessive high pressure sales tactics is most often a sure sign of a con artist at work.

• Assertions that the deal cannot be booked through a travel agent—it is an "exclusive" offer. (No reputable travel agent would touch it!)

• You must disclose your income, Social Security number, bank account number, or other private information. *Never!*

• You must pay using your credit card only. Fraudulent promoters demand a credit card number before disclosing any information about the vacation or travel offer or before explaining all the conditions. They will claim that a credit card number is required to "confirm your identity," "guarantee the opportunity," or "reserve your name on the list." Once they have your card number you have definitely fallen into the trip trap. Your account will be billed.

- You must wait more than 60 days before taking your trip. Most travel scam victims pay for their free trips using their credit card; scam artists know that you must dispute any credit card charge within 60 days. If they can persuade you to wait more than 60 days, you could be prevented from challenging the charge.
- The solicitation says that you were "specially selected" or chosen using very selective criteria to receive the offer. You have been "awarded" or won a trip or prize in a contest you never entered.
- Watch for official-looking embossed seals—usually gold—featuring an eagle with spread wings and arrows (you can purchase these at many stationery suppliers) or words in large bold type such as "Certificate of Guarantee"—a meaningless description.
- There are likely to be an impressive array of pictures of exotic travel destinations but no mention of specific dates or prices for the various packages. There are likely to be exciting descriptions of what your travel package includes, such as a "gala cruise," "thrilling shows," "glittering casinos," or "elegant resort accommodations"—all on unnamed cruise lines or at undisclosed resorts.
- They make vague references to "all major airlines" or "all major hotels"—again, unnamed.
- The company cannot provide the names of references, or the references you may call repeat nearly verbatim the claims of the travel provider.
- You must call a 900-number to confirm the travel prize or offer, or to obtain full details.
- Be alert for a phrase in the fine print that states that in order to qualify for one part of the package—airfare for example—you are required to purchase another part—such as your hotel room or land travel.
- Stated low rates on air travel require you to purchase an additional ticket for a companion—at a much higher rate.
- You must make a payment in advance to collect your prize or take advantage of the offer.

- The fraudulent promoters offer "unbeatable" bargains, but refuse to put any of the details in writing unless you pay first.
- They offer to send a courier to your home to pick up your payment. (They are trying to avoid detection and charges of mail or wire fraud.)

Tips on How to Protect Yourself

To help you avoid unpleasant and costly surprises, the FTC offers these tips:

- Be wary of "great deals" and low-priced travel offers. Legitimate travel companies cannot afford to give away products and services, or substantially undercut other companies' prices.
- Don't be pressured into buying. A good offer today usually will be a good offer tomorrow. Legitimate businesses do not expect customers to make snap decisions.
- Try to buy your vacation travel package from a travel company you know to be reputable. If possible, deal with agencies that belong to professional associations such as the American Society of Travel Agents, the National Tour Association, or the United States Tour Operators Association. Each has a website. If you're not familiar with a company, get its complete name, address and local telephone number and check it.
- Be cautious if the names of the seller and travel provider differ. You may be dealing with a telemarketer who has no responsibility to you after the sale.
- Be wary if have to attend a seminar (sales presentation) to qualify.
- The best way to defend yourself against these scams, other than to hang up, is to ask to have all the details sent to you in writing before you agree to commit yourself. Insist that these include a copy of the cancellation and refund policies. Ask detailed questions.
- Once you receive the written information, make sure it reflects what you were told over the phone and the terms you agreed to. Verify all of the agreed-upon arrangements before you pay. lGet the names, addresses and telephone numbers for the

hotels, airlines, and cruise ships you'll be using. Don't accept vague terms such as "major hotels" or "luxury cruise ships." Verify specific reservations.

- Don't buy part of the package, e.g. the air fare or hotel stay, separately from the rest. If the deal is not what you expected, it may be difficult to get your money back for the part of the package you purchased.
- Ask if the travel company has trip insurance and determine whether or not you should purchase cancellation insurance.
- Don't send money by messenger or overnight mail. If you pay with cash or a check, rather than a credit card, you lose your right to dispute fraudulent charges under the Fair Credit Billing Act.
- The FTC advises that you use a credit card whenever possible, although using a credit card is not a surefire way to protect yourself if you don't get what you paid for. However, if you act quickly, you can dispute the charge and perhaps avoid paying for a scam.
- Be wary of prepaying for long-term arrangements. Timeshares, campgrounds or travel clubs may offer to sell membership vacation accommodations for five years or more, or until you resell your interest. Unless you're certain you'll stay healthy, both physically and financially, and that the company selling the memberships will stay in business, prepaid vacations may not be right for you. In addition, annual membership and maintenance fees may rise. If the seller claims the fees will stay the same, beware. Beautiful properties today may be run-down in five or ten years without sufficient maintenance. If you decide to buy a timeshare or membership in a vacation club, understand that resales can be difficult, if not impossible because there may be no secondary market. As for timeshares as investments, they may never appreciate in value.
- Be suspicious of companies that require you to wait at least sixty days before taking your trip. They could abscond in that time. If in doubt, say "No!" You may have doubts—even if the offer sounds legitimate. In that case, trust your instincts. It's less risky to turn down the offer and hang up the phone (Sources: United States Federal Trade Commission, "Traveler's Advisory," 2000, and "Telemarketing Travel Fund," 1999).

Viaticals

Viaticals Defined

A viatical is defined as the discounted, pre-death sale of an existing life insurance policy. They are also referred to as "accelerated benefits," "living benefits," or "viatical settlements." In a typical transaction, the person holding a life insurance policy sells it to a third-party broker in return for a cash payment of a predetermined percentage of the policy's face value—typically 60 percent to 70 percent. His or her projected life expectancy is the primary factor in determining the percentage to be received. The shorter that time, the higher the amount— and conversely.

The broker then sells the policy, or shares of it, to third-party investor(s), who pay a percentage of the face value of the policy and assume full responsibility for all remaining premiums. The insured who has sold the policy as a viatical is under no further financial obligation to the insurance company that issued the policy to them. The investors in the viatical acquire the beneficiary rights of the policy and collect a share of the policy's benefits in full when the policy "matures"—that is, when the original policyholder, the viator, dies. The earlier the viator dies, the larger the return on the investment. Even when investors purchase viatical policies from people who really are terminally ill, there is no guarantee that person will die "on time." "The risk is high with viaticals, and investors need to ask themselves if the potential reward is worth the burden of hoping someone will die quickly so they can maximize their return" (North American Securities Administrators Association, "Risky 'Death Futures' Draw Warning," 2002).

Viaticals, which have been around since the early 1900s, are based on a legitimate economic and fiscal concept: They allow a terminally ill person to receive a partial payment of a policy's benefits in advance while he or she is still alive and at a time when he or she may desperately need funds for medical care or to support family. "There are few, if any, things more expensive than the costs related to a life-threatening illness. In addition to all the usual costs of daily living—from mortgages and utilities to food and transportation—the terminally ill often face staggering medical expenses.... And these individuals often are unable to earn a living because of their illness. Increasingly, people in these circumstances are turning to viatical settlements to provide a modicum of financial security during their last months or years" (Caughey, "Viaticals Help Face Terminal Illness," 1988).

Life or Senior Settlements

In a new twist, viatical companies and insurance brokers are now marketing a variation, a spin-off, of viatical settlements—interests in the death benefits of healthy older people. These are known as "life" or "senior" settlements. In these, the investor is offered a viatical on a person age 65 or older who believes that he or she no longer needs an existing life insurance policy as such, but may be in great need of the cash value it represents.

Investors are persuaded that they are providing financial assistance to senior citizens by providing them with funds they need to live comfortably in their old age. The National Association of Insurance Commissioners confirms that the licensing and disclosure laws, rules, and regulations that apply to viaticals do not always apply to senior settlements, leaving them effectively unregulated in many states.

A 1999 study by the Conning Corporation, a Connecticut-based research and investment management firm, noted that the potential market for senior settlements could, at that time, be "conservatively" estimated at over $100 billion (Source: North American Securities Administrators Association, "Risky 'Death Futures' Draw Warnings," 2002). AARP has stated: "Authorities are advising consumers to be cautious about senior settlements, an investment that is gaining popularity but in some cases may be tainted by fraud" (AARP, "Viaticals: Watch Out!").

Fraud is not the only way to lose in a viatical investment, however. Financial planners say investing in even a legitimate deal is risky. Though the profit can be considerable, so can the loss. For example, if the seller of a policy lives longer than expected, the investor may find it necessary to keep paying premiums much longer than anticipated just to keep the policy in force. As a result, the profitability of the investment markedly declines with each year the seller lives past his or her projected time of death. Rapid advances in medical science and technology mean persons in our society, even those with serious illnesses, are living longer, so betting your life savings on someone else's death is risky business. If the investor is elderly, the seller of the viatical policy, a healthy and robust fellow senior, could outlive them!

Viatical Fraud

There's an old saying: "The only sure things in life are death and taxes." Viatical salesmen play on that maxim. In February 2002, the North American Securities Administrators Association, citing deceptive marketing practices and numerous instances of fraud, warned that investors should not be misled by claims that viatical settlements offer safe, guaranteed returns such as those offered by certificates of deposit. "Viaticals contracts are legitimate products, but state securities regulators have two concerns. First, that the inherent risk of viatical investments—gambling on when someone will die—aren't being adequately disclosed, and second, many investors have been outright defrauded by some viatical companies or their sales agents.... Securities regulators from 21 states report bringing actions on behalf of thousands of investors nationwide who were defrauded of more than $400 million over the past three years" (North American Securities Administrators Association, "Risky 'Death Futures' Draw Warning," 2002).

Fraud in the marketing of viaticals is well documented. Insurance industry regulators and law enforcement authorities have reported that an overwhelming majority of investors in viaticals have lost all or part of their life savings as a result of misrepresentation on the part of salespersons and viatical brokers who guaranteed generous returns on their investment with minimal risk. Many of these investors report that they were told that their initial investment was all that would be required of them. Later they received letters from the viatical company demanding payment of monthly or annual premiums in order to maintain the policy they purchased or face the prospect of cancellation of the policy and forfeiture of their investment.

Viaticals are a business, an investment enterprise that has been largely unregulated by the federal government or—until recently—by many states. Because of the prevalence of fraud in the viaticals industry in the mid to late 1990s, a confederation of federal law enforcement officials and agencies formed a task force in a continuing effort to combat it.

There are several reasons why so many investors have become victims of this type of fraud.

- The life insurance industry is one of the oldest and most trusted in our nation. For generations, people have trusted in life insurance and faithfully paid their premiums, only to receive what was due upon the death of the insured. Most investors recognize the risk associated with speculative investments. However, when you discuss life insurance, most people think of it as a safe, secure investment. The distinction between the insurance industry and the viatical settlement industry may not be fully appreciated or understood by most investors.
- The investment in viatical settlements also appeals to the humanitarian side of the investor. They perceive themselves as helping a terminally ill person pay for the medical attention needed and to live as comfortably as possible in his or her final days. Such altruism can be costly.
- Finally, because of the nature of the fraud, and the obvious need to keep information about the insured private, there is reluctance by investors to follow-up or ask a lot of questions about their investment. When the investment does not pay off due to the death of the insured, they are most often reluctant to gripe because in effect they would be complaining that the insured did not die as projected—a crass action (Source: United States Postal Inspection Service, "Testimony of the U.S. Postal Inspection Service on Viatical Fraud," no date).

The Elderly as Victims of Viatical Fraud

The elderly are at highest risk for viatical fraud. Like thousands of other consumers in the United States, senior citizens have invested in a multi-billion-dollar business enterprise that has known widespread fraud. Senior citizens are often targeted by fraudsters and unfortunately end up as victims when misrepresentations are made by the viatical settlement companies about life expectancies of insured parties and guaranteed rates of return. Viatical settlement fraud is particularly insidious, as it frequently entices its elderly victims into investing their life savings.

The U.S. Postal Inspection Service reports:

[V]ictims have lost hundreds of millions of dollars investing in fraudulent viatical settlements. Older people seem to be the biggest victims.... They've taken money out of IRAs or they've cashed in certificates of deposit and they've converted to these investments and they've lost their life savings. Most of the fraud cases [USPIS] has worked on involved older people who are persuaded that buying into viaticals is a "humanitarian" gesture and great investment opportunity. They're told that buying this policy now gives [viators] money to help them live. But the more they think about it ... they think it's morbid, because they're waiting on this person to die—for this policy to mature. These investors rarely know who they're investing in. They're usually kept in the dark [cited in Fleck, "Consumer Alert on Viatical Fraud," 2001].

Competent financial consultants and conscientious advocates for the elderly consistently advise older people to stay away from this kind of investment. AARP's consumer protection unit cautions

Viaticals are not an investment for the typical consumer looking for a place to roll over their IRA or safely invest their money. Why invest in something so risky and so complicated when there are much safer investments available?.... Investing money in a way that supposedly helps a terminally ill person. Sounds good, doesn't it? But things are not always what they seem. Falling for these investments may be a good way to lose your money. When you hear "viaticals," watch out! What can go wrong with this type of investment? Lots! And most of what can go wrong will cost the investor a lot of money. The North American Securities Administrators Association calls viaticals one of the top ten investment scams [AARP, "Viaticals: Watch Out!" no date].

What Are the Risks?

Here are some of the ways an investor can lose in viaticals:

- Sometimes the insured person is not ill—let alone terminally ill—at all, so the investor can be forced to pay insurance premiums for many years or the original investment is forfeited.
- The scenario described above can effect a significant reduction in the anticipated rate of return on the investment and tie up your capital for a time much longer than you expected. Viaticals are not liquid investments, so you will not be able to access the cash benefits of the policy until the insured dies and the insurer pays.

• Investors have realized that they have been duped after the life insurance or viatical company discovered that the policy it issued was fraudulently obtained by the insured. When such fraud is discovered, an insurance company will rescind and or contest the policy and refuse to pay the death benefits settlement—effectively making the policy worthless to the investor. Costly and prolonged legal action may be the only recourse. If fraud can be proven, no payout!

• There could be interminable and frustrating delays in receiving death benefits under a policy should the policyholder's heirs challenge any changes made to it—especially as they may affect them as beneficiaries.

• The insurance company or viatical settlement company may suddenly be liquidated and cease to exist—as will your investment.

• Some disreputable insurance brokers may "guarantee" a specified rate of return on your investment, or affirm that the viatical has the same protections and financial benefits as an IRA. Neither assertion is true.

• There may be no life insurance policy at all. It can be an elaborate hoax based on a non-existent insured viator.

• Or there is a policy. However, an unscrupulous broker has sold the same policy to a number of unwitting investors. When the insured dies, they discover that the total benefits will be apportioned among all of them!

• Because of the nature of viatical fraud, and elements of confidentiality and privacy regarding the insured, investors may be very reluctant to pursue the issues. When the investment fails to yield the expected return, they may be unwilling to resort to complaining because the insured has not kept their part of the bargain—dying as expected—timely, conveniently, and profitably!

AARP advises, "The bottom line: Be very cautious of viaticals and life or senior settlements. They're very risky!" (AARP, "Viaticals: Watch Out!" no date).

A Final Comment

The greatest victim of such fraud is altruism. "Perhaps just as sad as the loss of money is the loss of faith in trying to do good for one another. These investments are marketed with the idea that the investor is helping someone in need of financial help—whether that's a terminally ill person or an older person. When the scam unfolds, the investor can be left hoping that a person dies soon in order to save their investment, and that's not a good feeling for anyone" (AARP, "Viaticals: Watch Out!" no date).

Work-at-Home

Retirees often have a great deal of time on their hands but, conversely, limited income. To relieve boredom and supplement modest means, many are tempted to turn to work-at-home (or work-from-home) opportunities. On July 14, 1998, the Federal Trade Commission released a consumer alert entitled "FTC Unveils Dirty Dozen Spam Scams," those that the FTC had identified as being the most likely to arrive in consumers' e-mail. Number four on the list was work-at-home schemes which typically "offer the 'chance to earn money in the comfort of your own home.' Two of the most popular versions pitch envelope stuffing and craft assembly. But nobody will really pay you for stuffing envelopes and craft assembly promoters usually refuse to buy the crafts produced claiming the work does not meet their 'quality standards'" (United States Federal Trade Commission, "FTC Unveils Dirty Dozen Spam Scans," 1998). It doesn't matter how the information gets to you, these types of schemes are always scams.

The U.S. Postal Inspection Service confirms this: "Advertised opportunities to earn money by doing work in your home are frequently nothing more than fraudulent schemes and, at best, rarely result in any meaningful earnings. The targets of the work-at-home con artists are those who need extra money but who are not able to work outside their homes. Victims typically include ... the elderly ... and people with low incomes" (United States Postal Inspection Service, "Work-at-Home Schemes," 2002). AARP concurs: "Con artists see [work-at-home schemes] as an opportunity to get your money.... [They are] a favorite way ... to exploit people. The schemes appeal to so many of our desires—earning more money, not having a boss, working fewer hours, commuting less. When things are too good to be true, it usually means they are not true. Work-at-home jobs are no exception" (AARP, "Work-at-Home Scams," 2002).

In 1999 the National Fraud Information Center, an agency of the National Consumers League, reported that work-at-home schemes were the number one telemarketing fraud reported in 1998. In 2002 online auction fraud was the overwhelming leader, and work-at-home schemes had dropped to sixth place with less than 0.1 percent of the complaints reported by consumers (Source: National Fraud Information Center, "2002 Top Ten Frauds," 2002). The National Consumers League has affirmed that consumers who pay for work-at-home schemes are likely to lose money, not make it. Telephone con artists have no qualms about taking advantage of vulnerable consumers by guaranteeing them large profits from working at home.

The Come-ons

We are overwhelmed by advertisements in newspapers, magazines, e-mail, and even those ubiquitous signs tacked illegally on utility poles promoting the ease and joy of working at home. These ads typically promise a "large income" for working on projects "in great demand." "You can make a fortune!" they say. These offers and claims may sound very attractive, particularly if you are unable to leave your home to work. However, you are advised to be very cautious about such employment proposals, especially those that promise large profits in a short period of time, or with minimum effort. While some work-at-home plans are legitimate, very many are not; these schemes are among the oldest and most prevalent kinds of consumer fraud.

Those tempted by the advertisements send money for information about starting a home-based business. The details are scant but the promises are abundant. They will include assurances that "we will provide all the training you need." The catch? They will relentlessly try to sell you more information and materials about this "special" training and the "support systems" they provide to "guarantee" your success—perhaps including a "personal coach." While the advertisements purport that you will be starting your own home-based business immediately, most of these scams involve selling consumers information about different ways that they can supposedly make money working from home. The operators are making money from the packet of information they are marketing and are not assisting anyone to find legitimate work-at-home opportunities.

What many of these advertisements fail to say is that you may have to work many hours before you see any return on your investment—if you ever do. There also may be substantial hidden costs. Many work-at-home schemes require you to spend your own money to place advertisements in newspapers, make photocopies, or purchase postage, envelopes, paper, and other supplies or equipment you will need. The one characteristic common to all of these schemes is that you are required to purchase something from the *promoter*—information or materials—before you are able to start working in your home. Or you may also be required to buy a "membership" fee or remit regular payments in order to receive "updated" instructional materials or necessary supplies. Many consumers have been taken in by these schemes and lost thousands of dollars and wasted thousands of hours.

The word "home" conveys the idea that such a work setting is convenient, easy, and ideal. On the contrary, working at home, or from home, can be a very challenging venture. Realistically, if getting rich quick working at home were such an easy task, we would all be home-based entrepreneurs. In reality, the only people who make a great deal of money from these schemes are the ones selling them (Source: United States Federal Trade Commission, "Work-at-Home Schemes," 2001).

Red Flags

The United States Postal Inspection Service advises that you be alert to some of these red flags for a work-at-home scam.

Language

Advertisements for work-at-home schemes typically feature common pitches.

- "Every day thousands of people just like you are getting started working at home!"
- "Earn hundreds [thousands] working only a few hours a week in your spare time in the comfort of your own home. You can be the next [sucker]. Let us tell you how." Avoid any program that asserts "we will do the work for you."
- "The work is easy." Realistically we know these schemes seldom live up to their promises of easy money. If they really worked

as well as claimed, why would the promoters sell their "sure fire" lucrative ideas to complete strangers such as you?
- "This offer is unique." Not in the annals of scams—it's hoary!
- "There is no investment risk." "Minimal or no investment is required." Translation: "We'll take you for all your worth!"
- "No experience is needed." "People from all walks of life have succeeded with no special training!" Translation: We have suckered everyone who has responded to this ad!
- "A vast potential market for your work already exists and is just waiting for you!" "Businesses all over the country are waiting to use you as an independent home worker." No one is waiting for you but the scammer.
- "Our guidelines have helped thousands of people like you get started working at home." They have scammed thousands of people (Source: United States Postal Inspection Service, "Work-at-Home Schemes," no date).

Or the advertisements scream out in bold-face type, in capital letters loaded with exclamation marks:

"MAKE EXTRA CASH AT HOME!"
"THESE SURE-FIRE OPPORTUNITIES ARE PROFITABLE AND EASY!!"
"WORK IN THE COMFORT OF YOUR OWN HOME!!!"
"WIDE SELECTION OF TOP PAYING JOBS!!!!"
"DON'T MISS THIS EXTRAORDINARY OPPORTUNITY. ACT NOW!!!!!"
"THIS COULD EASILY CHANGE YOUR LIFE FOREVER!!!!!!"
Indeed it will.

OTHER CLUES

Other tips in spotting a work-at-home scam include:

- Vagueness—the ads are very appealing but never indicate exactly what the so-called "opportunity" entails. The operators are totally nebulous about what you'll do, but aver untold riches for doing it—whatever it is. Stay away from any company whose ad doesn't come right out and tell what it is offering. And if you are called, or make a call as instructed, and hear a vague spiel, hang up and don't waste any more of your time.

- You are instructed to call a 900-number for details of the offer. You will be billed for seeking and listening to useless information. And 800-numbers should also raise a red flag. Most local companies don't use 800-numbers in local ads.

- An assurance that, for a fee, you will receive a long list of businesses that are looking for home-based workers. The list came from a telephone directory. None of them will be looking.

- You are pressured to make a decision immediately. High-pressure tactics are common to all scams. Seminars are an ideal way for a promoter to get potential victims excited about making money with their products or services. High-pressure sales pitches can mask the fact that the information they provide for a fee can be easily found free on the Internet and at your local library, or at least more cheaply at a book store.

- An up-front cash investment is required. Legitimate programs will not require any monetary investment on the strength of their promises. Their promoters should tell you—in writing, and at no cost—what is involved in the program. If you are considering a work-at-home opportunity that requires "no cash investment" or "minimal cash investment," you should be careful. Most such opportunities never deliver on their promises. Most of these schemes will eventually require you to spend money.

- Your initial investment must be made in cash, or by check or money order. Payment by credit card will not be acceptable— this would provide the potential victim an opportunity to get this money back—something that scam artists simply cannot allow.

- The address to which you are to remit the funds is in another state or another country, such as Canada. The farther away the scam operator the more difficult it can be to take remedial action when you discover the fraud.

- If the advertisement has been received in the mail, note the return address. Be cautious if the return address indicates a commercial mail receiving agency (CMRA). CMRAs are identified by a pound sign (#) in the return address. CMRAs are not business offices; they are non-post office mail drops where mail is deposited in private mailboxes. As a general rule, avoid any company that does not have a street address (not just a P.O. box) or a phone number. (The party listed for virtually any telephone number can be verified without calling it by using any of the several reverse telephone directories available on the Internet.)

• Be aware that fraudulent work-at-home businesses routinely set up fake names and rent post office boxes to begin business in a new area. By the time local law enforcement or the Attorney General's office learns about the scheme, the company has already moved on. Work-at-home scam businesses are usually transient, moving from town to town, stealing consumers' money along the way.

Examples of Work-at-home Scams

Here are several of the most common and long-lived work-at-home scams.

ASSEMBLY OR CRAFT WORK

Advertisements for opportunities in home assembly or craft work abound on the Web, on the pages of magazines, tabloids, and newsletters, in the classified ads of newspapers, and on the bulletin boards of supermarkets and shopping malls. Such an advertisement may read: "Assembly work-at-home: Earn easy money assembling craft items. No experience necessary."

Respondents to these offers usually must sign a contract which obligates them but does not obligate the promoter in any way. Quite often these offers are intended only to sell such equipment as sewing or sign-making machines or various "kits." These schemes typically require you to purchase from the fraud promoter only—at highly inflated prices—all the supplies, instructional materials, and equipment that you will need to assemble a product or produce a craft item. You will be given a "guarantee" from the promoter that once the product is completed, the company will purchase it from you and resell it, or you will be assured that there is a ready market for the products you will produce. On the basis of these promises you will spend a great deal of your time, effort, and money.

However, after you've purchased the supplies or equipment and performed the production work, these fraudulent operators will not buy anything from you. In fact, most consumers have had companies refuse to pay for their work because the finished product, unfailingly, did not meet undefined "standards of quality." Unfortunately, none of the work you will ever do will be "up to standard," leaving you with relatively expensive equipment, a basement or garage filled with supplies, and boxes of products that will be difficult if not impossible to sell—to customers that you yourself must find. You will be stuck with inventories of products for which there is virtually no market and will have no opportunity to recoup your investment.

DISPLAY RACKS AND VENDING MACHINES

The FTC has referred to fraudulent display rack and vending machine businesses as "the perennial plague of vending opportunities sold as sure-fire money-makers" (United States Federal Trade Commission, "Operation Vend Up Broke," 1998). Arguably, many of these ventures are franchises—a business concept that has been described in detail in the section entitled "Business Opportunities." However, since most are operated out of the individual's home rather than at an outside site of operations, we will included them in work-at-home scams.

Over the years, the FTC has investigated hundreds of consumer complaints about these schemes and their promoters. In a very recent case, as part of "Project Busted Opportunity," in August 2003 the FTC agreed to settle charges that Global Vending Services, Inc., headquartered in Las Vegas, had failed to provide the pre-sale disclosure documents required by the FTC's Franchise Rule to prospective purchasers of their snack and soda vending machine business opportunities. The defendants allegedly told consumers who responded to nationwide advertisements that they could earn specific amounts of money by buying the vending machine opportunity and that the defendants would help place machines in lucrative locations. Respondents received an information packet that included fact sheets on vending machines, machine specifications, and descriptions. The FTC alleged that he information packet did not include the disclosures required by the Franchise Rule.

The settlement with Global Vending, announced on August 11, 2003, prohibited the defendants from misrepresenting the income, profit, or sales volume that a purchaser is likely to achieve, or actually achieved by prior purchasers; the length of time that it is likely to take a purchaser to recoup the entire purchase price; the independence or authenticity of any third party references; the availability or existence of profitable locations in a purchaser's geographic area; and the terms and conditions of any refunds or guarantees of profitability that relate to any location service or company to which the defendants refer purchasers (Source: United States Federal Trade Commission, "Global Vending Serivces, Inc.," 2003).

In 1998, the FTC conducted "'Operation Vend Up Broke'... because that's exactly what happens to vulnerable consumers victimized by the promoters' false claims.... Every year, thousands of consumers literally end up broke after investing in purportedly lucrative vending opportunities" (United States Federal Trade Commission, "Operation Vend Up Broke," 1998).

Complaints detailing the alleged law violations in the cases the FTC has referred to the courts for prosecution are a compendium of nearly identical schemes. The defendants all place advertisements in newspapers or other media touting part-time distributorships involving display racks or vending machines. Many of the ads explicitly targeted individuals who want to "earn $100,000 or more." Such advertisements can be very alluring, especially for those who might be looking for part-time employment to supplement their income. Caution and skepticism are in order. While some business opportunities involving vending machines or display racks are legitimate, many are not, and you may lose your investment. So if you're thinking about investing in a display rack opportunity, the FTC has a message for you: "Check out their claims to avoid going to display rack and ruin."

The FTC has advised that entrepreneurs who invest in business opportunities like these rarely make the big money they're promised. Promoters often supply undesirable merchandise—for example, outdated products that may never have captured the public's attention—and offer unprofitable locations. In fact, would-be business owners generally lose their entire investment.

The promoters will assert that for an investment of as little as $5,000 to $15,000 (or whatever the market will bear), all you have to do is purchase, set up, and restock machines or displays in profitable high-traffic locations such as malls, shopping centers, supermarkets, airports, gift shops, convenience stores, drug stores, or other public venues. The promoters typically assure their potential victims that they will offer full support in setting up and operating the business. They promise to:

- Provide vending machines or display racks already placed in "highly desirable" locations or find such locations for you;
- relocate the machines or racks to more profitable locations at your request; or
- provide immediate repair or replacement for damaged machines or display racks.

"Despite typical claims that distributors will sell hundreds of dollars worth of products every month, investigations have turned up dozens of victims who have sworn in court documents to have made only pennies a day, or lost money, on investments typically ranging from $10,000 to $20,000. We [FTC] estimate that consumers have lost in excess of $50 million to these scams since the beginning of 1995. The villains in these dramatic scenes are the opportunists who exploit a recognized corporate name to sell an unworkable business" (United States Federal Trade Commission, "Trade Name Games," 1997).

The obvious question in all of this promotion: If such a business is so easy, why are so many companies selling display racks and vending machines? Why wouldn't they just place these units themselves in the "highly desirable" and lucrative locations? Answer: Because they're making far more money selling the schemes to unwitting investors than the dupes will ever realize from the venture.

The vending business is really a small franchise with a great deal more work. At least with a franchise you most likely have a fixed location and some kind of name recognition. Not in the vending business. Such ventures do not fail because of products being vended on display racks or by machines. They fail because of location! Finding profitable locations for the racks or machines is the greatest challenge. Owners of many potential sites demand a kickback or a fee before they will allow vending machines or display racks to be placed on their premises. Some may counter such a proposal by saying that they could simply acquire and set up the racks or machines themselves; why would they need you? Then there is always the problem of theft and vandalism. You will not be able to protect your investment at every location, at every minute.

Be aware that a homeowner's policy will not likely cover such instances. Alternative and adequate insurance coverage can be costly. Potential product liability lawsuits are another major consideration.

SIGNS OF A VENDING SCAM

There are certain common signs of a scam in these ventures.

- Large sums of money promised for very little work;
- very little information given up front about the business; and
- support services, money, and good placement locations promised, but no specific or written information is given to you prior to your involvement.

COMMON COMPLAINTS ABOUT VENDING VENTURES

Among the complaints the FTC has received from consumers who have bought into vending scams:

- There was a gross misrepresentation of earnings claims.
- Promoters failed to deliver the promised merchandise, machines or display racks.
- Promoters failed to find the type of locations promised.
- The machines were relocated to different, but not more profitable locations.
- Promoters failed provide support services as represented in their sales presentation.
- Promoters would not arrange for repair service or refused to replace badly damaged equipment. Investors were required to pay these expenses themselves.
- Promoters reneged on guarantees of refunds (Source: The 'Lectric Law Library, "Business Opportunity Scams," 1994).

ENVELOPE STUFFING

Envelope-stuffing promotions are perennial and pervasive scams. On December 16, 2003, the FTC, U.S. Postal Inspection Service, States, and Council of BBBs announced a crackdown on deceptive pitches for work-at-home envelope-stuffing business opportunities. The coordinated effort was dubbed "Operation Pushing the Envelope." It targeted the purveyors of fraudulent envelope-stuffing business opportunities who are taking money out of consumers' pockets with their deceptive pitches for work-at-home opportunities. "Stuffing is fine for turkeys and stockings, but envelope-stuffing scams deserve a lump of coal," said Howard Beales, Director of the FTC's Bureau of Consumer Protection. Educating potential victims is key to curbing the outreach of con artists who perpetrate these "easy-income, no-experience-necessary" frauds. Many of their victims are unemployed, disabled, or elderly consumers who hoped to earn an income working from home. The text of the FTC alert can be found online at the URL shown in the sources.

This most common and enduring work-at-home scam advertisement promises that, for a minimal amount of work, you'll earn a steady income for stuffing envelopes. For example, you're promised you'll earn $2 to $5 each time you fold a brochure, stuff it, seal it in an envelope, and mail it. Promoters usually advertise that, for a "small" fee, they will tell you how to take advantage of this employment opportunity. The U.S. Postal Inspection Service has confirmed that they have never seen such an advertisement placed where a respondent actually made the amounts of income alleged. These are always scams, and one of the most long-running scams at that.

In fact, there never is any real envelope stuffing employment available. Instead, you pay the fee (usually around $30—pure profit for the scam operator) to "register" to get started in the business. Later—when it's too late—you find out that the promoter never had any real employment to offer. Instead, for your fee he will send you the details which turn out to be instructions on how you are to place the same kind of ad the scam promoter ran in the first place in newspapers or magazines (all this at your expense) or to send the ad to others. Pursuing the plan may require spending several hundred dollars more for advertising, postage, envelopes, and printing. The promoter's instructions will include a copy of the advertisement you originally responded to, along with the draft of text for a similar advertisement telling people about how much money they can make stuffing envelopes, and to send a self-addressed stamped envelope and a fee to you for all details of the opportunity. This system feeds on continuous recruitment of people to offer the same plan to others—a classic pyramid.

If, and when, you receive the SASE (if you have a .25 percent response rate you will be doing very well), you send out the same material you initially received from the promoter. Of course the postage is free on the SASE, but you have had to pay for the printing of the mailing piece and the cost of placing the advertisement in magazines or newspapers—an expensive option. But technically you have stuffed an envelope and you have received an amount of money in return, but not enough to cover your costs.

In a common variation of the scheme you send the required registration fee and in return receive a package which contains all of the materials the operator incorporates in one of his own mailings to people like you. Your assigned task is to fold the brochures and stuff them in the envelopes supplied according to the enclosed instructions—always *very exact* instructions that will assure compliance with their "standards." Having done so, you send the envelopes you have prepared back to the operator expecting to be paid for your efforts. Of course none of the materials that you have assembled will ever meet their standards. Or there will be some other excuse for not paying you. None of this will prevent them from sending out the materials you have prepared for them for free! You have been scammed and unwittingly have become a scammer!

Envelope stuffing and bulk mail processing has become a highly mechanized operation using sophisticated mass mailing techniques and equipment which obviates the need for individuals doing this type of work at home—and any possible profit in attempting to do so. Realistically, if there is computer-operated equipment that will handle over 10,000 envelopes an hour, what company will pay anyone $1, let alone $5, to stuff a single envelope? These machines can stuff envelopes faster, better and far cheaper than hiring individuals to work at home. There are a few companies that have recurring special mail handling needs, and they will contract to hire temporary employees to meet these needs. However, they will hire locally—usually through agencies—and they will pay "envelope-stuffing rates," which will likely be minimum wage.

The envelope-stuffing business is just another variation of an illegal pyramid scheme. If you earn any money, it will be from the new victims you entice. Regardless of what the ads may claim, these schemes can not only cost you money, but they can cause you serious legal problems. You are actually promoting a scam, so in that sense you can be both the victim and the perpetrator. You could go to prison!

MEDICAL BILLING

The FTC has received hundreds of complaints from consumers about medical billing opportunities whose promoters have advertised far more than they've delivered. In a review of websites and print advertisements by the FTC and the BBB in summer 2001, investigators found more than 500 promotions for medical billing opportunities, most of highly dubious merit. The FTC has brought charges in the courts of proper jurisdiction against a number of promoters of medical billing centers for misrepresenting the earnings potential of their businesses and for failing to provide key pre-investment information that the law requires.

In one of the most recent cases, the FTC announced it had secured a stipulated final court judgment and order which was entered on April 22, 2003, in the U.S. District Court for the Central District of California against several California-based defendants who allegedly pitched bogus medical billing opportunities to thousands of consumers nationwide. The action ended the FTC's litigation against Electronic Medical Billing, Inc., a Nevada corporation. "These promoters made promises about earnings and marketability that sounded too good to be true— and they were.... The reality is that few consumers who pay for medical billing opportunities find clients or make any money, let alone earn the promised substantial income" (United States Federal Trade Commission, "Defendants Permanently Barred from Selling Work-at-Home Opportunities," 2003). Consumers who buy into medical billing business proposals should not expect to earn a substantial income from their investment. In fact, the chances of making the money claimed are slim to none.

According to the Commission's complaint, in the above cited case, which had been filed in April 2002, the defendants used deceptive means to market and sell medical billing work-at-home business opportunities to consumers, promising an annual income of between $25,000 and $50,000. According to the FTC, consumers, who paid $325 each after responding to either a classified or Internet ad, were unable to earn any money from the program. The FTC contended that, between late 1999 and the summer of 2002, the defendants falsely promised consumers they would provide them with everything necessary to perform medical billing from home, including a list of doctors in need of home-based medical billers, training, and the software necessary to perform the work. However, consumers who paid the fee invariably discovered that the doctors on the lists they were provided either were impossible to reach or did not need help with medical billing (Source: United States Federal Trade Commission, "Defendants," 2003).

THE COME-ONS IN MEDICAL BILLING

Fraudulent medical billing business opportunities are a type of work-at-home scheme advertised on the Internet and the classified sections of local newspapers and "giveaway" shopper's guides. In the "Help Wanted" classified sections, the ads often appear alongside legitimate ads for medical claims processors, leading consumers who respond to think they're applying for a job, not buying a business opportunity. They might have a special attraction for retired nurses, medical office assistants, or others who have had careers in health care or medical records management.

Typically, the ads tout sure-fire "opportunities" and lure consumers with promises of high income working at home full-time or part-time— "no experience required." An example of such an advertisement might look like this:

> You can earn from $800 to $1000 weekly processing insurance claims on your home computer for health care professionals such as doctors, dentists chiropractors, and podiatrists. Over 80 percent of providers need your services. Learn how in one day! [Source: Better Business Bureau, "Work-at-Home Schemes," 2003].

In such ads, consumers are encouraged to call a toll-free number for more information. The call exposes you to a relentless sales pitch. Or you may be invited to a seminar. Should you elect to respond, as a member of a captive audience you will be:

- Urged to buy software programs and even computers at exorbitant prices; a program selling at a software store for under $70 might cost you several thousand dollars;
- told that your work will be "coordinated" with insurance companies by a central computer;
- required to pay for expensive training sessions available at a "current special rate" that will increase in the future; and or

•pressured to make a decision immediately (Source: Better Business Bureau, "Work-at-Home Schemes," 2002).

Most likely, the expensive training sessions will be cursory discussions, and the highly touted potential market for your services is virtually nonexistent. From either a telemarketer or at a seminar you'll get a sales pitch that will try to convince you that there's "a crisis" in the health care system, due partly to the overwhelming task of processing paper claims. The medical billing market is "wide open"; "there is no competition." In reality, competition in the medical billing market is fierce, especially for those who are new to it and have no experience or no contacts, and the market revolves around a number of large and well-established firms. There is no place for the inexperienced novice medical biller working at home.

And the clincher: "If you are not completely satisfied, you may return the materials within 30 days for a full refund!" The money-back "guarantees" often prove worthless. Even after making repeated calls to the promoter or complaining to credit card companies, government agencies, or consumer groups, only a few victims actually obtain refunds.

How the Medical Billing Scam Works

Most of the victims who were targeted in this scheme came from small towns across the United States. Almost without exception, those who bought into the scam found that there simply was *no* market for their services. "And after investing thousands of dollars in 'medical billing center' software and services, many consumers don't even end up with one customer and most don't even recover their original investment" (United States Federal Trade Commission, "Medical Billing Opportunities," 2002).

The operators promise that for your investment (typically $2,000 to $8,000) they will provide everything necessary to conduct a medical billing business in your home, including a list of potential clients— physicians who "need" such services. They will tell you that many doctors who process claims in their offices want to outsource their billing operations to save money. They will provide clients eager to contract for your services, or that their qualified marketing staff will find many clients for you. These promoters rarely provide experienced sales staff or have contacts within the medical community. The reality: You will have to sell aggressively to unreceptive prospective clients.

Most often the client lists they provide are derived from out-of-date databases. The victim soon discovers that the list of physicians provided them was inaccurate, obsolete, or that the physicians listed did not want or need at-home billing help. The same names and addresses—current and accurate—are readily available on the American Medical Association website or from a telephone directory. (None of them will need or want your services either!) Although many physician's or dentist's offices process their own medical claims, the fact is that most of these professionals outsource their billing and they use established firms—not small, unproven, start-up companies and certainly not individuals working in their homes.

The scam operator promises to supply the necessary computer software, training, and technical support. The software has usually proven useless, or may not have been properly authorized and therefore is illegal copyright infringement. The software programs do little if anything to help consumers succeed. If the promoter provides another company's software, check with that company to determine whether company representatives know of any problems with the medical billing promoter.

HOW TO PROTECT YOURSELF FROM MEDICAL BILLING SCAMS

Medical billing opportunities may not be what the doctor ordered. Taking certain precautions can help you minimize your risk of losing money to this scam. For consumers considering a medical billing venture, the FTC offers this advice:

> Talk to other people who have bought into the program. Ask the promoter to give you the names of many or all previous purchasers. Then you pick and choose whom to call. Interview these references in person and ask for the names of their clients and a description of their operations. If the promoter wants to provide only a few references, be wary. The promoter may be serving up "shills"—people who are paid to endorse the program. Consult with organizations for medical claims processors or medical billing businesses and with local doctors. Ask them about the medical billing field: How much of a need is there for this type of work? How much work does medical billing entail? What kind of training is required? Do they know anything about the promotion or promoter you're interested in? [United States Federal Trade Commission, "Medical Billing Opportunities," 2002].

Questions to Ask About All Work-at-Home Opportunities

There are a number of questions you should ask regarding any work-at-home offer.

- What tasks will I be required to perform? Request a detailed list.
- What is the total cost of the work-at-home program, including supplies, equipment, and membership fees? What will I get for my money?
- Will I get a refund for materials and supplies if the job does not work out?
- Can I get a refund for up-front fees?
- Does the company buy back the unused materials you have purchased?
- Will I be paid a salary or on commission?
- Who will pay me?
- How much, when, and how will I get paid?

The answers to these questions may help you determine whether a work-at-home program is appropriate for your circumstances, and whether or not it may be legitimate. If it is, its promoter should readily answer these questions—in writing.

Precautions About All Work-at-Home Opportunities

Despite the scams, many work-at-home businesses are reputable and have helped retirees, families, homemakers, and single parents achieve greater financial independence. If working at home is your goal, do your homework and associate yourself with only a legitimate company. At this point, you should have some ideas about how to discriminate the scams from the legitimate opportunities, but there is more that you can do to prevent becoming a victim and possibly recoup your loss if you have been victimized. If you think you have an economically viable and feasible opportunity, you might want to check out the company with your local consumer protection agency, state AG and the BBB, not only where the company is located, but also where you live.

These organizations can tell you whether they have received complaints about the work-at-home program that interests you. But be wary: the absence of complaints doesn't necessarily mean the company is legitimate. Unscrupulous companies may settle complaints, change their names, or relocate their operations frequently to avoid detection and prosecution. Here are more tips.

- Review the FTC and AARP websites for consumer protection information on work-at-home and all other money-making schemes—on virtually all scams.
- Be extremely skeptical of past "success stories." Obtain references—as many as possible. Contact them all. But don't rely solely on the names given to you by the promoter. Be aware that references may be bogus. Fraudulent companies frequently hire "satisfied clients" to speak to potential investors and confirm exaggerated earnings claims they have been given.
- Do not believe everything that is stated about sales, profits or income. Demand all earnings claims in writing. Be sure the data include the number and percent of others who have earned at least as much as the promoter claims. If the promoter hesitates or refuses, walk away from the deal—fast!
- Search the Internet. You can also log on to message boards or chat rooms. Special cautions are in order here. The scamsters are lurking!
- Never pay by an online check. If the promoter will accept only online checks that should be a tip-off to a likely scam. Once you divulge your checking account information you are vulnerable to having your account cleaned out. If you have done so, your only recourse may be to close the account. If you believe you are too late, contact your bank and file a fraud report.
- Pay with a credit card, not a debit or check guarantee card. Credit card companies offer greater ease of getting your money back if you can demonstrate that are a victim of fraud. They may give you a charge-back if the alleged scam operator will not cooperate.
- It is very important that you confirm that the product and or services you intend to provide from your home are in conformity

with all applicable laws. The more they try to claim that everything is "perfectly legal," the more you should check into it.
Determine all of *your* legal requirements. For example, you
may need a license or certificate from a state or local authority to operate this business. Will it conform to zoning ordi-
nances in your community?

• As in *any* investment under consideration, consult an attorney,
accountant, or other business advisor before you sign any
agreement or make any payments upfront.

• And of paramount importance, if you have any unresolved doubts
or questions about the deal abandon the idea. You have nothing to lose and everything to save.

"Because there are so many fraudulent operators out there, it's critical that consumers interested in work-at-home opportunities keep their
eyes wide open and their wallets shut tight until they're absolutely sure
of what they're getting for their money" (United States Federal Trade
Commission, "Medical Billing Opportunities," 2002).

III

Where to Get Help

Resources

The consensus among consumer advocate groups and regulatory authorities is that a consumer should always try to resolve complaints with the business itself first. If that effort is not successful and you believe you have been defrauded, contact your local consumer protection agency and or your state Attorney General's consumer protection office. Depending on the nature and medium of the fraud, e.g. U.S. mail, you can then file a complaint with one or more of the agencies and organizations discussed here.

Attorney General (AG)

The office of a state Attorney General handles virtually every aspect of consumer protection. The individual state's Consumer Protection Agency is usually a department of the AG's office. To obtain the name, address, and telephone number of your state's AG, go the website for the National Association of Attorneys General (NAAG) and locate it on the master list. The website is at http://www.naag.org/ag/full_ag_table.php; you will also find the information in your telephone directory.

Better Business Bureau (BBB)

Better Business Bureaus are nonprofit organizations supported primarily by local businesses that are members. The focus of BBB activi-

ties is to promote an ethical marketplace by encouraging honest advertising and selling practices, and by providing alternative dispute reso-
lution. BBBs offer a variety of consumer services. For example, they
provide consumer education materials; business checks, particularly
whether or not there are unanswered or unsettled complaints; resolu-
tion of marketplace problems including mediation and arbitration services; and information about charities and other organizations that may
be soliciting donations.

BBBs usually request that a consumer complaint be submitted in
writing so that an accurate record exists of the dispute. The BBB will
then take up the complaint with the business involved. If the complaint
cannot be satisfactorily resolved through communication with the business, the BBB may offer an alternative dispute settlement process, such
as mediation or arbitration. BBBs do not judge or rate individual products or brands, handle employer/employee wage disputes, or provide
legal advice.

If you need help with a consumer question or have a complaint,
call your local BBB to ask about its services. Or you can contact the
BBB online for consumer fraud and scam alerts, and for information
about BBB programs, services and the locations of member BBBs in
your area. The BBB website is www.bbb.org.

Federal Trade Commission (FTC)

The FTC works for the consumer to prevent fraudulent, deceptive,
and unfair business practices in the marketplace, and to provide information to help consumers spot, stop, and avoid them. To file a complaint or to get free information on consumer issues, visit the FTC
website at www.ftc.gov or call toll-free 1-877-382-4357.

The FTC publishes a series of "Facts for Consumers" that describe
fraudulent sales practices, precautions consumers can take to avoid
becoming victimized, and consumers' rights under federal credit protection laws. These and other brochures are available online in the
FTC's "Best Sellers for Consumers" webpage at http://www.ftc.gov. An
online order form is also provided; the publications are free.

The Federal Citizen Information Center (FCIC) publication *The
Consumer Action Handbook* includes a list of "National Consumer Organizations" and the "Consumer Assistance Directory." The latter includes

the topics "After You Buy" and "File a Complaint." The *Handbook* is online at http://www.pueblo.gsa.gov/. The other topics are also online at: http://www.consumeraction.gov/caw_afterubuy_general_tips.htm and http://www.pueblo.gsa.gov/complaintresources.htm.

Regarding general inquiries and complaints, write to:

> Correspondence Branch
> Federal Trade Commission
> 6th & Pennsylvania Avenue NW
> Washington, D.C. 20580.

You can file a complaint online by using the "FTC Consumer Complaint Form," which is a hyperlink on the FTC website. Use this form to submit a complaint to the Federal Trade Commission Bureau of Consumer Protection about a particular company or organization. The information you provide is up to you. However, if you do not provide your name or other information, it may be impossible for the FTC to refer, respond to, or investigate your complaint or request.

Although the FTC generally does not intervene in individual disputes or directly resolve individual consumer problems, your complaint and the information you provide can assist the FTC's fraud investigators to identify a pattern of possible law violations requiring investigation. Following an investigation, the Commission may initiate an enforcement action if it finds "reason to believe" that the law is being violated. The Commission uses certain of its statutory powers to enforce both consumer protection and antitrust laws.

The FTC enters Internet, telemarketing, identity theft and other fraud-related complaints into Consumer Sentinel®, a secure online database available to hundreds of civil and criminal law enforcement agencies worldwide.

If you have a specific complaint about unsolicited commercial e-mail (spam), use the online form. You can forward spam directly to the Commission at uce@ftc.gov without using the complaint form.

The FTC collects complaints about identity theft from consumers who have been victimized. Although the FTC does not have the authority to bring criminal action, the Commission can help victims of identity theft by providing information to assist them in resolving the financial and other problems that can result from this crime. The FTC also refers victim complaints to other appropriate government agencies and private organizations for further action.

If you've been a victim of identity theft, file a complaint with the FTC by contacting the FTC's Identity Theft Hotline by telephone toll-free at 1-877-IDTHEFT (438-4338) or going online at http://www.consumer.gov/idtheft. You can also contact the FTC by mail at

> Identity Theft Clearinghouse
> Federal Trade Commission
> 600 Pennsylvania Avenue NW
> Washington, DC 20580

Other agencies and organizations also are working to combat identity theft. If specific institutions and companies are not being responsive to your questions and complaints, you also may want to contact the government agencies with jurisdiction over those companies.

United States Postal Inspection Service (USPIS)

Every year, illegal mail fraud schemes rob consumers, often elderly citizens, of their hard-earned life savings. For more information on mail fraud that targets senior citizens go to http://www.usps.com/postalinspectors/fraud/seniorwk.htm. If you believe you may be a potential or actual victim of mail fraud, or if any aspect of the situation involves the United States mail, you should contact the nearest U.S. postal inspector. Your local post office can assist you.

You can also contact the U.S. Postal Inspection Service by phone, toll-free, at 1-888-877-7644 or by e-mail at: www.uspsoig.gov. The USPIS can be contacted by mail at the following address:

> U.S. Postal Inspection Service
> Office of Inspector General
> Operations Support Group
> 222 S. Riverside Plaza, Suite 1250
> Chicago, IL 60606-6100

You are advised to save all documentation of the transaction, including letters, postcards, canceled checks, telephone bills, credit card statements, and mailing envelopes. If you believe your mail was stolen, report it immediately to your local postmaster or nearest postal inspector. You will be asked to file a formal complaint. Do not hesitate to do so.

The U.S. Postal Inspection Service provides an online mail fraud complaint form. The form can be found at: http://www.usps.com/postal-inspectors/fraud/MailFraudComplaint.htm

National Fraud Information Center and Internet Fraud Watch

Information about the consumer protection activities of these organizations can be found online at http://www.fraud.org/. They provide two ways to report fraud: a hotline at 1-800-876-7060, and an online complaint form at http://68.166.162.20/repoform.htm.

Resources for Specific Types of Fraud

Health Care Products and Services

If you have questions about a possibly fraudulent health care product or service, discuss the matter with your physician, particularly if you have had any injuries, or contact one of the following agencies.

Food and Drug Administration
HFE 88
5600 Fishers Lane
Rockville, MD 20857

The Food and Drug Administration answers questions about medical devices, medicines, and food supplements that are mislabeled, misrepresented, or in some way harmful.

U.S. Postal Service
Office of Criminal Investigation
Washington, D.C. 20260-2166

The U.S. Postal Service monitors quack products purchased by mail.

Magazine Subscriptions

Although the common magazine subscription scam is that people are enticed into buying something based on misrepresentations of savings, gifts, and appeals to help out a worthy cause, one of the most frequent consumer complaints involves non-delivery of the magazines ordered. Be aware that the magazine industry publishing standard regarding the time before a non-delivery complaint can be processed is usually ninety days. While many publishers do much better than this, it is likely that many of the non-delivery complaints they receive are due to the lead time that a publisher may require to send the first copy to the new subscriber. However, if you think you've been involved in a magazine subscription scam, contact your state AG, local consumer protection office, and or the FTC.

Nigerian Letter

If you receive an offer from someone claiming to need your help getting money out of Nigeria—or any other country, for that matter—but have *not* lost any money to this scheme, send a copy of the correspondence to the appropriate U.S. officials. If the offer comes via e-mail, forward it to the FTC at uce@ftc.gov. If it arrives via fax, fax a copy of the letter to the United States Secret Service at 202-435-5031.

If you have lost money to one of these schemes, forward appropriate written documentation to:

> United States Secret Service
> Financial Crimes Division
> 1800 G Street NW, Room 942
> Washington, D.C. 20223

Telephone Billing

Take the following actions if there are any charges listed on your telephone bill that you suspect are fraudulent:

- Immediately call the company that charged you for calls you did not place, or charged you for services you did not authorize or use. Ask the company to explain the charges. Request an adjustment to your bill for any incorrect charges.
- Call your local telephone company. FCC rules require telephone companies to place a toll-free number on their bills for customers to contact with billing inquiries. Explain your concerns about the charges and ask your telephone company to explain the procedure for having incorrect charges removed from your bill.
- If neither the local phone company nor the company in question will remove the incorrect charges you can file a complaint with the state regulatory agency that handles your particular area of concern.

Sources

AARP. July 15, 2003. *Off the Hook: Reducing Participation in Telemarketing Fraud.* http://www.aarp.org/press/2003/nr071503.html. Full text of report: http://research.aarp.org/consume/d17812_fraud.html.

_____. June 10, 2003. "Online Fraud on the Rise." http://www.aarp.org/bulletin/departments/2003/consumer/0610_consumer_1.html.

_____. March 21, 2003. "Reverse Mortgage: Basic Loan Features." http://www.aarp.org/revmort-basics/Articles/a2003-03-21-basicloanfeatures.html.

_____. October 4, 2002. "Phone Cramming: Watch Your Bill." http://www.aarp.org/consumerprotect-utilities/Articles/a2002-10-04-WiseConsumerPhone.

_____. October 2, 2002. "Online Auctions: Bidder Beware!" http://www.aarp.org/consumerprotect-wise/Articles/a2002-10-02-WiseConsumerOnlineAuctions.html.

_____. October 2, 2002. "Work-At-Home Scams." http://www.aarp.org/consumerprotect-frauds/Articles/a2002-10-02-FraudsWorkatHome.html.

_____. October 1, 2002. "Credit Card Fraud." http://www.aarp.org/consumerprotect-frauds/Articles/a2002-10-01-FraudsCreditCards.html.

_____. October 1, 2002. "Sweepstakes Action." http://www.aarp.org/consumerprotect-frauds/Articles/a2002-10-01-FraudsSweepstakes.

_____. April 2000. "Stock Frauds on the Rise: Boiler Room Rogues Turn on the Heat." http://www.aarp.org/bulletin/apr00/boiler.html.

_____. 1994. "Elderly Become Target of Scams." http://www.lectlaw.com/tcos.html.

_____. No date. "Evaluating Health Information on the Internet." http://www.aarp.org/confacts/health/wwwhealth.html.

_____. No date. "Home Improvement Fraud." http://www.aarp.org/confacts/money/homeimprovement.html.

_____. No date. "Travel Fraud: Go to Paradise Rather Than to the Cleaners!" http://www.aarp.org/confacts/money/travscam.html.

_____. No date. "The Pigeon Drop." http://www.aarp.org/confacts/money/pigeondrop.html.

_____. No date. "Viaticals: Watch Out!" http://www.aarp.org/confacts/money/viaticals.html.

Administration on Aging. 2002. "Consumer Protection & the Elderly." http://www.aoa.gov/naic/notes/consumerprotection.html.

_____. December 21, 2001. *A Profile of Older Americans: 2001.* http://www.aoa.dhhs.gov/aoa/stats/profile/2001/1.html.

Barrett, Stephen. 1997. "Ten Ways to Avoid Being Quacked." http://www.quack watch.org/01QuackeryRelatedTopics/avoid.html.

———. No date. "Quackery: How Should It Be Defined?" http://www.quackwatch.org/01QuackeryRelatedTopics/quackdef.html.

———, William T. Jarvis, Manfred Kroger, and William M. London. 2002. *Consumer Health*, 7th Edition, McGraw-Hill. http://www.quackwatch.org/chs/about/foreword.html.

Bendeich, Mark and Bernhard Warner. 2003. "Fraudsters Pose as UK Bankers in New E-mail Scam." Online content: http://www.reuters.com/newsArticle.jhtml;jsessionid=Q05GIK4VVDU4OCRBAEOCFEY?type=internetNews&storyID=3554828.

Better Business Bureau. 2003. "Work-at-Home Schemes." http://www.bbb.org/library/workathome.asp.

———. January 8, 2002. "Consumers Now Target of Nigerian Letter Scams." http://www.bbb.org/pubpages/nigerian.asp.

Blaylock, Bob. No date. "Pyramid Schemes, Ponzi Schemes, and Related Frauds." http://www.impulse.net/~thebob/Pyramid.html.

California Contractors State License Board. No date. "Traveler Tip Sheet." http://www.cslb.ca.gov/forms/travelerfacts.pdf.

Caughey, Andrea. September 3, 1998. "Viaticals Help Face Terminal Illness." http://www.seniorworld.com/articles/a19980903104435.html.

CBS News. April 14, 2003. "Costly Tax Advice." http://www.cbsnews.com/stories/2003/04/14/eveningnews/consumer/main549233.shtml.

CNN. February 14, 2000. "Investment Scams Targeting the Elderly." http://money.cnn.com/2000/02/14/senior_living/q_retire_scams/.

Consumer Action. *You Can Help Fight Phone Fraud*. http://www.consumer-action.org/English/library/telephone/1999_FightPhoneFraud/index.php.

The Consumer Law Page. November 1992. "Dance Studios." http://consumerlawpage.com/brochure/28.shtml.

Consumer News. September 26, 2002. "Home Improvement Scams Bloom in Spring." http://www.consumeraffairs.com/news/homeowner_scams.html.

Cooper, Porus P. October 8, 2002. "Officials again warn of money-transfer scam." *Philadelphia Inquirer*. http://www.philly.com/mld/inquirer/.

Crime Watch. 1996. "How to Protect Yourself: Dance Studios." http://www.consumersgroup.com/crimewatch/dance_studios.htm.

eBay. "Help: Buying." 2003. Webpage. http://pages.ebay.com/education/buyingtips/index.html.

———. "Help: Safe Trading." 2003. Webpage. http://pages.ebay.com/help/confidence/hub.html.

Federal Consumer Information Center. August 27, 2002. "High-Cost 'Predatory' Home Loans: How to Avoid the Traps." http://www.pueblo.gsa.gov/cic_text/housing/hcloans/cvrstry.html.

Federal Reserve Bank of San Francisco. No date. "Frauds and Scams: Protect Yourself and Your Money on the Phone, at the Door, Through the Mailbox, and Other General Precautions." http://www.frbsf.org/publications/consumer/fraud.html.

FirstGov for Seniors. No date. "AARP Launches Drive Against Unscrupulous Mortgage Lenders." http://www.seniors.gov/articles/0401/mortgage-lenders.html.

Fleck, Carole. September 2001. "Consumer Alert on Viatical Fraud: Buying: This

Insurance Can Leave You Poorer." http://www.aarp.org/bulletin/departments/2001/consumer/0805_consumer_1.html.

The Funeral Consumers Alliance. No date. *Prepaying Your Funeral: Benefits and Dangers*. http://www.funerals.org/personal/prepay.htm.

_____. No date. *Understanding the Tricks of the Funeral Trade*. http://www.funerals.org/personal/tricks.htm.

Goodstein, Ellen. 2003. "10 Things Funeral Directors Don't Want You to Know." http://www.bankrate.com/brm/news/cheap/20031118a1.asp.

Harrison, Mary N. July 2000. "Pyramids to Urns: Funeral Costs and Options." http://edis.ifas.ufl.edu/BODY_FY023.

_____. July 1999. "Don't Get Gypped." http://edis.ifas.ufl.edu/HE816.

Henderson, Les. 2000. Website. *Crimes of Persuasion*. www.crimes-of-persuasion.com.

Hopper, D. Ian. May 26, 2002. "An Old Scam Takes a New Form: E-mail." *Philadelphia Inquirer*. http://www.philly.com/mld/inquirer/news/nation/3340721.htm.

Identity Theft Resource Center. 2003. "Identity Theft Prevention and Survival." http://www.identifytheft.org.

International Cemetery and Funeral Association. Website. http://www.icfa.org.

Jarvis, William T. October 4, 1998. "Alternative Healthcare: Past, Present and Prospects." http://www.acsh.org/publications/priorities/1004/alternative.html.

_____, and Stephen Barrett. August 29, 2000. "How Quackery Sells." http://www.quackwatch.org/01QuackeryRelatedTopics/quacksell.html.

Lanford, Audri, and Jim Lanford. March 29, 2001. "Online Auctions: Deal or Steal?" http://www.scambusters.org/Scambusters43.html.

The 'Lectric Law Library. 1994. "Business Opportunity Scams: Vending Machines and Display Racks." http://www.lectlaw.com/tcos.html.

_____. No date. "Multi-Level Marketing: Legit Deal or Pyramid Scheme?" http://www.lectlaw.com/files/cos67.htm.

Martin-Worley, Barbara. February 7, 2002. *The Truth About Elder Fraud*. http://www.ext.colostate.edu/pubs/columnha/ha0007.html.

McKay, Carol. August 6, 2002. "Credit Card Scams Bump Prizes and Sweepstakes as #1 Telemarketing Fraud." http://www.nclnet.org/fraudweek1.htm.

McLeod, Don. May 1995. "High Tech Swindlers Filch Millions." http://www.lectlaw.com/files/cos09.htm.

Merriam-Webster. 1996. *Merriam-Webster's Dictionary of Law*. http://www.refdesk.com.

Mr. Kenyada's Neighborhood. Website. http://www.kenyada.com/senior.htm.

MSNBC. April 12, 2002. "Investment Fraud against the Retired: Advice on How to Not Make Yourself a Target." http://www.msnbc.com/news/737161.asp?cp1=1.

_____. March 1, 2002. "Home Improvement Scams." http://www.msnbc.com/news/715657.asp?cp1=1.

Myers, Lisa. March 25, 2002. "Older Americans Targeted for Scams." http://www.msnbc.com/news/729202.asp?cp1=1.

National Center for Victims of Crime. July 21, 1999. "Elder Fraud: Remarks by Susan Herman Before the Senate Judiciary Committee." http://www.ncvc.org/MAIN/Susan/ef.htm.

National Consumer Law Center. March 2000. "Home Improvement Scams Alert." http://www.consumerlaw.org/seniors_initiative/home_improv.htm.

_____. August 1999. "Advice for Seniors About Credit Cards." http://www.consumerlaw.org.

_____. 1998. "Understanding Living Trusts and Avoiding Living Trust Scams." http://www.consumerlaw.org/seniors_initiative/98livtru.html.

_____. No date. "Helping Elderly Homeowners Victimized by Predatory Mortgage Loans." http://www.consumerlaw.org/initiatives/seniors_initiative/helping_elderly.shtml.

National Consumers League. March 25, 2003. "Online Auctions Dominant Consumer Fraud." http://www.natlconsumersleague.org/internetfraud02.htm.

_____. No date. "Understanding Your Phone Bill." http://www.natlconsumersleague.org/phonebill/index.html.

The National Fraud Information Center. 2002. "2002 Top Ten Frauds." http://www.fraud.org/2002intstats.htm.

National Institute on Aging. 1994. "Health Quackery." http://www.nia.nih.gov/health/agepages/healthqy.htm.

Nightly Business Report. March 20, 1996. "When It Comes to Living Trusts, You Can't Always 'Trust' What You Hear." http://www.lectlaw.com/files/est08.htm.

North American Securities Administrators Association. February 26, 2002. "Risky 'death futures' draw warning." http://www.nasaa.org/nasaa/abtnasaa/display_top_story.asp?stid=245.

Pew Internet & American Life Project. July 16, 2003. *Internet Health Resources.* http://www.pewinternet.org/reports/toc.asp?Report-95.

Quackwatch. Website. http://www.quackwatch.org.

Seniors.gov. April 2001. "The Top 10 Investment Scams." http://www.seniors.gov/articles/0401/investment_scams.html.

_____. January 2001. "Charitable Donations: Give or Take." http://www.seniors.gov/articles/0101/charitable-donations.html.

SPRY Foundation. 2001. *Evaluating Health Information on the World Wide Web: A Guide for Older Adults and Caregivers.* http://www.spry.org/sprys_work/education/EvaluatingHealthInfo.html.

Sullivan, Bob. May 25, 2003. "Nigerian Scam Spam on the Rise." http://www.msnbc.com/news/756074.asp?0dm=T11OT&cp1=1.

_____. July 3, 2002. "Fake escrow sites lure auction users." http://www.msnbc.com/news/775457.asp.

Trinity University. No author. No date. "Economics of the Aging Revolution." http://www.trinity.edu/mkearl/ger-econ.html.

2ScamU! No date. "Magazine Scams!" http://www.2scamu.com/magazine.html.

United States Bureau of the Census. September 2001. "Home Computers and Internet Use in the United States: August 2000." http://www.census.gov/prod/2001pubs/p23-207.pdf.

_____. 2000. *Population Projections of the United States by Age, Sex, Race, and Hispanic Origin: 1995 to 2050.* http://landview.census.gov/mp/www/pub/pop/mspop06y.html.

United States Department of Housing and Urban Development. 1997. "Stop Reverse Mortgage Rip-Offs." http://www.hud.gov.

United States Department of Justice. 2002. "Identity Theft and Fraud." http://www.usdoj.gov/criminal/fraud/idtheft.html.

United States Federal Bureau of Investigation. April 9, 2003. "Internet Fraud Complaint Center Referred More Than 48,000 Fraud Complaints to Law Enforcement in 2002." http://www1.ifccfbi.gov/strategy/wn030409.asp.

_____. September 10, 2001. "Fraud Against the Elderly." http://www.fbi.gov/congress/congress01/lormel0910.htm.

_____. No date. "Senior Citizens Fraud." http://www.fbi.gov/majcases/fraud/seniors fam.htm.

_____. No date. "What is an Advance-Fee Scheme?" http://www.fbi.gov/majcases/fraud/fraudschemes.htm.

United States Federal Communications Commission. 2002. "Cramming." http://www.fcc.gov/cgb/consumerfacts/cramming.html.

United States Federal Trade Commission. December 16, 2003. "Take This Scheme and Stuff It: Avoiding Envelope-Stuffing Rip-Offs." http://www.ftc.gov/bcp/online/pubs/alerts/stufftalrt.htm.

_____. September 3, 2003. "FTC Releases Survey of Identity Theft in U.S." http://www.ftc.gov/opa/2003/09/idtheft.htm.

_____. August 21, 2003. "FTC Warns Consumers of Scammers Charging for Do Not Call Registration." http://www.ftc.gov/opa/2003/08/dncscammers.htm.

_____. August 11, 2003. "National Credit Repair." http://www.ftc.gov/opa/2003/08/nationwide.htm.

_____. August 11, 2003. "Global Vending Services, Inc." http://www.ftc.gov/opa/2003/08/globalvending.htm.

_____. July 24, 2003. "How Not to Get Hooked by a 'Phishing' Scam." http://www.ftc.gov/bcp/conline/pubs/alerts/phishingalrt.htm.

_____. July 3, 2003. "Protecting Yourself from Fund Raising Fraud." http://www.ftc.gov/bcp/conline/pubs/naps/naps_raising.pdf.

_____. May 2003. "Fraud on the Line: Avoiding 'Do Not Call' Scams." http://www.ftc.gov/bcp/conline/pubs/alerts/dncregalrt.htm.

_____. April 23, 2003. "Defendants Permanently Barred from Selling Work-At-Home Opportunities." http://www.ftc.gov/opa/2003/04/elecmedbilling.htm.

_____. April 2003. "Going, Going, Gone: When Online Auction Users Lose Out to Phony Payment and Escrow Services." http://www.ftc.gov/bcp/conline/features/onlauctions.htm.

_____. April 2003. "Internet Auctions: A Guide for Buyers and Sellers." http://www.ftc.gov/bcp/conline/pubs/online/auctions.htm.

_____. September 2002. "The 'Nigerian' Scam: Costly Compassion." http://www.ftc.gov/bcp/conline/pubs/alerts/nigeralrt.htm.

_____. July 18, 2002. "FTC Testifies on Identity Theft and the Impact on Seniors." http://www.ftc.gov/opa/2002/07/senioridtheft.htm.

_____. June 25, 2002. "Scam Artists Use Do Not Call Registry to Commit Fraud." http://www.ftc.gov/opa/2002/06/donotcallscam.htm.

_____. April 2002. "Medical Billing Opportunities: Not Exactly What the Doctor Ordered." http://www.ftc.gov/bcp/conline/edcams/bizopps/press.html.

_____. February 2002. _ID Theft: When Bad Things Happen to Your Good Name._ http://www.ftc.gov/bcp/conline/pubs/credit/idtheft.htm.

_____. September 10, 2001. "Health Fraud and the Elderly." http://www.ftc.gov/opa/2001/09/healthfraud.htm.

_____. March 2001. "Work-at-Home Schemes." http://www.ftc.gov/bcp/conline/edcams/bizopps/coninfo.html.

_____. October 2000. _Catch the Bandit in Your Mailbox._ http://www.ftc.gov/bcp/conline/pubs/tmarkg/bandit.htm.

_____. October 2000. "Credit Card Loss Protection Offers: They're the Real Steal." http://www.ftc.gov/bcp/conline/pubs/alerts/lossalrt.htm.

_____. August 10, 2000. "Fraud Against Seniors." http://www.ftc.gov/os/2000/08/agingtestimony.htm.

_____. August 8, 2000. "Fraud Against Seniors." http://www.ftc.gov/os/2000/08/agingtestimony.htm.

_____. August 2000. "Traveler's Advisory: Get What You Pay For." http://www.ftc.gov/bcp/conline/pubs/alerts/trvlalrt.htm.

_____. July 2000. "Prize Offers: You Don't Have to Pay to Play." http://www.ftc.gov/bcp/conline/pubs/tmarkg/prizes.htm.

_____. July 2000. "Living Trust Offers: How to Make Sure They're Trust-Worthy." http://www.ftc.gov/bcp/conline/pubs/services/livtrust.htm.

_____. June 2000. "Funerals: A Consumer Guide." http://www.ftc.gov/bcp/conline/pubs/services/funeral.htm.

_____. March 2000. *Franchise and Business Opportunities.* http://www.ftc.gov/bcp/conline/pubs/invest/franchse.htm.

_____. March 2000. *Guidelines for Managers of Telemarketing Enterprises Who Sell Magazine Subscriptions.* http://www.ftc.gov/bcp/conline/pubs/buspubs/magseller.htm.

_____. February 2000. "Identity Crisis: What to Do If Your Identity is Stolen." http://www.ftc.gov/bcp/conline/pubs/alerts/idenalrt.htm.

_____. January 2000. "Lotions and Potions: The Bottom Line About Multilevel Marketing Plans." http://www.ftc.gov/bcp/conline/pubs/alerts/lotionalrt.htm.

_____. January 2000. "The Gifting Club 'Gotcha'." http://www.ftc.gov/bcp/menu-seniors.htm.

_____. August 1999. "Easy Credit? Not So Fast." http://www.ftc.gov/bcp/conline/pubs/tmarkg/loans.htm.

_____. July 1999. "Telemarketing Travel Fraud." http://www.ftc.gov/bcp/conline/pubs/tmarkg/trvlfrd.htm.

_____. September 3, 1998. "Operation Vend Up Broke." http://www.ftc.gov/opa/1998/09/vendup2.htm.

_____. July 14, 1998. "FTC Unveils Dirty Dozen Spam Scams." http://www.ftc.gov/opa/1998/07/dozen.htm.

_____. May 13, 1998. "Pyramid Schemes." http://www.ftc.gov/speeches/other/dvimf16.htm.

_____. May 1998. "Reloading Scams: Double Trouble for Consumers." http://www.ftc.gov/bcp/menu-seniors.htm.

_____. May 1998. "The Seminar Pitch: A Real Curve Ball." http://www.ftc.gov/bcp/conline/pubs/invest/seminar.htm.

_____. February 1998. "Credit Repair: Self-Help May Be Best." http://www.ftc.gov/bcp/conline/pubs/credit/repair.htm.

_____. January 1998. "Avoiding Home Equity Scams." http://www.ftc.gov/bcp/conline/pubs/alerts/eqtyalrt.htm.

_____. August 1997. "Avoiding Credit and Charge Card Fraud. http://www.ftc.gov/bcp/conline/pubs/credit/cards.htm.

_____. August 5, 1997. "Trade Name Games." http://www.ftc.gov/bcp/conline/edcams/bizopps/press.html.

_____. July 1997. "Investment Risks." http://www.ftc.gov/bcp/menu-seniors.htm.

_____. January 1997. *Fighting Consumer Fraud: The Challenge and the Campaign.* http://www.ftc.gov/reports/Fraud/.

_____. November 1996. "Multilevel Marketing Plans." http://www.ftc.gov/bcp/con line/pubs/invest/mlm.htm.

_____. May 1996. "The Cooling-Off Rule." http://www.ftc.gov/bcp/conline/pubs/buy ing/cooling.htm.

_____. July 18, 1995. "Business Opportunity Scam Epidemic." http://www.ftc.gov/ bcp/conline/edcams/bizopps/coninfo.html.

_____. December 1994. A Consumer Guide to Buying a Franchise. http://www.pueblo. gsa.gov/cic_text/smbuss/franchise/franchise.htm.

_____. October 1993. Reverse Mortgages. http://www.ftc.gov/bcp/menu-seniors. htm.

_____. No date. "Break the Chain." http://www.ftc.gov/bcp/conline/edcams/chain mail/index.htm.

_____. Bureau of Consumer Protection. No date. "Catch the Bandit in Your Mail-box." http://www.ftc.gov/bcp/conline/pubs/tmarkg/bandit.htm.

_____. No date. "Consumer Fraud against the Elderly." http://www.ftc.gov/bcp/con line/pubs/services/apact/apact01.htm.

_____. Consumer Sentinel. Website. http://www.consumer.gov/sentinel/.

_____. No date. "Test Your Skills at Avoiding a Home Repair Nightmare." http:// www.ftc.gov/bcp/conline/edcams/homeimp/quiz2.htm.

United States General Accounting Office. February 14, 2002. "Identity Theft: Avail-able Data Indicate Growth in Prevalence and Cost." http://www.gao.gov (Search for report: GAO-02-424T.)

United States House of Representatives, Select Committee on Aging, Subcom-mittee on Health and Long-term Care. "Quackery: A $10 Billion Scandal." Washington, DC, 1984, U.S. Government Printing Office.

United States Internal Revenue Service. 2003. "IRS Updates the 'Dirty Dozen' for 2003." http://www.irs.gov/newsroom/article/0,,id=107493,00.html.

_____. 2002. "Types of Schemes: Testimony on Promoted Tax Schemes." http:// www.irs.gov/irs/article/0,,id=106063,00.html.

United States Postal Inspection Service. December 2002. 2002 Annual Report of Inspections. http://www.usps.com/postalinspectors/ar02/ar02text.htm.

_____. August 26, 2002. "Senior Citizens Targeted in National Fraud Awareness Campaign." http://www.usps.com/postalinspectors/NRsenior.htm.

_____. December 2001. 2001 Annual Report of Inspections. http://www.usps.com/postal inspectors/ar01text.htm.

_____. No date. "Chain Letters." http://www.usps.com/websites/depart/inspect/chain let.htm.

_____. No date. "Credit Card Schemes." http://www.usps.com/websites/depart/ inspect/consmenu.htm.

_____. No date. "Distributorship and Franchise Fraud." http://www.framed.usps. com/websites/depart/inspect/distrib.htm.

_____. No date. "The Free Vacation Scam." http://www.usps.com/websites/depart/ inspect/consmenu.htm.

_____. No date. "Government Look-Alike Mail." http://www.usps.com/websites/ depart/inspect/consmenu.htm.

_____. No date. "Sweepstakes and Lotteries." http://www.usps.com/websites/depart/ inspect/consmenu.htm.

_____. No date. "Testimony of the U.S. Postal Inspection Service on Viatical Fraud." http://www.quatloos.com/viaticals_usps.htm.

_____. No date. "Work-at-Home Schemes." http://www.usps.com/websites/depart/inspect/workhome.htm.

United States Secret Service. 2002. "Advance Fee Fraud Advisory." www.secret service.gov/alert419.shtml.

United States Securities and Exchange Commission. November 15, 2001. "Internet Fraud: How to Avoid Internet Investment Scams." http://www.sec.gov/investor/pubs/cyberfraud.htm.

United States Senate Special Committee on Aging. July 9, 2002. "Buyer Beware: Public Health Concerns of Counterfeit Medicine." http://frwebgate.access.gpo.gov/cgi-bin/getdoc.cgi?dbname=107_senate_hearings&docid=f:82326.wais.

United States Federal Trade Commission. 2003. "Internet Auction Fraud Targeted by Law Enforcers." http://www.ftc.gov/opa/2003/04/bidderbeware.htm.

United States Treasury Department. No date. "Tax Fraud Alerts." http://www.ustreas.gov/irs/ci/tax_fraud.index.htm.

Wasik, John F. "Fraud in the Funeral Industry." September/October 1995. *Consumers Digest*, 34 (5). http://business.accesscomm.ca/jbyggdin/articles/cdsep95.htm.

Index